D0896704

More True Canadian Ghost Stories

Other Books by John Robert Colombo

True Canadian Ghost Stories

True Canadian UFO Stories

The Midnight Hour

Haunted Toronto

Mysterious Canada

Ghost Stories of Ontario

Ghost Stories of Canada

More True Canadian Ghost Stories

John Robert Colombo

PROSPERO
B·O·O·K·S

To Liedewy and Tony Hawke

Copyright © 2005 by John Robert Colombo

All rights reserved. No part of this work covered by the copyrights hereon may be reproduced or used in any form or by any means—graphic, electronic or mechanical, including photocopying, recording, taping or information storage and retrieval systems—without the prior written permission of the publisher, or, in the case of photocopying or other reprographic copying, a licence from Access Copyright, the Canadian Copyright Licensing Agency, One Yonge Street, Suite 1900, Toronto, Ontario, M6B 3A9.

Library and Archives Canada Cataloguing in Publication

Colombo, John Robert, 1936–

   More true Canadian ghost stories / John Robert Colombo.

 ISBN 1-55267-691-9

1. Ghosts—Canada. I. Title.

BF1472.C3C655 2005   133.1'0971   C2005-900132-1

This collection produced for Prospero Books.

Key Porter Books Limited
6 Adelaide Street East, 10th Floor
Toronto, Ontario
Canada M5C 1H6

www.keyporter.com

Text design: Peter Maher
Electronic formatting: Jean Lightfoot Peters

Printed and bound in Canada

05 06 07 08 09 5 4 3 2 1

Contents

Preface

More *True Canadian Ghost Stories* offers you close to three hundred pages of thrills and chills. Each page unlocks a door, opens a window, lifts a veil…to permit you to peer beyond the real…into the unknown!

Here you have an invitation and an opportunity to think about such weighty matters as the existence of ghosts and spirits, ghouls and monsters, near-death experiences, life after death, the return of the dead from their graves to haunt people and places today.

Here is your chance to ponder the mysteries of life and death, and the wonders of fate and destiny.

Told as True

The incidents described in this book, like those in its predecessor, *True Canadian Ghost Stories*, are "told as true." They are not offered as works of fact. They are not fiction. Each informant or narrator assures us that these events and experiences occurred. There is no proof that this is so, or that any details have been suppressed or added for effect, except for the heartfelt assurances of the witness. A few of these tales seem close to folklore, others might be delusions, and a tiny number could be willful deceptions. We have to take many things on faith, so why not these stories? Like the efficacy of megavitamins, a ghost story is one of those things we take on faith—or, in the words of the poet, Samuel Taylor Coleridge, with "the willing suspension of disbelief."

These episodes are Canadian because they took place here or happened to Canadians. We might not have a manse as haunted as England's Borley Rectory, nor a suburban bungalow as bedevilled as New Jersey's Amityville Horror. But right across Canada, there are hundreds of haunted sites, each one with a story of its own—a story that can hold an audience. At the same time, it is good to bear in mind that many of the disturbances reported at Borley were earlier reported in Amherst, Nova Scotia, and indeed even originated there. We might also concede that the so-called horror at Amityville was the pipe dream of a journalist turned novelist. We have our own hauntings, bizarre sites to call our own. No foreign ghosts are summoned. No branch-plant hauntings for us!

Most of the fifty-four episodes described in these pages involve what we call ghosts. The word "ghost" means, well, "rage." That is, in German. In English, it has come to mean "spirit" and to refer specifically to two things: the principle of life and the soul of a dead person. Among the general public, the word conveys the notion of some mysterious force, power, entity, personality, or being that haunts the living—mindlessly, mischievously, or malignantly. There are reports that ghosts appear to warn or forewarn. There are reports that spirits materialize to bless the living and assure them that "There is no death" and that "Death is not the end." There are also reports of appearances and disappearances of ghosts and spirits that make no sense at all, motivated perhaps by a mindless malignancy. Varied is the world of the spirits.

We cannot summon a spirit at will, but we can willingly recall the story of a haunting. In English, the word "story" has two meanings. One meaning is "a true account of an event or experience." Another is "a fictional description of an imaginary event or experience." But whether it's true or fictional, someone tells a story to entertain someone else, perhaps for the purpose of frightening the listener.

One curious psychological fact is that people who recount the tales of eerie events or unusual experiences that have happened to them, in all honesty and without a trace of delusion or dementia, do so candidly, with no desire to deceive. But, at the same time, they do not necessarily believe in the existence of ghosts. They are telling us what happened to them, what they experienced. It seems *something* has happened, and it fits into the category of the traditional weird tale or the contemporary ghost story. Indeed, ghosts belong to the category of experience, not belief.

This raises the question, Do ghosts actually exist?

The Existence of Ghosts

If ghosts exist, they do not exist in the way that physical objects exist. Perhaps they exist in the way that electricity or radio waves or the World Wide Web exist. Both seen and unseen forces are real enough. The German philosopher Immanuel Kant devoted an essay to the status of ghosts. In "Dreams of a Spirit-Seer" (1766), he made this assessment: "The same ignorance makes me so bold as to absolutely deny the truth of the various ghost stories, and yet with the common, although queer, reservation that while I doubt any one of them, still I have a certain faith in the whole of them together."

More than two centuries ago, Samuel Johnson noted the range of opinions held by people about the existence of spirits. He said, "It is wonderful that five thousand years have not elapsed since the creation of the world, and still it is undecided whether or not there has ever been an instance of the spirit of any person appearing after death. All argument is against it; but all belief is for it."

Dr. Johnson made that observation to his biographer and companion, James Boswell, on April 3, 1778. Twelve days later, Dr. Johnson went on to assure Boswell that the question of the existence of ghosts and spirits was not a frivolous one, but a question that remained "whether in theology or philosophy, one of the most important that can come before the human understanding."

The question is as interesting today as it was then. Marshall McLuhan once wrote, "Technology is the most human thing about man," and his observation can be applied to the immaterial world—our curiosity and concern about spirits sheds more light on human nature than it does on the twilight world of the spirits. So ghosts represent knowledge of the self and prompt us to ask questions about epistemology and reality. Sigmund Freud described the experience of the spirit world as the sense of "the uncanny"; that is, the breakdown of the sense of self and the fear of possession, of losing control, that we are less "real" than we were. "The fantastic is the real that most people want to ignore," noted Robertson Davies. The things we fear are the things we want to ignore. And, as William James noted, "The first maker of the gods was fear." Fear is an emotion, a sensation, and a notion—it moves us mightily.

The Swiss psychologist Carl Jung was fascinated throughout his life with the enigma of ghosts and spirits. As a young physician, he wrote:

> These parapsychic phenomena seem to be connected as a rule with the presence of a medium. They are, so far as my experience goes, the exteriorized effects of unconscious complexes. I for one am certainly convinced that they are exteriorizations. I have repeatedly observed the telepathic effects of unconscious complexes, and also a number of parapsychical phenomena. But in all this I see no proof whatever of the existence of real spirits, and until such proof is forthcoming I must regard this whole territory as an appendix of psychology.

As the wise sage, he had reason to rethink his words. When it came time, half a century later, to reprint the passage above, he found his position had shifted from mild scepticism to warm acceptance, so he added the following observation in a footnote:

> After collecting psychological experiences from many people and many countries for fifty years, I no longer feel as certain as I did in 1919, when I wrote this sentence. To put it bluntly, I doubt whether an exclusively psychological approach can do justice to the phenomena in question. Not only the findings of parapsychology, but my own theoretical reflections, outlined in "On the Nature of the Psyche," have led me to certain postulates which touch on the realm of nuclear physics and the conception of the space-time continuum. This opens up the whole question of the transpsychic reality immediately underlying the psyche. (C.G. Jung, "The Psychological Foundations of Belief in Spirits," 1920, in *Psychology and the Occult*, translated by

R.F.C. Hull. Princeton. NJ: Princeton University Press,
Bollingen Series, 1977.)

In other words, Jung had come to the mature conclusion that spirits
could "exteriorize."

Limitations of Belief

I like to say that I do not believe in ghosts, and I do not disbelieve in
ghosts, but I do believe in ghost stories. I accept the fact that ghostly
episodes have been reported in all climes, cultures, and times, and that
the majority of informants are telling the truth as they perceive it. While
there is no proof that these accounts are totally truthful, there is no evidence that they have been falsified either. No lie detector has yet been
invented that will separate truth-tellers from lie-tellers. I have no doubt
there are people who "make up" credible-seeming stories. Yet there is
little to gain from admitting to a ghostly encounter; indeed, in modern
society, all that is gained by gabbing about ghosts is ridicule.

I hold that ghosts belong to the category of experience, not to the category of belief. Little is to be gained as well by arguing about the
reality, pro or con. Who am I to deny that such things have occurred as
described? The themes of the stories and their details have much in
common, and these are interesting cultural and important psychological facts. So more may be learned about these stories by studying them
than by scoffing at them.

In the meantime, the simplest thing to do is enjoy them.

Visit Ghostly Sites

Do you want to visit a ghostly site? Try a Ghost Walk.

A ghost walk is a great way to see a city, your own city or another,
especially during off hours, and particularly those areas that are off the
beaten track. If the guide who leads the ghost walk is knowledgeable,
you will learn the history of the buildings in an older part of town and
the idiosyncrasies of their inhabitants, historical and legendary. These

walks are usually scheduled for early evening in the summer and fall, and their number and the number of people they attract increase to mark the approach of Halloween on October 31. The following Canadian cities have well-publicized ghost tours:

British Columbia: Vancouver, Victoria
Alberta: Calgary, Edmonton
Manitoba: Winnipeg
Ontario: Brockville, Burlington, Hamilton, Kingston, Niagara-on-the-Lake (at Fort George), Ottawa, Parry Sound, Thunder Bay, Toronto
Quebec: Montreal, Quebec City
Nova Scotia: Halifax
Newfoundland: St. John's

Toronto offers several tours (both walking and biking). The Ontario town of Fergus may have no guided tour of its own—after all, its population is a mere 8,000 souls—but the Fergus and District Chamber of Commerce filled the breach in 1994 by producing a sixteen-page booklet called *Ontario's Only Self-Guided Ghost Tour*. Written by local historian Pat Mestern, it guides visitors up and down the town's streets to view its haunted houses, of which there are a surprising number. Mestern offers the following advice to all ghosthunters: "Be alert, be sensitive, and have a great time." On a per-capita basis, Fergus is Canada's most haunted community, followed by Ontario's Niagara-on-the-Lake. Both places seem to have interesting inhabitants—dead or alive!

Many communities with no regular ghost walks sponsor special events around Halloween that involve telling ghost stories and staging scary skits. These are sometimes called spirit dinners and are great fun, as well as fine charity fundraisers. Many communities also sponsor one-off annual events that are very popular, like the ghost walk of the Discovery Harbour, the former naval and military installations at Penetanguishene, Ontario. Across the country, every summer camp for youngsters has its own ghostly figure or eccentric hermit. And then there are Ontario's "boo barns" and "haunted hayrides." Farmers' families and their hired help do their darndest to scare school-age children (and not a few parents!), using their tractors and barns and rides through the woods to creaky and creepy effect.

Throughout the country, and indeed around the Western world, local tourism offices distribute brochures that advertise such events and attractions. The conductors of these walks are usually ghost-lore enthusiasts, history students, or local historians. The best walk of the many I've taken was my first. My wife, Ruth, and I took it in 1974, and it covered parts of England's historic walled city of York. Such a creepy place at dusk! I took my second-best tour in 2001, and it covered the Inner Harbour of Victoria, British Columbia. Both tour guides placed a premium on local history and interesting personalities, all the while alluding to the local traditions and rumours about the buildings and their occupants. The guides encouraged their customers to speculate on matters of life and death. No tour guide will guarantee that on your early evening stroll you will spot a ghost or experience a poltergeist-like effect, but, then, no tour guide will ever guarantee that you will *not* be scared by such things... you simply never know!

Check the Internet

If you enter the word "ghosts" in a search engine, you might be surprised. When I did that on Google on January 23, 2005, the word "ghosts" produced 5,750,000 hits and the word "spirits" 8,010,000. The word "poltergeists" resulted in only 81,900 hits: Is the Internet poltergeist-poor? I have no doubt that when I next try, there will be even more hits.

The numbers are bound to increase as people realize that the web is a wonderful source of information on such matters. And it's free. Enthusiasts should visit the websites established by psychics and others; then be sure to check out the websites hosted by local and national sceptical groups.

The leading Canadian website, and a very respectable one, is maintained by the brother and sister team of Matthew James Didier and Jennifer Krutilla. In October 1997, they launched what is now known as the Toronto Ghosts and Hauntings Research Society, **www.torontoghosts.org.** The site is very popular, and its postings are reflective of the enthusiasm of correspondents and the restraint of its webmasters. The society sponsors evenings of special talks and walks to explore sites of particular interest. Links lead users to dozens of related Canadian sites and then to thousands (indeed, hundreds of thousands) of web pages outside the country.

Let me add a note about scepticism. The world's leading sceptical group is the Committee for the Scientific Investigation of Claims of the Paranormal (CSICOP), founded in 1976 by philosopher and humanist Paul Kurtz and others on a site adjacent to the State University of New York at Buffalo. The web address is **www.centerforinquiry.net** and there are "affiliated organizations" in Vancouver, Calgary, Toronto, Ottawa, and Montreal. The largest such group is Ontario Skeptics, which was founded by magician Henry Gordon and others and is now managed by editor Eric McMillan as the Ontario Skeptics Society for Critical Inquiry (OSSCI), **www.skeptics.ca**. Local groups generally attract youngish, technology-minded people with a "sense of wonder" about the universe and man's illusions, delusions, and belief systems. The groups hold public meetings, and speakers discuss paranormal subjects, such as ghosts, but also subjects of social interest such as chiropractic, the status of lie detectors, fringe science, fundamentalist beliefs, psychic fraud, and alternative therapies, to name a few.

I have attended meetings of both the sceptical study groups and the psychical research groups, where I made the observation that the pointed discussions at the meetings of the sceptical groups are generally more relevant to an understanding and appreciation of psychical phenomena than the rambling discourses delivered by spiritualists and professed believers in psychical research circles or schools. Let me give an illustration.

Some years ago, I was asked to address a meeting of the Toronto

Humanists on the subject of superstitions. The meeting was scheduled for Halloween. I checked Google for the word "superstition" and came up with more than 200,000 hits. I did not click on all of them or I'd still be clicking, but I did check the top twenty sites. To my surprise, I discovered that seventeen of the top twenty were sponsored by sceptical groups, not by psychical groups. The sceptical webmasters were anxious to debunk superstitious beliefs, customs, and practices! From them, I was able to learn a lot about superstitions from other cultures, ideas that were entirely new to me and my audience... and also the reasons why such beliefs, customs, and practices are of limited or of no value whatsoever. (Few of the sites, whether pro or con, shed much light on the psychological value of such behaviour.) The discussion at the Humanists was characterized by curiosity about the use that people make of elaborate belief systems and mankind's continuing need for them. Groups interested in psychical matters, I found, attract credulous people who wish to believe something—anything—everything!

Books, Television, and Film

Every bookstore, newsstand, and public library in the country has a section devoted to popular books on the supernatural, paranormal, and occult, and these sections are steadily increasing to represent the stream of well-researched new books on sceptical approaches to "the unknown." There are many excellent books, but the field is overrun by the shoddy titles. Yet even these may be rewarding. Many a reader first learned about the genuinely curious Nazca Lines in the desert of Peru after reading Eric von Däniken's *Chariots of the Gods*, or about shipping lanes in the Atlantic after encountering Charles Berlitz's *The Bermuda Triangle*. But how many readers even know there are scholarly studies that take theories of "ancient astronauts" and the "hoodoo seas" far more seriously than did their authors by rigorously checking the sources for the individual claims? I am thinking now of folklorist Thomas E. Bullard's article "Ancient Astronauts" in *The Encyclopedia of the Paranormal* (1996), edited by Gordon Stein, and librarian Larry

Kusche's *The Bermuda Triangle Mystery—Solved* (1975), which is a spirited examination of what evidence exists for Berlitz's assertions and suggestions. In their own way, the critical books do more than debunk popular theories; they demonstrate the working of the scholarly method and offer instances of critical thinking.

It seems that every night on television there are entertaining programs about the paranormal—particularly scary ones about hauntings, possessions, demonic powers, etc. They range from dramatic (and melodramatic) series such as the old *X-Files* (currently in reruns) to series or specials devoted to true-life stories such as *Unsolved Mysteries* and *Supernatural Science* (composed of dramatic reconstructions with sombre voice-overs). Then there are screenings of classic and more current horror movies such as *Nosferatu* and *The Sixth Sense* (the best of the modern lot). Indeed, I like to say that the best place to see a ghost is in a movie theatre or on your television screen— watching *The Sixth Sense*.

Happy haunting, happy encounters!

PART I
GREAT GHOSTS OF THE PAST

L et us return to the past... to meet some of the famous ghosts and celebrated spirits of yesteryear. I like to think there is a ghost for every community in the country. And when a community has an independent local newspaper, there is likely to be a ghost story—if not a spirit—lurking about! During the Victorian period, the newspapers were a lot more lively than they are today, since they were truly local and not yet links in various newspaper chains. In their columns, "his ghostship," to use one of the wry terms of the period, customarily took up residence in the oldest structure in town, whether it was a log cabin, a pioneer farmstead, a courthouse, a church, a churchyard, or the cemetery. Some of this lore has survived into our own time, preserved in the columns of the local newspapers.

We can attribute the sparseness of traditions of ghosts and hauntings in English Canada during the 18th and 19th centuries to a number of causes. One is that the educated people in the community—the doctors and lawyers, businessmen and bankers—scoffed at intangibles like spirits. Intangibles couldn't be bought or sold, so they had no "net worth" and they couldn't be assessed and taxed. You might think that the clergymen of the day would be sensitive to "spiritual presences," but that wasn't the case. From the pulpit, the minister and the priest regularly denounced what were dismissed as superstitious beliefs and practices. It was suggested that such "remnants" of pagan thought were "the works of the devil," and hence right-thinking people would avoid them at all costs.

Another reason that the knowledge of traditional hauntings tended to disappear is that most episodes were local affairs and not known outside their communities. These were often sporadic occurrences rather than recurrent hauntings. Farmer Brown saw the spectre of his dead son in the upstairs room of his farmhouse, the bedroom to the right of the stairs. Or groups of neighbours were drawn to the McDonald farmhouse because of reports of poltergeist-like activity there: Mysterious fires broke out, red-hot nails fell from the ceiling, crockery flew about, weird sounds were heard, eerie messages appeared on walls, and so on. Then, abruptly, everything returned to normal. The haunting might be a one-day affair or a seven-day wonder. No matter its duration, the occurrences were rooted in the region, on the quarter-section perhaps, and the distances to the next crossroads were measured in furlongs and then miles. Such was the local and limited fame of the ghost or the poltergeist in 19th-century Canada.

Despite the scepticism of the local populace and the remoteness of many of the communities, before the turn of the 20th century there were some hauntings in the country that were notable at the time and remain so to this day. These early hauntings attained a level of fame (or infamy), a degree of note (or notoriety), that few if any hauntings have subsequently attained. Some of them were known nationally and even throughout the British Empire.

The six early hauntings featured in this first section are appreciated by connoisseurs of true ghost stories throughout the English-speaking world. These stories occurred in Canada in the 18th and 19th centuries and are among the most thrilling in the present collection. They are classic tales and are accepted as true ghost stories by ghosthunters, psychical researchers, parapsychologists, psychologists, sociologists, and folklorists. Five are reprinted from the columns of 19th-century newspapers. The sixth, "The Mackenzie River Ghost," seems not to have been reported or recalled in a newspaper during the Victorian period, so it appears here as it appeared in a 19th-century book of travel.

A crisis apparition occurs when the spirit or apparition of a dying person appears to a relative or friend in another part of the world at the point of dying or great stress. There is much literature on Canada's most famous crisis apparition—the so-called Wynyard apparition. The account that appears here suggests that it is little more than folklore, what today we might call an urban myth. Indeed, it does seem to be a well-travelled tale. Yet, in its classic form, it is well documented. It concerns Lieutenant (later General) Wynyard and Captain John C. Sherbrooke (later Lieutenant-Governor of Nova Scotia and still later Governor General of Canada). It took place at approximately four o'clock in the afternoon of October 15, 1785, in the officers' quarters of the British garrison in Sydney, Nova Scotia. Here it is treated as a traditional ghost story, one that grows in the telling and that shifts ground a lot. But it also appears in the standard biography of Governor General Sherbrooke written by A. Patchett Martin.

A poltergeist is generally described as "a noisy ghost." It goes unseen but is known by its effects. "The Baldoon Mystery" concerns the poltergeist-like activities that took place on the McDonald farm near Baldoon, a Scottish farming community located northwest of Chatham, Ontario. All manner of disturbances were reported by farmer John McDonald, family members, members of the farming community, and travellers and mediums during the three-year period from 1829 to 1831. The disturbances included a hail of bullets, stones, lead pellets, water, and sporadic fires. It is said that at one point the small wooden farmhouse heaved from its very foundations. One fateful night, it was consumed in flames and burnt to the ground. These disturbances were never satisfactorily explained, though many fanciful tales were told about the cause of the disruptions, including the curse of a witch, followed by the summoning of a witch doctor. The account that appears here has never before been reprinted.

The fame and fascination of "The Great Amherst Mystery" spread far and wide because professional interest in the matter was shown by a touring New York actor named Walter Hubbell. A man of curiosity and invention, he read newspaper accounts of the poltergeist-like activities that were taking place in 1878 and 1879 at the Cox family cottage in Amherst, Nova Scotia, and decided to visit the site. He boarded at the cottage, wrote an account of some of the happenings, and in the process coined the phrase "the great Amherst mystery." He did his best to publicize and popularize the disturbances, first through a roadshow starring himself and the poor young woman, Esther Cox, and second through writing a booklet titled, inevitably, *The Great Amherst Mystery.*

Hubbell would be surprised to learn that the effects he described as taking place in the Cox cottage would, fifty years later, through a stroke of fate—call it serendipity—be replayed in the haunting of Borley Rectory, Sussex. In its day, Borley Rectory was known as "the most haunted house in England." If that is indeed so, the Cox family cottage could be considered to have been, in its day, "the most haunted house in Canada."

The case of the Binstead haunting, widely discussed in the late 19th century, has been all but forgotten in the early 21st century. The account of the haunting appeared in the prestigious *Journal of the Society for Psychical Research* as part of the section titled "On Recognised Apparitions Occurring More than a Year after Death" (*JSPR*, July 8, 1889). The Society for Psychical Research had been founded by a group of British scientists to conduct psychical research, study mediumship, document hallucinations, and investigate what was quaintly called "spirit-survival." The author of the account is identified, also quaintly, as "Mrs. Pennée, of St. Anne de Beaupré, Quebec, daughter of the late Mr. William Ward (a Conservative M.P. for London), and sister of the late Rev. A.B. Ward, of Cambridge." The calm of the estate, located outside East River, Prince Edward Island, was compromised by events that took place in its past; they led to the appearance of "a woman with a baby" in one arm who stirred ashes in the fireplace with the other.

The text of the account printed here (with some additional comments by the *JSPR*'s editor) is based on the version that appeared in the journal rather than the one that was published in the newspaper. The newspaper's account was headed "A Real Ghost!" and began with the following words: "The English Society for Psychical Research is still vigorously pursuing its investigations and is about to publish part XV of its proceedings, containing articles on apparitions, duplex personality, and séances with the celebrated medium, D.D. Home, &c." Minor variations in punctuation and spelling were noted, but the principal difference between the versions is that the newspaper story is shorter than the journal story. The newspaper story ends before the introduction of the second and third letters. The full version is the one featured here.

"The Dagg Poltergeist" is the case of a ruckus caused by "an invisible inhabitant of the woodshed" on the Dagg family farm in Shawville, on the Ottawa River, in 1889. There are at least three interesting features to this lively story. First, the effects of the poltergeist-like spirit were observed by many members of the community in the Ottawa Valley, who swore on oath that the manifestations occurred precisely as described. Second, it features Percy Woodcock, an ambitious reporter who offered readers of the *Brockville Recorder and Times* exclusive, eyewitness accounts of happenings on the farm before giving them exposure across North America. Third, the story was dramatized by the National Film Board of Canada, and it includes an interview with the country's leading psychical researcher, R.S. Lambert.

"The Mackenzie River Ghost," the most famous true ghost story of the Northwest, received its greatest exposure through its appearance in *Lord Halifax's Ghost Book* (1936), an influential and widely read compilation of English ghost stories prepared by Charles Lindley, Viscount. The events themselves took place in the Great Northwest in 1853 and 1854: a fur trader, accompanying a corpse by dogsled from Fort McPherson, in the Mackenzie River District, to Fort Simpson, heard the corpse utter the command *"Marché!"* at times that turned out to be critical to the survival of the group.

It is told here in the words of Roderick MacFarlane (1835–1920), Fellow of the Royal Geographical Society and a fur trader in the Northwest Territories for over forty years. It was MacFarlane who established Fort Smith in 1874, and it was at his instigation that the first steamship for travel on the Mackenzie River was constructed in 1886. MacFarlane was the principal witness to the eerie experiences recorded in this account and recalled what he had observed at the request of a scholar at Oxford University in 1883. The full account appeared as "Ghost Story" in *The Beaver*, December 1986–January 1987. (That account is the original one, and it is reproduced here.) It was given semi-factual, semi-fictional treatment by the British officer and explorer Sir W.F. Butler in *Good Words* (1877) and was retold by Ernest Thompson Seton in *Trail and Campfire Stories* (1940). Noted ghosthunter R.S. Lambert, in *Exploring the Supernatural: The Weird in Canadian Folklore* (1955), called the story "the most convincing of all Canadian apparitions."

So here are six of Canada's classic spooks!

The Wynyard Apparition

MONTREAL HERALD
NOVEMBER 6, 1822

Sir John Sherbrooke and George Wynyard were, as young men, officers in the same regiment, which was employed on foreign service. They were connected by similarity of taste and studies, and spent together in literary occupation, much of that vacant time which was squandered by their brother officers in those excesses of the table, which some forty years ago, were considered among the necessary accomplishments of the military character. They were one afternoon sitting in Wynyard's apartment. It was perfect light, the hour was about four o'clock; they had dined but neither of them had drank wine, and they had retired from the mess to continue together the occupations of the day—I ought to have said, that the apartment in which they were had two doors in it, the one opening into a passage, and the other opening into Wynyard's bedroom. There were no other means of entering the sitting room but from the passage, and no other egress from the bed-room but through the sitting room; so that any person passing into the bed-room must have remained there, unless he returned by the way he entered. This point is of consequence to the story. As these two young officers were pursuing their studies, Sherbrooke, whose eye happened accidentally to glance from the volume before him towards the door that opened in the passageway, observed a tall youth, of about 20 years of age, whose appearance was that of extreme emaciation, standing behind him. Struck with the presence of a perfect stranger, he immediately turned to his friend, who was sitting near him, and directed his attention to the guest who had thus strangely broken in upon their studies. As soon as Wynyard's eyes were turned towards the mysterious visitor, his countenance became suddenly agitated. "I have heard," says

Sir John Sherbrooke, "of a man's being as white as death, but I never saw a living face assume the appearance of a corpse, except Wynyard's at the moment. As they looked silently at the form before them—for Wynyard, who seemed to apprehend the import of the appearance, was deprived of the faculty of speech, and Sherbrooke, perceiving the agitation of his friend, felt no inclination to address it—as they looked silently upon the figure, it proceeded slowly into the adjoining apartment, and in the act of passing them, cast its eyes with an expression of somewhat melancholy affection on Wynyard. The oppression of this extraordinary presence was no sooner removed than Wynyard, seizing his friend by the arm, and drawing a deep breath, as if recovering from the suffocation of intense astonishment and emotion, muttered in a low and almost inaudible tone of voice: "Good God! My brother!"

"Your brother," repeated Sherbrooke, "what can you mean, Wynyard? There must be some deception—follow me," and immediately taking his friend by the arm, he preceded him into the bed-room, which, as I before stated, was connected with the sitting room, and into which the strange visitor had evidently entered. I have already said that from this chamber there was no possibility of withdrawing but by the way of the apartment through which the figure had certainly passed, and as certainly never had returned. Wynyard's mind had received an impression at the first moment of his observing him that the figure whom he had seen was the spirit of his brother. Sherbrooke still persevered in strenuously believing that some imposition had been practised. They took note of the day and hour in which the event had happened; but they resolved not to mention the occurrence in the regiment, and gradually they persuaded each other they had been imposed upon by some of their fellow officers, though they could neither account for the reason, or suspect the author, or conceive the means of its execution. They were content to imagine anything possible rather than admit the possibility of a supernatural appearance. But though they had attempted these stratagems of self-delusion, Wynyard could not help expressing his solicitude with respect to the safety of the brother whose apparition he had either seen or imagined himself to have seen, and the anxiety which he exhibited for letters from England, and his frequent mention of his fears for his brother's health, at length awakened the curiosity of his comrades, and eventually betrayed him into a declaration of the circumstances which he had in vain determined to conceal. The story of the silent and unbidden visitor was no sooner bruited abroad than the destiny of Wynyard's brother became an object of universal and painful interest to the officers of the regiment; there were few who did not inquire for Wynyard's letters before they made any demand after their own, and the packets that arrived from England were welcomed with more than usual eagerness, for they brought, not only remembrances from their friends at home, but promised to afford a clue to the mystery which had happened among themselves. By the first ship no intelligence relating to the story could have been received, for they had all departed from England previously to the appearance of the spirit. At length the long-wished-for vessels arrived; all the officers had letters except Wynyard. Still the secret was unexplained. They examined the several newspapers; they contained no mention of any death, or of any other circumstance connected with his family, that could account for the preternatural event. There was a solitary letter for Sherbrooke still unopened. The officers had received their letters in the mess room at the hour of supper. After Sherbrooke had broken the seal of his last packet, and cast a glance on its contents, he beckoned his friend away from the company, and departed from the room. All were silent. The suspense of the interest was now at its climax; the impatience for the return of Sherbrooke was inexpressible. They doubted not but that letter had contained the long-expected intelligence. At the interval of one hour Sherbrooke joined them. No one dared be guilty of such rudeness as to enquire the nature of his correspondence; but they waited in mute attention, expecting that he would himself touch upon the subject. His mind was manifestly full of thoughts that pained, bewildered and oppressed him. He drew near the fireplace, and leaning his head on the mantle piece, after a pause of some moments, said, in a low voice, to the person who was nearest to him, "Wynyard's brother is no more." The first line of Sherbrooke's letter was, "Dear John, break to your friend Wynyard the death of his favourite brother." He had died on the way and at the very hour on which the friend had seen his spirit pass so mysteriously through the apartment.

It might have been imagined that these events would have been sufficient to have impressed the mind of Sherbrooke with the conviction of their truth; but so strong was his prepossession against the existence, or even the possibility, of any preternatural intercourse with the souls of the dead, that he still entertained a doubt of the report of his senses, supported as their testimony was by the coincidence of vision and event. Some years after, on his return from England, he was walking with two gentlemen in Piccadilly when, on the opposite side of the way, he saw a person bearing the most striking resemblance to the figure which had been disclosed to Wynyard and himself. His companions were acquainted with the story, and he instantly directed their attention to the gentleman opposite as the individual who had contrived to enter and depart from Wynyard's apartments without their being conscious of the means. Full of the impression, he immediately went over and at once addressed the gentleman; he now fully expected to elucidate the mystery. He apologized for the interruption, but excused it by relating the occurrence which had induced to this solecism in manners. He had never been out of the country, but he was the twin brother of the youth whose spirit had been seen.

This story is related with several variations. It is sometimes told as having happened in Gibraltar, at others in England, at others in America. There are also differences with respect to the conclusion. Some say that gentleman who Sir John Sherbrooke afterwards met in London, and addressed, as the person whom he had previously seen in so mysterious a manner, was not another brother of General Wynyard, but a gentleman who bore a strong resemblance to the family. But however, the leading facts in every account are the same. Sir John Sherbrooke and General Wynyard, two gentlemen of veracity, were together present at the spiritual appearance of the brother of General Wynyard; the appearance took place at the moment of dissolution; and the countenance and form of the ghost's figure were so distinctly impressed upon the memory of Sir John Sherbrooke, to whom the living man had been unknown, that on accidentally meeting with his likeness, he perceived and acknowledged the resemblance.

If this story be true, it silences the common objections that ghosts always appear at night and are never visible to two persons at the same time.

The Baldoon Mystery

THE GLOBE (TORONTO)
SEPTEMBER 8, 1894

Unsolved Mystery
Haunted House of the Baldoon Settlement
A Tale of Forty Years Ago
Missiles Thrown by Unseen Hands
Beds that Rocked and Rose in the Air
Strange Behaviour of a Musket
Unaccountable Phenomena
(Special Correspondent of The Globe*)*

Just at the present time, when the haunted schoolhouse in Grey is exciting attention, it seems proper to recall another mystery, which, happening more than forty years ago, has never been satisfactorily explained, unless, indeed, we fall back on the ever-present doubt, inherent in us all, that, despite our outward and often thrust-forward scepticism, there may indeed be unseen forces around us—a spirit world in which we have no part, and of which we rarely witness manifestations.

For myself, I am a sceptic of sceptics—brought up by my Scotch ancestors to disbelieve in the existence of such phantoms—nay, trained rather to look on the discussion of which even to rank heresy, I entertain a well-grounded distrust of ghost stories in general, and for my own part have never seen anything to shake that prejudice. But when one converses with a man whose word has never been doubted, and he relates a circumstantial story of spooks with the matter-of-fact air which precludes doubt, it kind of staggers one's firm belief.

When, moreover, one inquires further and learns that a whole community, or the older people at least, implicitly believe this story, and that there are still several living witnesses, believable in all other affairs of life, it gives one's preconceived notions another and more severe jar, and one naturally questions himself: Can these things be true?

Such was my experience a few days ago in the pleasant Town of Wallaceburg, where I first heard of what has been called "The Baldoon Mystery"—a mystery which made much noise thereabouts some forty-odd years ago. And first, let me tell you where Baldoon is.

At the beginning of the present century, Lord Selkirk, in passing up our noble chain of lakes and rivers to his Red River settlement, noticed the beauty of a little peninsula, formed by the junction of the Sydenham and St. Clair Rivers. With an eye ever on the lookout for choice sites for his hardy Scotch settlers, he saw that this would be a splendid field for growing corn and other supplies for his colony scattered along the Red River of the north, for at that time it was supposed that none of the food grains could be grown so far north.

Just above the peninsula the green woods of Walpole Island—peopled then and now with dusky red men—divided the blue waters of the St. Clair and the current, clear and sparkling, which flowed past to meet the muddy Sydenham, which had been christened by the early French explorers "Chenail Ecarté"—the lost channel—because it does not mix with the turbid Sydenham, but plunges under it, too proud to soil its lovely waters. This beautifully poetic name just now locally degenerated into the home-spun title of "The Sny," whatever that means.

Origin of Baldoon

At the "meeting of the waters," on the rich alluvial soil carried down by the two rivers, Lord Selkirk in 1804 founded the Baldoon settlement. On the extreme point of the peninsula, where the snow-flowing Sydenham met the limpid St. Clair, he erected a huge wind-mill, so that every field could be supplied with water, and on the Sydenham side extensive sheep-folds testified to the thrift of his settlers. Every season long boats, propelled slowly by oars called "batteaux," came down from the other settlement on the Red River, nearly a thousand miles away, and took back the surplus corn, wood, etc., of the Baldoon settlers.

Most of these settlers came from Argyleshire, and four family names were especially conspicuous, McDonalds, McDougalls, McGregors and McLeans. They had been specially chosen by Lord Selkirk for their physique and are described as models of womanly and manly beauty. At the present day their descendants, now scattered over a wide area, may be distinguished by their generous, open faces and lordly bearing. As the families intermarried and increased, it became difficult to distinguish the names apart, so that it was customary to call them "Farmer" McDonald, "Tailor" McDonald, etc., from their trade, or for any particularity, even.

Just outside the Baldoon settlement proper, and up the Chenail Ecarté about half a mile, there stood in 1829 a small log house, fronting the river, inhabited by a man named John McDonald, though he usually was called John "Tailor," as tailoring was his business, and many of his customers never knew that McDonald was his real name. This man was not from Argyleshire, like the other surrounding settlers, but from the islands of Arran off the Scottish coast. Subsequent developments caused his past history to be looked into rather carefully, but the most searching inquiries failed to discern anything discreditable.

Early in the spring of that year his modest little home acquired a notoriety, through strange manifestations which suddenly made their appearance. Perhaps the story may best be told by Mr. L.A. McDougall of Wallaceburg, a very old gentleman, but remarkably intelligent. Here it is as I gathered it from him a few days ago at his residence in the town:—

A Strange Story

"You are one of the original Baldoon settlers, I believe, Mr. McDougall," I asked.

"No, not exactly, for I was born six years after my father settled there, and I am now 84," he answered, in the deep bass of a Highlander.

"But you remember distinctly what was called the Baldoon mystery?" I persisted.

"Oh, yes; that was only about forty years ago"—as if forty years were only a slight gap.

"Would you mind telling me the particulars of that affair, Mr. McDougall?"

"Not at all, not at all," but turning quickly towards me, so that the light streamed full across his wrinkled but still handsome face. "Have you read the book they published about it some years ago?"

Upon my answer that I had not, he said, half to himself: "Just as well, just as well; most of it was lies, anyhow."

Then, settling himself back more comfortably in his chair, he resumed. "I was going up the river to Algonac one day that spring in my boat, with another man, and when we were opposite the tailor's house I noticed the women run out of the house screaming, as if frightened, and looking back again and again. We rowed into the shore, and asked them what was the matter. They said stones were coming in through windows. 'Stones?' we asked them again. 'Yes, stones from the bed of the river.' We ran over to the house and, sir, it was just as they said. Big and little stones were lying on the floor, and the windows were all broken. While we were looking more stones came crashing through, and we ran outside to see who was throwing them, but there was not as much as a bush in front to hide in, and nobody in sight. The river, about half a mile wide, ran directly in front of the house."

"Did these stones come from any great force, Mr. McDougall?"

"Not particularly," he answered. "They broke the windows and rolled across to the opposite wall, where they lay in little heaps."

"Did you pick them up and examine them?"

"Oh, yes; they were ordinary river stones of all shapes."

"Did you see any other uncanny signs then, Mr. McDougall?"

"Not at that time; but about two weeks after, hearing that they were still going on"—he invariably referred to the manifestations as "they"—"I went up and stopped over Sunday. The family had returned to the house, and I slept with one of the tailor's sons. During the night the bed began to wave back and forth in the air, as if we were at sea. My companion was sleeping soundly, so I woke him up and asked him did he feel the motion of the bed. He drowsily answered, 'Yes,' but said he was getting used to that sort of thing—that every night he heard carriages rolling across the roof before he went to sleep, and often the bed was up against the roof. In a short time he was again asleep, but I tell you I did not sleep much, for, besides the bed, once in a while a stone would come bang against the house."

There Was No Ghost

"Did you see anything ghostly, Mr. McDougall?" I asked.

"Nothing at all," he answered, "though I watched closely. We all went to church Sunday morning, and, coming home, one of the girls went ahead and unlocked the door of the house. Instantly she came screaming back to us, and on going up we found all the furniture, bedding, stoves and everything, piled up in a window from one corner to the other."

"How long did these things continue, Mr. McDougall?" I asked him.

"For nearly a year, and people came from Chatham and all over to see them go on," he answered. "The Catholics said that if a priest was brought he could stop them; but one did come from Chatham, and stayed for a week, but it was no use. They got worse, if anything, and the house began to get on fire, a dozen times a day, now, besides the stones. Many people took lead balls, and, marking them, threw them out as far as they could in the river, but in a moment they would be back again in the room. At last they boarded up the windows, but as soon as a door was opened they came in there, and the house itself used to be bombarded day and night. One day a stranger came along on horse-back—there were scarcely any taverns then—and asked the tailor could he stay all night. The tailor answered, yes, if he was not afraid of spir-its. While they were talking at the door an old musket which hung on the opposite wall came down, and after going around the room it came and stood directly in front of the stranger's horse. 'If that's the kind of people you are, I'm away,' said the man in a frightened voice, as he drove the spurs into his horse."

"How did the people generally account for these things, Mr. McDougall?"

"Some said the tailor sold one of his children to the devil in the old country, but I never believed that story, for he always seemed a respectable, quiet man. Some others blamed a schoolmaster in Wallaceburg, and he lost his position through it, and went away, but they kept right on. At last, after the house had taken fire hundreds of times, they took out their furniture and let it burn down. They put up another, but it always could take fire day or night, and often right in the room where you were sitting the wall would blaze up. Finally, the tai-lor and his family moved to another house near Wallaceburg, but the same things happened—stones came through the windows, etc.—and they moved back again, as their landlord did not want them to remain."

"How did it end at last, Mr. McDougall?" I asked.

"It ended as suddenly as it began; they simply stopped themselves, and it became like any other house after a year of excitement."

Now, reader, you will naturally ask me, "Are these strange stories true?" That question I will not try to answer. You have them as I heard them from this courteous and respectable old gentleman, and draw your own conclusions. If at any time you visit the pretty little town of Wallaceburg, you can question for yourself; but, speaking generally, I may say this: they are usually believed there to be gospel truths, for they are vouched for by men of the highest standing. I may also add that one of "the tailor's" sons lives now in Marine City, Michigan.

The Great Amherst Mystery

THE BORDERER (AMHERST, NOVA SCOTIA)
DECEMBER 4, 1878

A Nova Scotia Mystery

Running in a southerly direction from Church Street, Amherst, and parallel with Main Street, is a thoroughfare which leads in the direction of the railway station. A short distance below Church Street corner is the house occupied by Mr. Daniel Teed, a respected resident of the town, who holds a position in the Amherst Shoe Factory. The house is an ordinary two-storey dwelling. In the rear is a barn, to which we shall refer. The occupants of the house are Mr. Teed, his wife and infant, Miss Esther Cox, and Miss Jane Cox. The last named are sisters of Mrs. Teed, and are young women past twenty years of age. Miss Esther is the central figure in the story. Her health has been good, and she has lived until recently undisturbed by mysterious influences, and in ignorance of the theories of practices of spiritualistic mediums. The first indication of anything unusual was a mesmeric trance, by which she was overcome during her early illness, eight weeks ago. One night she retired to bed with her sister Jane, and scarcely had she done so when a noise was heard in a pasteboard box, containing scraps of cloths, which was under the bed. Little attention was paid to this, as it was supposed to be the work of a mouse, nor were the girls much disturbed when they heard it in the straw of the ticking. They went to sleep and their slumbers were not interrupted. On the following night they again retired, and again the mysterious noise was heard. This time it was of a more positive character, for the box was violently overturned. Much alarmed, the sisters called their brother, who responded to their call, righted the box, placed the cover on it, and set it in the middle of the floor. The effect was most surprising, for not only was the box again overturned, but the cover flew through the air and landed on top of the table. As often as the test was made, so often did the same result follow, and as was natural enough, much alarm was felt at these extraordinary manifestations. The unknown (we hardly know the term to apply to it) now entered upon its work in earnest, and for four nights it continued its freaks, varying its method on each occasion. When the girls went to bed, it would seize the quilts and drag them to one corner of the bed, pillows would be pulled from under Esther's head by the invisible influence, and with such force was this done that she was unable to hold on and prevent the articles moving. Strange rappings were next heard in various places where Esther was, and during the day as well as night. Mr. John White went to the house one morning and as Esther went out to the barn a terrific pounding, which is described as resembling a one hundred and fifty-six pound weight falling in succession on the roof, commenced at once, and continued until Esther ran back to the house. This pounding has always been loud when she has gone to the barn, but it has been fully as loud around the house. When Esther goes into the cellar it sounds as if a colossal fist were pounding on the beams with the fury of a demon. In order to test Esther's good faith, her hands have been tied behind her back, but the pounding was instantaneous and as loud as before. Other persons have accompanied her and have satisfied themselves that the noise was made by no human agency visible to mortal eye. Sometimes the pounding is in one room and sometimes in another. It is as heavy as the blows of an axe would be, but has more of a dead sound, as if it were a flesh-covered fist. Rapping commenced in the early history of the case. It resembles a drumming on a board with the fingers and nails of a person's hand. It was first heard on the slats under the bed, on the wall and around the bedpost. To an unpracticed ear it is suggestive of telegraphy, but it is not that, and is more like the tippy-tip-tap of an impatient boy. Dr. Carritte, as the medical attendant, has endeavoured to trace the noise to some agency, but has failed to do so. Esther has been placed sitting on the top of the bedclothes, where the slightest motion of her body could be observed, but though she has remained motionless the noise has continued. She has been seated on a chair placed on thick rugs in the middle of the floor, and the rapping was as if someone were tapping on the wall with the knuckles. Sometimes it taps on the legs of a table, a chair, a shelf—anything so long as Esther is present. More than this, it is musical. It beats the measure of "Yankee Doodle" and "Somebody Tapping at the Garden Gate" while it regularly keeps time with anyone [who] whistles or sings. During Esther's sickness it frequently slapped her in the face, causing much pain and leaving a conspicuous red mark. Esther is not a facile writer, but when she takes a pencil in her hand and places it against the wall, it is guided by an influence which she cannot resist, and writes sentences of which she has not the remote thought. We are sorry to say that some of these sentences are very wicked ones and are most horribly profane. The writing is not at all like Esther's, but it is said to be exactly like that of a certain young man. Not only is the language far from choice, and such as Esther is not capable of using, but the spelling is most atrocious. "I ded rit to her Cister," is intended to signify "I did write to her sister." The sentences are incoherent, but they have declared that they are from the man in question, and his latest proclamation is that there will be great sport in three weeks' time. On one occasion, the unknown is said to have scratched a word on the plaster when no one was present. A Mr. Campbell was in the house, and the name "Cammal" was scratched on the wall as if with a pin. The word is there, however it got there. The scratching noise, like nails scratching over a smooth board, is heard frequently, and is enough to send a chill down the backs of nervous persons. The bed on which Esther has slept is marked in various places, as if a hot iron was rapidly passed over it in an irregular manner. On one occasion, when twelve persons were in the room, Esther lay in bed, with her hands outside the cover-lid. The bed clothes were violently agitated; but the pillow acted as if literally "possessed of a devil." It would leap towards Esther's head, strike her and bound back, and this it continued to do several times. Two persons then took hold of the corners of it and stood several feet away from the bed. The pillow straightened itself out horizontally in the direction of Esther, and those who held it declare that a weight of twenty-five or thirty pounds seemed pulling against them. When it could not get away it elongated itself to its utmost capacity just as a piece of elastic rubber would do, and wriggled and squirmed like a leech in a jar of water. A hat placed on the bed stood on the edge of its rim and pirouetted and danced around as if suspended by a string. This was witnessed by at least a dozen persons, several of them being ladies of high respectability.

On Saturday last, we are told, Esther felt the influence at work on her shoe string, and in another moment, though the string had been tied in a hard knot, the boot was unlaced. Later manifestations are in the nature of chair and table tippings. A few days ago the cradle in which the baby was lying was rocked for some time by invisible hands. An ordinary wooden chair on which Esther was sitting, with her feet on the rug, began to tip backwards and forwards, and she was rocked as if in a rocking-chair. Chairs follow her. She went to the street door, and a chair followed her the entire distance. She went into the pantry, closing the door after her, and when she came out every chair in the kitchen had piled itself against its neighbour at the door, as if seeking admittance. On Tuesday, when she was walking through the cellar, a basket of beets took a notion to follow her, and travelled actively over the floor, accommodating itself with great ease to any irregularities in the planking. Another curious thing, at times, is the action of the water in its pail when Esther is present. The water will be violently agitated into a whirlpool, and will foam like the waves of the tide.

Among the clergymen who have visited the house are Rev. Messrs. Temple, Jarvis, and Sutcliffe, of Amherst, and Rev. Edwin Clay, M.D., of Pugwash. The latter well-known gentleman is a biologist and is thoroughly versed in what is known as psychology and animal magnetism. He came under the impression that he could put an end to the disturbance, but after devoting the best part of two days to the effort he went away baffled, and wholly unable to account for the manifestations, of the existence of which he had such positive face-to-face proof.

The *Yarmouth Herald*, referring to the mystery, says: "A similar case in Yarmouth about seventy years ago attracted much local attention, and has been familiarly known as the 'Rub-a-dub.' There are persons still living who remember the excitement it created at the time."

The Binstead Haunting

DAILY EXAMINER (CHARLOTTETOWN, PEI) NOVEMBER 28, 1889

XIV—The following case, which we owe to the kindness of Mr. Wilfrid Ward (and of Lord Tennyson, for whom it was first committed to writing some years ago), is sent by Mrs. Pennée, of St. Anne de Beaupré, Quebec, daughter of the late Mr. William Ward (a Conservative M.P. for London), and sister of the late Rev. A.B. Ward, of Cambridge.

WESTON MANOR, Freshwater, Isle of Wight, 1884—It was in the year 1856 that my husband took me to live at a house called Binstead, about five miles from Charlottetown, Prince Edward Island. It was a good-sized house, and at the back had been considerably extended to allow for extra offices, since there were about two hundred acres of farm land around it, necessitating several resident farming men. Although forming part of the house, these premises could only be entered through the inner kitchen, as no wall had ever been broken down to form a door or passage from upstairs. Thus the farming men's sleeping rooms were adjacent to those occupied by the family and visitors, although there was no communication through the upstairs corridor.

It was always in or near the sleeping apartment immediately adjacent to the men's that the apparition was seen, and as that was one of our spare bedrooms, it may have frequently been unperceived.

About ten days after we had established ourselves at Binstead, we commenced hearing strange noises. For many weeks they were of very frequent occurrence, and were heard simultaneously in every part of the house, and always appeared to be in close proximity to each person. The noise was more like a rumbling which made the house vibrate than like that produced by dragging a heavy body, of which one so often hears in ghost stories.

As spring came on we began to hear shrieks, which would grow fainter or louder, as if someone was being chased around the house, but always culminating in a volley of shrieks, sobs, moans, and half-uttered words, proceeding from beneath a tree that stood at a little distance from the dining-room window, and whose branches nearly touched the window of the bedroom I have mentioned.

It was in February (I think), 1857, that the first apparition came under my notice. Two ladies were sleeping in the bedroom. Of course, for that season of the year a fire had been lighted in the grate, and the fireplace really contained a grate and not an American substitute for one.

About two o'clock, Mrs. M. was awakened by a bright light which pervaded the room. She saw a woman standing by the fireplace. On her left arm was a young baby, and with her right hand she was stirring the ashes, over which she was slightly stooping.

Mrs. M. pushed Miss C. to awaken her, and just then the figure turned her face towards them, disclosing the features of quite a young woman with a singularly anxious pleading look upon her face. They took notice of a little check shawl which was crossed over her bosom. Miss C. had previously heard some tales concerning the house being haunted (which neither Mrs. M. nor I had ever heard), so jumping to the conclusion that she beheld a ghost, she screamed and pulled the bedclothes tightly over the heads of herself and her companion, so that the sequel of the ghost's proceedings is unknown.

The following spring I went home to England, and just before starting I had my own experience of seeing a ghost. I had temporarily established myself in the room, and one evening, finding my little daughter (now Mrs. Amyot) far from well, had her bed wheeled in beside mine that I might attend to her. About twelve o'clock I got up to give her some medicine, and was feeling for the matches when she called my attention to a brilliant light shining under the door. I exclaimed that it was her papa and threw open the door to admit him. I found myself face to face with a woman. She had a baby on her left arm, a check shawl crossed over her bosom, and all around her shone a bright pleasant light, whence emanating I could not say. Her look at me was one of entreaty—almost agonizing entreaty. She did not enter the room but moved across the staircase, vanishing into the opposite wall, exactly where the inner man-servant's room was situated.

Neither my daughter nor myself felt the slightest alarm; at the moment it appeared to be a matter of common occurrence. When Mr. Pennée came upstairs and I told him what we had seen, he examined the wall, the staircase, the passage, but found no traces of anything extraordinary. Nor did my dogs bark.

On my return from England in 1858 I was informed that "the creature had been carrying on," but it was the screams that had been the worst. However, Harry (a farm-servant) had had several visits but would tell no particulars. I never could get Harry to tell me much. He acknowledged that the woman had several times stood at the foot of his bed, but he would not tell me more. One night Harry had certainly been much disturbed in mind, and the other man heard voices and sobs.

Nothing would ever induce Harry to let anyone share his room, and he was most careful to fasten his door before retiring. At the time, I attached no importance to "his ways," as we called them.

In the autumn of the following year, 1859, my connection with Binstead ceased, for we gave up the house and returned to Charlottetown.

I left Prince Edward Island in 1861, and went to Quebec. In 1877 I happened to return to the Island, and spent several months there. One day I was at the Bishop's residence, when the parish priest came in with a letter in his hand. He asked me about my residence at Binstead, and whether I could throw any light on the contents of his letter. It was from the wife of the then owner of Binstead, asking him to come out and try to deliver them from the ghost of a young woman with a baby in her arms, who had appeared several times.

After I went to live in Charlottetown, I became acquainted with the following facts, which seem to throw light on my ghost story.

The ground on which Binstead stood had been cleared, in about 1840, by a rich Englishman, who had built a very nice house. Getting tired of colonial life, he sold the property to a man whose name I forget, but whom I will call Pigott (that was like the name). He was a man of low tastes and immoral habits, but a capital farmer. It was he who added all the back wings of the house and made the necessary divisions, &c., for farming the land. He had two sisters in his service, the daughters of a labourer who lived in a regular hovel, about three miles nearer town. After a time each sister gave birth to a boy.

Very little can be learnt of the domestic arrangements, since Pigott bore so bad a name that the house was avoided by respectable people; but it is certain that one sister and one baby disappeared altogether, though when and how is a complete mystery.

When the other baby was between one and two years old, Pigott sold Binstead to an English gentleman named Fellowes, from whom we hired it, with the intention of eventually buying it. The other sister returned to her father's house, and leaving the baby with Mrs. Newbury, her mother, went to the States, and has never returned. Before leaving she would reveal nothing, except that the boy was her sister's, her own being dead. It was this very Harry Newbury that we had unwittingly engaged as a farm-servant. He came to bid me farewell a few months after I left Binstead, saying he would never return there. In 1877, I inquired about him, and found that he had never been seen since in Prince Edward Island.

In another letter dated September 24th, 1887, Mrs. Pennée adds:

Another fact has come to my notice. A young lady, then a child of from five to ten, remembers being afraid of sleeping alone when on a visit at Binstead on account of the screams she heard outside, and also the "woman with a baby," whom she saw passing through her room. Her experience goes back some ten to fifteen years before mine.

In a further letter, dated St. Anne de Beaupré, Quebec, January 23rd, 1889, Mrs. Pennée gives additional facts, as follows:

(1) Mrs. Pennée interviewed Father Boudreault, the priest sent for by the C. family to exorcise the house. Father B., however, was on his death-bed; and although he remembered the fact that he had been sent for to Binstead for this purpose, he could not recollect what had been told him as to apparitions, &c.

(2) Mrs. M., who first saw the figure, has gone to England, and cannot now be traced. Mrs. Pennée adds: "The lady in question told several people that she saw a woman with a baby in her arms when she slept at Binstead; and, like myself, she noticed a frilled cap on the woman. The woman whose ghost we imagine this to be was an Irish woman, and perhaps you have noticed their love of wide frills in their head-gear."

(3) Mrs. Pennée revisited Binstead in 1888, and says, "The tree whence the screams started is cut down; the room where all saw the ghost is totally uninhabited; and Mrs. C. would not let us stay in it, and entreated us to talk no further on the subject. From the man we got out a little, but she followed us up very closely. He says that since the priest blessed the house a woman has been seen (or said to have been

seen, he corrected himself) round the front entrance, and once at an upper window."

The list of cases cited in this and the previous paper, while insufficient (as I have already said) to compel conviction, is striking enough to plead for serious attention to a subject which will never be properly threshed out unless the interest taken in it assumes a scientific rather than an emotional form.

The Dagg Poltergeist

OTTAWA FREE PRESS
NOVEMBER 25, 1889

A Disincarnated Being
The Clarendon Spirit Tells Who He Is to a Psychist
Voices from the Other World
A Sworn Report Concerning the Strange Doings at Dagg's House

The enterprise shown by the *Free Press* in despatching a reporter to personally enquire into the strange proceedings at the house of George Dagg, a farmer residing at Clarendon Front, Pontiac County, has attracted general attention to that spirit-haunted locality, and the result has been a general rush of curiosity seekers to investigate these phenomena. Those who went could make nothing out of the matter and for the most part laughed at the whole affair and attributed the alleged supernatural occurrences to human agency. A correspondent apparently a past master in black art did explain the cause of the persecution of the Dagg family but in too vague a manner to satisfy the general public. It has remained therefore for Mr. Percy Woodcock, an adept in psychological matters, to act as the medium between the spirits, who, he claims, are the cause of all the trouble and an unbelieving public. That gentleman's adventures are little else than marvellous and the sworn testimony he exhibits seems to prove satisfactorily that there actually exist airy spirits beyond the ken of mortal eye. Mr. Woodcock, who is well known as an artist in Ottawa, Montreal, New York and Paris, spent three days with the Dagg family and certainly did not waste his time. The spirits "cottoned" to him at once, for he had hardly arrived at the house before an invisible inhabitant of the family woodshed addressed the artist as follows: "I am the devil; and I'll have you in my clutches." Mr. Woodcock declined to be scared, and therefore the spirit called him opprobrious names.

A conversation then ensued between Mr. Woodcock, the voice and Mr. George Dagg, who afterwards joined them, lasting for five hours without a break. Mr. Woodcock took the position that he had to deal with an invisible personality, as real as though there in the flesh, and on this basis endeavoured to shame him into better behaviour and stop persecuting the Daggs, who had admittedly done him (the voice) no harm. On the other hand the voice resisted for a long time, but finally seemed to yield to the expostulations of Mr. Woodcock and Mr. Dagg and agreed to cease the use of obscene language and finally admitted that it had been actuated solely by the spirit of mischief, of having fun, as it termed it, and had no ill will against anybody except Woodcock and the little girl Dinah, to whom he seemed to have a decided antipathy. Mr. Woodcock's later experiences are of the same remarkable nature. In order to convince the outside world that there was no humbug in the matter, he drew upon a "report" which seventeen responsible citizens of the neighbourhood signed. This document sets forth that the curious proceedings treated of being on the 15th of September and were still in progress on the 17th November. The events chronicled are, briefly, that fires broke out spontaneously in different parts of the house; that stones were thrown by invisible hands through the window; that various household articles were thrown about by invisible agency; that a mouth organ was heard to be played and seen to move across the floor; that a rocking chair began rocking, that when the child Dinah is present, a deep gruff voice like that of an aged man had been heard at various times, both in the house and outdoors, and when asked questions answered so as to be distinctly heard, showing that he is cognizant of all that has taken place, not only in Mr. Dagg's family but also in the families in the surrounding neighbourhood; that he claims to be a disincarnated being who died twenty years ago, aged eighty years; that he gave his name to Mr. George Dagg and Mr. Willie Dagg, forbidding them to tell him; that this intelligence is able to make himself visible to Dinah, little Mary and Johnnie, who have seen him under different forms at different times, at one time as a tall, thin man with a cow's head, horns, tail, and cloven foot, at another time as a big, black dog, and finally as a man with a beautiful face and long white hair, dressed in white, wearing a crown with stars on it.

The above document is signed by the following: John Dagg, Portage du Fort, Quebec; George Dagg, Portage du Fort, Quebec; William Eddes, Radsford, Quebec; William H. Dagg, Arthur Smart, Charles A. Dagg, Bruno Morrow, Portage du Fort; Benjamin Smart, William J. Dagg, Shawville, Quebec; Robert J. Peever, Cobden, Ontario; R.H. Lockhart, John Fulford, Portage du Fort; George G. Hodgins, Richard E. Dagg, Shawville; George Blackwell, Haley's, Ontario; William Smart, John J. Dagg, Portage du Fort.

After Mr. Woodcock left on Sunday night the following extraordinary manifestation is said to have been given. The voice requested that some persons whom it named should be sent for. As these gentlemen were far away, Rev. Mr. Bell, a Baptist clergyman, was persuaded to come. Mr. Bell read a chapter from the Bible, the voice accompanying him through it and occasionally going in advance of the clergyman. When they knelt to pray the voice responded. Mr. Bell prayed for the family, whom he said had brought the trouble upon themselves by trampling the Bible underfoot, or words to that effect, and finally exorcised the spirit, commanding him in the name of the Saviour to depart, whereupon the spirit laughed and said it was all words, that Mr. Bell had better stick to photography. Mr. Bell left without directly speaking to the voice at any time.

Afterwards the voice sang a hymn in so beautiful a manner as to cause the women present to shed tears. On Monday morning Mr. Woodcock went over to the house again and whilst there the three children came rushing out of the house wild-eyed and fearfully excited, saying that they had seen a beautiful man dressed in white with gold things on his head and stars in it, and that the man spoke to them. The child Dinah said she heard the man say that Woodcock had said that he was not an angel, but that he would show that he was. Thereupon the apparition went up in the air in a blaze of fire and disappeared. This final transformation scene is supposed by Mr. Woodcock to be the last of the mysterious events at the Dagg mansion. It seems a pity that Mr. Woodcock's visit and the ghastly pranks should cease at the same time.

The Mackenzie River Ghost

RODERICK MACFARLANE

On the 15th day of March, 1853, Augustus Richard Peers, a fur trader and post manager in the service of the Hudson's Bay Company, departed his life at Fort McPherson, Peel's River, in the Mackenzie River District, Arctic America. Although he had occasionally complained of ill health, his death after a few days' sickness at the comparatively early age of thirty-three years was entirely unexpected. He was of Anglo-Irish origin, an able officer, much esteemed by his friends and popular among the Indians. During a residence of, I think, eleven years in that remote district, he had been stationed for two or three Outfit seasons at "Head-quarters," Fort Simpson, and afterwards at Forts Norman and McPherson. In 1849, Mr. Peers was married to the eldest daughter of the late Chief Trader John Bell of the Hudson's Bay Company. They had two children. In 1855 the widow remarried the late Alexander McKenzie, who succeeded Mr. Peers at Fort McPherson.

While a resident of both Norman and McPherson, the deceased had been heard to express a strong dislike, in the event of his death, that his bones should rest at either spot. Mr. Peers was thought to have made a holograph will some time previous to his demise; but if so, he must have mislaid or destroyed it, as no such document ever turned up.

Having entered the service of the Company in 1852, I was appointed to the Mackenzie River District the following year, and reached Fort Simpson five months after Mr. Peers's death, where I met his widow and infant children. In the autumn of 1859, at the urgent request of Mrs. McKenzie and her husband, it was decided that the long contemplated transfer of the remains of Mr. Peers from their place of interment at Peel's River to Fort Simpson, on the Mackenzie, should be carried out that winter. Mr. Charles P. (now Chief Trader) Gaudet, then in charge of Fort McPherson, agreed to convey the body by dog train to my trade post at Fort Good Hope, a distance of three hundred miles, while I undertook to render it at its final destination, some five hundred miles further south.

Fort McPherson is situated about one degree north of the Arctic Circle. The soil in its neighbourhood is marshy, and frost is ever present at a shallow depth beneath the surface. On being exhumed by Mr. Gaudet, the body was found in much the same condition it had assumed shortly after its burial. It was then removed from the original coffin, and placed in a new and unnecessarily large coffin which, secured by a moose skin wrapper and lines on a Hudson's Bay dog sled or train, made it an extremely awkward and difficult load for men and dogs to haul and conduct over the rugged masses of tossed-up ice which annually occur at intervals along the mighty Mackenzie River, especially in the higher and more rapid portion of its course towards the northern ocean.

On the first day of March, 1860, Mr. Gaudet arrived at Good Hope and delivered up the body to my care, and I set out for Fort Simpson. The coffin was fixed on one team or train of three dogs conducted by an Iroquois Indian from Caughnawaga, near Montreal, named Michel Thomas (since deceased), while the second train carried our bedding, voyaging utensils and provisions. I myself led the march on snowshoes, and after seven days of very hard and trying labour, owing to the unusual depth of the snow and much rugged ice, the first two hundred miles of our journey to the nearest point (Fort Norman) from Good Hope, was successfully accomplished. At this place Mr. Nicol Taylor (now deceased) strongly pointed out that unless the coffin was removed, and the body properly secured on the train, it would be almost impossible to travel over the vast masses of tossed-up ice which were sure to be encountered at certain points between here and Fort Simpson. As I had previously gone twice over the ground in winter, and had already had some experience of bourdons, I acted on his advice, and we had subsequently good reason for congratulation on having done so.

After one day's rest at Norman, we started on the last and longest portion of the journey. There was no intervening station at that time, and we met few Indians. The Iroquois Thomas remained with the body train. The baggage train and man from Good Hope were exchanged at Norman for fresh animals and a new driver named Michel Iroquois. Mr. Taylor also assisted me in beating the track for the party, he having volunteered to accompany the remains of his former master and friend, Mr. Peers.

A full description of winter travelling in this country may be learned from the pages of Franklin, Back, Richardson and Butler. Here it may be briefly stated that we got under way by four o'clock in the morning, dined at some convenient spot about noon, and after an hour's rest, resumed our march until sunset, when we laid up for the night, generally in a pine bluff on the top or close to the immediate bank of the river. Clearing away the snow to the ground for a space of about ten feet square, cutting and carrying pine brush for carpeting the camp and collecting firewood for cooking and warming purposes, usually occupied us for about an hour. Another hour would see supper over and the dogs fed, and by the end of the next sixty or more minutes, most of the party would be sound asleep. Except on two occasions to be presently mentioned, the train carrying the body of the deceased was invariably hauled up and placed for the night in the immediate rear of our encampment, and except also on the first of the said occasions, our dogs never exhibited any desire to get at same, nor did they seem in the slightest degree affected by its presence in our midst.

About sunset on the 15th day of March, 1860, the seventh anniversary of poor Peers's death, we were obliged to encamp at a short distance from Roche qui trempe a l'eau, the rock by the riverside of Sir Alexander Mackenzie, as there was no better place within reach. The banks here were high, rocky and steep, and we had to leave both trains on the ice; we experienced much difficulty in scrambling up the bank with our axes, snowshoes, bedding and provisions for supper and breakfast. The dogs were unharnessed and remained below, while the weather was calm and comparatively fine and mild. The bank rose about thirty feet to the summit where, on a shelving flat some thirty feet beyond, we selected a position for the night. All hands then set about making the camp, cutting and carrying the requisite supply of pine brush and firewood.

After being thus busily employed for ten or twelve minutes, the dogs began to bark and we at once concluded that Indians were approaching us, as this was a part of the river where a few were frequently met with. We, however, continued our work, the dogs still barking, though not so loudly or fiercely as they usually do under similar circumstances. Neither the dogs nor sleds were visible from the camp, but only from the summit of the river bank. While talking with Mr. Taylor about the expected Indians, we all distinctly heard the word *"Marché!"* (I may remark that French terms are almost universally applied to hauling dogs and their work in the Northwest Territories of Canada.) It seemed to have been uttered by someone at the foot of the bank who wished to drive away the dogs in his path, and we all left off work in order to see who the stranger was; but as no one appeared in sight, Michel Thomas and myself proceeded to the aforesaid summit, where, to our astonishment, no man was visible, while the dogs were seen surrounding the body train at a distance of several feet, and still apparently excited at something. We had to call them repeatedly before they gave up barking, but after a few minutes they desisted and then somehow managed to ascend the bank to our encampment, where they remained perfectly quiet for the night, and thereafter continued as indifferent as before in respect to the deceased's body.

It struck me at the time I heard it that the word *"marché"* was enunciated in a clearer manner than I had ever before known an Indian to do so, as they seldom get beyond a *mashé* or *massé* pronunciation of the term.

On the 18th day of March we were compelled to travel two hours after dark in order to find a suitable encampment, and although we discovered a tolerably good place near the head of a large island on the Mackenzie, yet it was not an easy matter to ascend a perpendicular bank of some twelve feet in height. The baggage train being now rather light, by tying a line to the foremost dog, we managed to drag it and them to the top. The same plan answered with the dogs of the body train; but we considered it beyond our power to get it up, and we were therefore reluctantly obliged to leave it below. After cutting a trail through thick willows for about thirty or forty yards, we reached the edge of a dense forest of small spruce, where we camped. The customary operations were at once attended to, and when most of the work was over I turned up with some firewood from a distance where I had been collecting a lot for the night.

Mr. Taylor then asked me if I had heard a very loud call or yell twice repeated from the direction of the river.

I said, "No," as my cap ear protectors were closely tied down owing to the cold wind, and the thicket very dense.

The two Iroquois corroborated Mr. Taylor's statement, but to settle the matter and find out if any Indian had followed our tracks, we all proceeded to the bank, where nothing could be seen or heard, and we at once decided on having the body train hauled up by sheer force, and it proved a tough job to do so.

We remembered our experience of the 15th of March, and when we set out early next morning we had reason to congratulate ourselves on taking this trouble, as on reaching the spot from which we had removed the body train, we discovered that a *carcajou* or wolverine had been there during the night. To those who know the power of this destructive animal, I need not say that he would have played havoc with the aforesaid remains.

Fort Simpson was at length reached without a recurrence of anything of an unusual nature, in the forenoon of the 21st of March, and the body was duly buried in the adjacent graveyard on the 23rd of that month. Shortly after my arrival, Mr. Taylor and I recounted everything to Chief Trader Bernard R. Ross (since deceased), the district manager, who had been an intimate friend and countryman of Mr. Peers. Mr. Ross was a good mimic and had an excellent memory. He was asked to utter the word *"marché"* in the voice of the deceased, and while I at once recognized the tone as similar to that heard by us at our encampment of the 15th of March, Mr. Taylor had no doubt whatever on the subject.

During my stay at Fort Simpson, I occupied a shakedown bed in the same room with Mr. Ross, and at a distance from his of some eight or ten feet. On the first or second night after retiring and extinguishing the candle light, while conversing on the subject of the rather remarkable occurrences narrated herein (including the supposed disappearance of his will) relating to the deceased, I became overpoweringly conscious of what struck me then and since to have been the spiritual or supernatural presence of the late Mr. Peers. The feeling, however, came on so very suddenly that I instantly covered my face with the blanket and remained speechless. After an interval of perhaps only a few seconds Mr. Ross (whose voice had also ceased) in a somewhat excited tone asked me if I had experienced a very peculiar sensation. I answered that I had and described the feeling, which he assured me agreed exactly with what he himself had just undergone. I know from experience what nightmare is; but while it is most unlikely that two individuals who were carrying on a conversation in which they felt a deep interest should be thus attacked simultaneously, it may be stated that neither of us had partaken of any wines, spirits or anything else which could have brought on a nightmare.

I leave it to others, if they can, to give a reasonable account or explanation of the facts I have here stated; but if it be assumed as an axiom that the spirits of some of the dead are occasionally permitted to revisit former scenes and to take more or less interest in their discarded bodies, then from what we have incidentally learned of the late Mr. Peers's sentiments in respect to the final disposition of his remains, what other or more natural course would the spirit of such a man be expected to take with the view of preventing any unnecessary desecration of them than that apparently adopted on the nights of the 15th and 18th of March, 1860?

From the position of our camp of the 15th of March, it may be taken for granted that it was almost impossible to have hauled the body train up such a steep and rugged rocky bank. Dogs are invariably hungry at the end of a long day's travel and, as the weather was fine that day, they may have scented the still fresh and perfect remains, and probably desired to get at them, while their barking at and position around the sled would, on any other hypothesis, be at least equally strange and unaccountable. Of course, there was danger from wolves and wolverines, but it is presumed that spirits know more than mortals. On the night of March 18, however, although the bank was very difficult of ascent (to get up one had first to raise and push a man till he laid hold of the root of a stout willow by which he hoisted himself to the top, and then threw us a line which aided the rest) it was not insurmountable; and as a most vicious and destructive animal actually visited the spot where we intended leaving the body train for the night, but for the calls and yells referred to, I again ask what other course than that mentioned would any man or spirit possessed of future knowledge be likely to take? And as to the extraordinary feeling experienced by Mr. Ross and myself at the moment when we were talking about the deceased and his supposed will, if it be possible for spirits to communicate with mortals, might this not have arisen (as I actually felt at the time) from a desire on his part to convey some information to us who evinced so deep an interest in the matter but which, from losing our presence of mind, we missed the opportunity of ascertaining?

The foregoing facts made so indelible an impression on my mind that I firmly believe that my present account of them does not in any material point differ from what I communicated to Mr. Ross at the time, and repeatedly since to others. I also distinctly remember the occasion on which I gave similar details to General Sir William F. (then Captain) Butler, K.C.B. It was at Green Lake Post, North West Territories, in the month of February, 1873. Captain Butler soon after proceeded to Ashanti, where he experienced a very severe attack of illness, and he, moreover, wrote me that he had taken poetical licence with my narrative, and this will naturally account for the discrepancies between the statements I have given in this paper and his story of same in *Good Words* for 1877.

PART II
CREEPY FARMHOUSES

The French philosopher Gaston Bachelard once said that everyone lives in a house. We live in a house whether we inhabit a single detached dwelling, a row house, an apartment, a flat, a condo, a co-op, a cottage, a log cabin, a ranch, or a shack. We do so imaginatively because we feel there is a damp basement beneath us, a dry attic above us. In addition, there is the indispensable dining room, the recreation room, the kitchen, the bathroom, and the bedroom. There is thus plenty of room in the psychological house in which we dwell for ghosts that haunt us from the past and spirits to direct us towards the future. Bachelard was speaking metaphorically, of course, but he also felt that every house we occupy is haunted by our hopes and our fears.

Here are some haunted farmhouses, including a camp, a cabin, a shack, and some other forms of accommodation, largely located in the backwoods. They house our hopes and fears... along with hosts of ghosts and spirits!

Colonel Reagan's Ghost

OTTAWA FREE PRESS
FEBRUARY 18, 1900

Prospectors live by hope and often by superstition. "Colonel Reagan's Ghost" appeared in the Ottawa Free Press *of February 18, 1900. The story was apparently reprinted from the* Dawson Weekly News.

◆ ◆ ◆

Colonel Reagan's Ghost
Incident in the Life of an Old Cassiar Miner in the Winter of '72

The *Dawson Weekly News* of January 26 has the following: J. Reagan is a typical old-time prospector. He has followed the fortunes of many mining camps since the early '50s in California and now that he has reached the ripe old age of seventy-five winters with hardly a friend to lend him a helping-hand his lot in life seems gloomy and despair has helped to break his once robust frame and subdue his once indomitable spirit. He came to Dawson in the rush of 1898 from the Cassiar mining district, but in the hurly-burly rush for desirable ground he was pushed aside and lost in the scramble. The old-time method of prospecting and then recording was not the way of the Klondike to make a success and so his funds have run short, and he now depends upon a few old-time friends to give him shelter and provisions. He has been living in a little cabin on the hillside but his wood becoming exhausted and his provisions about gone he has found a temporary shelter at the Flannery hotel.

In the early '70s, when the Cassiar mining district was in its heyday of prosperity, Colonel Reagan was well-to-do, having a rich paying claim on Tibbett Creek. In those days of frontier hospitality no man came to Reagan's cabin without receiving food or shelter. He was known all over the diggings as an eccentric character, devout in the observance of his religious duties and lavish in his gifts when called upon to help a fellow miner. He was held in considerable reverence by the Indians as a great medicine man, having cured several of the tribe of their prevailing sicknesses.

He was a good talker, and the story he tells of meeting a ghost during the last years of his life in the Cassiar mining district is interesting. He never tires of telling it, for he says that that experience has taught him that this manifestation of the unknown in the spirit world proves to him the existence of a hereafter and the truth of the immortality of the soul. He is a very little man—about five feet four inches in height, attenuated in form, with a large head covered with grey straggling locks and bright eyes that mark him as a man of an iron resolution ready to battle with the vicissitudes of life as long as he had a breath in his body. As he narrated, at the Flannery hotel last night, the story of meeting with the stranger in the lone cabin, the fire of zealous belief kindled in his eyes and seemed to bring back the scene of twenty-eight years ago. He said:

"It was a cold and bitter night in the winter of 1872 when I crossed over the ridge and came to Dick Willoughby's cabin at Buck's Bar, on the Cassiar River. It was full of miners and they directed me to an empty cabin across the stream which was said to be haunted. I pulled my sled over to the shelter and entered, finding two rooms, one of them containing a fireplace which had not been used for some time. I started a fire and fried a little bacon and made some tea. As I was eating I looked up and found a stranger by my side. I did not hear him come through the doorway and was naturally surprised. He was an Englishman, smartly dressed and wore no coat. He had his arms folded across his breast and gazed upon me. His eyes seemed to look through me and I felt very uncomfortable.

"Finally I addressed him and asked him if he owned the cabin. He shook his head and said no. I asked him where he came from and he pointed to a number of graves standing white on the hillside. I had now become thoroughly alarmed and asked him if he was going to stay for the night.

"He pointed to the graves and beckoned me to follow him. As he was dressed in a strangely fashioned suit foreign to our miner's clothes, I was puzzled and began to believe that he was a supernatural being, a genuine ghost. I finally pulled myself together and offered him some of my bacon, bread and tea, but he silently left the room without a sound of footsteps. When he had disappeared the fire blazed up into a flame and roared up the chimney, my frying pan rattled and banged on the floor and finally balanced in the flames while the bacon turned to a deep blood red hue. I almost swooned with fright. Then all of a sudden the fire subsided and I was alone with my thoughts. I looked at the bacon and it had still the blood-red hue and to this day I could never solve the mystery."

Ghost Story

FREE PRESS (ACTON, ONTARIO)
MARCH 6, 1879

The contest between the farmer and the mysterious stranger (who may be the devil in disguise) is a familiar motif to folklorists. It is the basis of Stephen Vincent Benét's celebrated short story "The Devil and Daniel Webster," which has been filmed a number of times and even turned into an opera. The motif of the devilish duel was also known to pioneers and settlers, who learned a lot about the wiles of Mr. Scratch, the devil incarnate, from their preachers and from the pages of their Bibles.

Here is one such story.

◆ ◆ ◆

A stout Yorkshire farmer of the name of James Wreggit, having emigrated to Canada, settled himself and family on a good farm which he rented in one of the townships. He was considered fair-dealing and honourable in all transactions with his neighbours, and in every respect bore a most excellent character. In the farmer's house was a first-floor sitting room with a large fire-place. In this room the children slept, but from the first night evinced the greatest dislike to going to bed there, screaming with terror, and saying that a man was in the room with them. For a long time the parents paid no attention to their complaints. During harvest time a change was made, and the farmer himself slept in this room, as it was cooler and more convenient. The first night he slept there he was about to rise almost before the break of day, when, glancing towards the fire-place, he saw standing there a stranger of a dissipated drunken appearance. "Ha'lo! What's thee doing there?" was his very natural exclamation. Receiving no reply, "Won't thee speak? I'll make thee speak!" and picking up one of his heavy boots from the bedside he was preparing to throw it at the intruder, when the man, suddenly raising his arm as if to ward off the blow, vanished in a moment from before his eyes. Wreggit, unable to get this matter out of his head, brooded over it till the next day, when about noon he entered into conversation with a neighbour who was working with him, and asked him to describe the former tenant of the farm, who had died from excessive drinking. The description so entirely resembled the man he had seen in the room that he at once exclaimed, "I saw him last night!" Wreggit recounted this to some old friends near whom he had lived before taking the farm, and it is from the dictation of one of his auditors that I have written down this remarkable circumstance. At the time neither Wreggit nor his friend had the slightest belief in apparitions.

Remarkable Phenomena

THE GLOBE (TORONTO)
SEPTEMBER 6, 1880

It was mentioned earlier that the word "poltergeist" is German for "noisy spirit," a mischievous, often boisterous sprite that is intent on disturbance and disruption. Perhaps it is best to refer to "poltergeist-like effects" in terms of a rash of inexplicable disturbances that arise spontaneously and inexplicably withdraw. In effect, a poltergeist might well be described as a ghostly presence that is known by its effects alone.

Accounts of rural life in the days of the early settlers are rich in stories of this sort, and here is a short but detailed account of the activity of a poltergeist in an Ontario farmhouse near Crosshill, in Wellesley Township. It was titled "Remarkable Phenomena" when it appeared in Toronto's Globe in 1880.

◆ ◆ ◆

Remarkable Phenomena
*The Windows of a Farmer's Dwelling Repeatedly Shattered to Pieces,
And the Inmates Drenched with Water*

WELLESLEY, September 6—A very extraordinary story having gained currency in this section of the country that Mr. George Manser, a very respectable and well-to-do farmer residing near the village of Crosshill, in the township of Wellesley, had with his family been driven out of his dwelling by the mysterious breaking of his windows and showering down of water in dry weather, your correspondent took occasion today to visit the place and interview Mr.

Manser and his family in regard to the report in circulation. On approaching the house he noticed the windows, six in number, closed up with boards, which still further excited his curiosity and gave reason to believe that there must be some ground for the report.

The house I found to be a large one-and-a-half-storey hewed log building, rather old but in a very good state of repair, situated a short distance from the highway on the most elevated part of the farm. On stating the object of my visit, Mr. Manser very kindly showed me through the building and gave me the following facts:

About a month or six weeks ago the glass in the windows began to break, several panes bursting out at a time. These were replaced with new ones only to meet the same fate. A careful examination was then made to ascertain the cause. It was at first supposed that the house being old and getting a little out of shape might affect the windows, but the sash was found to be quite easy and even loose in the frames. Then the family are surprised and put to flight with a shower of water, saturating their beds, their clothing, in fact everything in the house, whilst the sun is shining beautifully in the horizon, and outside all is calm and serene. Nothing daunted, Mr. Manser repairs to the village store and obtains a fresh supply of glass, and even tries the experiment of using some new sash, and utterly failing to discover the mysterious cause of either the breaking of the glass or the sudden showers of water, all taking place in broad daylight. His neighbours are called in, and whilst they are endeavouring to solve the mystery, a half dozen or more panes of glass would suddenly burst, making a report similar to that of a pistol shot. Mr. Manser states that he inserted more than one hundred new lights of glass and then gave it up, and boarded up the windows, first taking out the sash and setting them aside, but on account of the continued bursts of water, they were compelled to remove all their beds, some to the wood-shed and others to the barn, leaving only those things in the house that are not so liable to be damaged by the showering process to which he has been so repeatedly subjected. He has commenced the erection of a new dwelling, hoping thereby to escape those remarkable tricks of nature, or whatever it may be, which seem to continue their operations to the old house. If these strange occurrences had taken place at night, one would suspect that Mr. Manser was the victim of some mischievous people, but occurring in the daytime in the presence of the family and other witnesses, and in fine weather, it seems very difficult of solution. Various theories have been put forward, but none of them seem sufficient to account for the double phenomena of the sudden showers of water under a good roof in fine weather, and the oft-repeated bursting out of the windows. Perhaps you or some of your scientific readers can crack the nut.

I Never Saw Anything Like It

IRISH CANADIAN
NOVEMBER 29, 1883

Usually, ghost stories are not really stories as much as they are sketchy accounts of sensations, impressions, suppositions, conjectures, and speculations. A ghost story, to be a good story, should have a beginning, a middle, and an end, as well as some characterizations, setting, and plot. Here is a good one. Few accounts of wraith-like visitors are as detailed as this one, which was contributed by P.A. O'Neill, an upper-school teacher, to the Irish Canadian *in 1883.*

◆ ◆ ◆

A Genuine Ghost Story
How the Spirit was "Laid"
By P.A. O'Neill

An article in the *Fortnightly Review*, entitled "Phantasms of the Living," has induced me to relate here the circumstance of an apparition which I myself saw, and to the fact of seeing which I am prepared to make affidavit. I will premise by saying that I by no means belong to the superstitious class. On the contrary, I am strongly inclined to skepticism, and was at that time.

In 1877 I was engaged to teach in the third district of Ennismore, Peterboro' County, Ontario. As was customary at that time, and is yet, the school teacher boarded round. But in this particular case a widow, possessor of a small farm, undertook the business of boarding the schoolmaster. After remaining with her for some time, she told me that she had concluded to rent or sell (I forget which) her small farm; consequently I should have to look out for another place to board. I was naturally a little perplexed, for upon the condition of boarding permanently with her during my engagement, I had accepted the situation.

However there was nothing for it but to acquiesce. So, next Sunday, I set out for mass to the one parish church of Ennismore. I knew there was a farmer living four miles distant, with a comparatively small family, who had a very large farm house. Originally it had been intended for a country tavern, with a row of horse stalls, large dance hall, etc., after the manner of the time. But through some cause, generally attributed to the dullness of the times, the house had fallen back to the rank of an ordinary farm house—a giant among its neighbours.

After mass it is a custom—especially an Irish custom—to assemble for some time and gossip in front of the church before driving home; and you may be sure that Ennismore marks no exception to the general rule. After the usual courtesies had been exchanged I broached the subject of board for the school teacher to my friend, Mr. —— (the only name which shall be held sacred in this relation). He said that, particularly for the sake of his two boys, nothing would suit him better than to board me; but he had no sleeping room for me. I naturally wondered at this, and frankly told him that a man living in the largest farm house in the township, with a comparatively small family, could not be hard pressed for sleeping room.

"Well," said he, "I don't own the farm; I merely lease it from the owner. But one-half of the house is entirely useless to me, except the lower half, which I use as a granary; for in the upper half is a very large room with a very fine bed in which no one will sleep."

Said I: "Did you ever try to sleep there yourself?"

"God forbid!" was the reply.

I was somewhat surprised at this remark, and begged to know the cause of the trouble, but all the information he would volunteer was that the room was haunted. It was the only available room he had in the house for a stranger, and he could scarcely offer hospitality to anyone in it, when nobody could sleep in it. The end of it was that I laughed down my worthy friend's superstition; occupied the next day the haunted room; congratulated myself upon having so large, cool and fine a room in hot July weather; ate generously of a most bounteously furnished table—nothing better in the world than in Ennismore—and altogether rejoiced in my good luck in the change from the scrimpy widow's board to the generous farmer's cuisine; and enjoyed many a quiet laugh at the ghost's expense.

My first experience of her ghostship was while sitting on a rail fence in a warm August day at twilight, talking to a friend at a considerable elevation above the house. My friend, who seemed to know the room I occupied, suddenly, with an exclamation of surprise, turned to me and said:

"Look, Daly, there's someone in your room, and it's a woman, too."

I looked in the direction indicated, and sure enough there was a light in the room and a shadow upon the window curtains showed a woman moving to and fro. Of course I was somewhat nonplussed, but I accounted for the circumstance by thinking that some of the girls of the house were engaged in the room in the performance of the ordinary domestic duties. Still I thought this a little strange, knowing the abhorrence entertained by every member of the family of entering the so-called haunted room.

On returning that evening I congratulated the farmer's wife on her courage in once more throwing open the room. She stared at me with blank astonishment. She wouldn't, for all the world, have anything to do with the room. Why, did I suppose she had? I told her what I had seen. There had been nobody there, as far as she knew. I went upstairs; the door was locked, the lamp unlit, the wick as I had left it, no evidence in the world that anybody had been there since morning. I considered the whole thing an optical illusion, and went to sleep. My dreams were not disturbed.

Three or four nights after, however, operations began. I awoke about the witching hour of night—so my watch admonished me—feeling chilly. The covering was all off the bed. I jumped up and found that the bedclothes had been removed and placed on the floor in a heap below the foot-board. I replaced them, deeming I had kicked them off, and thought no more about it. But the same thing occurred several successive nights, so that it became a worry to me; and at last I got worked up to such a nervous pitch that I could not sleep at all. Towards the middle of the night I distinctly felt the bedclothes begin to move downward. I clutched at them grimly, and quite an exciting struggle for their possession began. But my invisible antagonist proving the stronger, I saw everything disappear slowly but surely through the open space between the foot-rail and the floor-board.

Meanwhile, I had turned on the light, and leaping from the bed exclaimed: "Now I've got you!" in no enviable frame of mind, either. I seized a stout cudgel and explored the foot of the bed, and everywhere in the room; found the door securely locked and bolted. Not a single vestige of my nocturnal visitant except the heap of bedclothing on the floor. To say the least, I was awed as well as puzzled; and not knowing what other deviltry might be forthcoming, I took care to keep the light burning the rest of the night.

I need not say I slept no more but lay awake thinking. What could it be? Nevertheless, a bright thought struck me. I was not going to be driven out of my comfortable quarters by any ghost who played such a shabby track as this, for by this time I began to think it was a ghost, after all. Still, if stealing bedclothes was all it could do it wasn't much of a terror; and I'd fix that. The next morning I procured a wide slat and nailed it securely across the open space at the foot of the bed. Several nights passed; no more annoyance from that source.

I had then, and still have, a habit of placing my boots at the side of the bed before retiring for the night. One night, at the usual hour, I was awakened by a sound as loud as a pistol shot succeeded by dead silence. I immediately jumped up, and upon investigation found one of my boots missing. Looking around I espied it under the bed close to the wall, against which it had been thrown with such violence that it chipped off some of the plaster. Certainly my nocturnal visitant exhibited a strange inclination for working close to the ground.

By this time I was in a towering passion, and seizing the remaining boot I sent it flying with an oath accompanying it in the direction the other had apparently come from. I listened for a reply, but none coming, I got up on the bed. Scarcely had I lifted my legs from the floor when the boot was thrown back with such force that I felt the wind strike my leg as the missile passed it. Had it struck me it would surely have broken the limb. My investigations ceased for that night. I lay still and let the boots alone. Yet, after that, not wishing to undergo the same experience, I took the boots to bed with me, and nothing more of that kind occurring, I began to flatter myself on having laid the spirit. Besides, I was strengthened in my opinion by the congratulations of my neighbours, who looked upon me as a man of extraordinary moral courage, and, as my landlord had laughingly remarked, "undoubtedly ghost-proof." Of course I mentioned my experience to no one. I feared ridicule, in fact, and really believed that I would solve the mystery, and prove the ghost theory to be all nonsense.

Nothing occurred for several weeks afterward. I enjoyed the old farmer's hospitality meanwhile, taught my school and made my mind easy. One night, however, I was rudely disturbed from this happy frame of mind. I awoke with a feeling of terror. My usual resource, I at once turned on the light. Then I beheld a sight which filled me with mingled fear and amazement. There stood, evidently, my ghostly visitant, staring at me—a woman, pale and wan, yet with traces of beauty on her face. She was dressed in an ordinary black dress, with a black ribbon around her throat. But the thing which riveted my attention most was the expression of dire sorrow and awful despair upon her countenance. I never saw anything like it, not even in the faces of those condemned to an ignominious death. Once or twice the lips parted as if to speak; then, I suppose, as the expression of horror upon my countenance increased, there was a slight frown. With a strange fascination I continued to gaze for what appeared to be a minute. Then I made a movement towards the woman, when she appeared to go through the doorway. I examined the door, however, but found it locked as usual, and bolted. I listened, but heard no footsteps or other sounds on the stairs.

Then, returning to my couch, I concluded, as I am now thoroughly convinced, that I had seen a spirit. I received, however, a severe nervous shock, which was plainly visible to my kind host at breakfast next morning. He questioned me, and I related to him the circumstances herein set forth. From him I ascertained the name of the owners of the farm, and when vacation occurred I hied me to Peterborough, where Mr. Sullivan lived, to get an explanation of the mystery. Of course I slept no more in the haunted room.

Mr. Sullivan was quite friendly in his manner. "Yes," he said; "that woman was my wife's sister. She died in that bed in that room of consumption. We did all we could for her in her last sickness. She had the priest with her, received the last sacraments, but, though suffering terribly from disease, seemed terribly unwilling to die. Yet, why she should not rest with the multitude who sleep in Christ, and rest in peace, we do not know. We did all we could to make her comfortable, and in return she has driven us from our farm. She appeared to my wife one night, shortly after death, and so terrified the woman that she came near joining her ghostly visitant in the other world. Nothing would ever induce my wife to sleep in the house again, so I had to move here, engage in another occupation and rent my farm. She has never troubled us here, but seems to confine her visits to the room where she died. To me the whole thing is unaccountable."

I assured him it was equally so to me, and took my departure.

Now, why was this spirit so spiteful against anybody sleeping in the bed she died on? Why did she visit the scene of her demise at all? Rev. Mr. Searless, in the *Catholic World*, says if the spirit of the friend appears to us and gives "reasonable proofs of his identity we may of course put faith in what he may tell us of his experience since his departure." But no such faith is needed in this essay, as the apparition will never be called upon for proofs of identity, or spoken to at all. The poor spirit may abandon hope. The scene is the heart of an exclusively Irish settlement, and there is not a man, woman or child who would dare to speak to it. It is graven upon the Irish mind, the superstition—coming, it is said, from druidical days—that he who speaks to a spirit shall surely die within a year.

The old house may sink and rot and pass away, and the day of judgement come, but in Ennismore it never will be known why this uneasy spirit revisits the "glimpses of the moon."

Perhaps, however, some adventurous stranger, bolder than I am, or rather with more presence of mind, may wish to undergo my experience and solve the mystery. The house is there yet; is easily accessible; the door of the room locked, and the room itself abandoned to its ghostly tenant.

A Thrilling Adventure

CANADIAN STATESMAN
DECEMBER 24, 1889

"They change their skies and not their hearts who travel across the seas" is an old adage that applies (somewhat) to the present tale, which appeared under the above title in 1889. The tale is told in the first person, but nowhere is the name of the narrator given, though the reader is given assurances that he (and not she) is a new—and marked—person following the mysterious events that occurred that night in the unnamed tavern in the backwoods of Ontario. Yet the narrator seems to be quite impressionable, judging by early references to "a secret shudder" and an "awful doom." Does the reader suppose that the narrator was any less so after the events related here? Whatever the answer, the account makes lively reading today!

◆ ◆ ◆

A Thrilling Adventure
A Pedlar's Startling Experience at a Backwoods Tavern in the Early Days of Ontario

In all my travels, over thousands of miles of country, I was never really terrified but once; and then I confess I had a fright which I did not recover from for weeks, and which I still never recall without a secret shudder. My life might be said to have hung on a bare thread; and nothing but heaven's kind providence, interposed in a most miraculous manner, saved me from the awful doom.

In the regular pursuit of my vocation, I was travelling through Western Canada, when, towards evening of one hot, sultry, summer day, I found myself passing through a long stretch of swampy woodland, along what might much better have been denominated a horse-path than a road. I had taken a rather obscure by-way, in the hopes, if I found few customers, to find those who would pay well; but I had made a serious mistake, in that I had discovered none at all. In a walk of eight tedious miles, I had seen only three dwellings, and these miserable shanties, one of which was unoccupied, and the other two with ragged families who had no money for trade. At the last house, I inquired the distance to the next, and I was informed that four miles further on I would come to a main road, where there was an inn for travellers; and towards this I was now making my way, with the intention of putting up there for the night.

I came in sight of the road and the inn just as the sun was setting behind a drift of clouds that seemed to betoken the gathering of a storm. Tired and hungry as I was, with night setting in upon me in such a lonely country, I was very glad to come in sight of a place of rest, and went forward in comparatively good spirits.

The inn was a brown stone building, two storeys in height, and quite respectable looking for that region of country. As I came up to it, however, I fancied it had a certain air of gloom, which had a rather depressing effect upon my spirits; but then this, I thought, might be caused by the absence of sparkling lights and bustle, and seeing it at the hour of twilight. No one met me at the door; nor did I perceive a human being in or about it till I had entered the unlighted bar room, where a man, who was sitting in a corner, rose and came forward, with a slight nod of salutation.

"Are you the landlord?" I inquired.

"I am," was the answer.

"I suppose I can put up with you for the night?" I said.

"Certainly," he answered, glancing at my trunks. "Shall I take care of them for you?"

"I will merely set them behind your bar till I retire for the night, and then I will take them to my room. I suppose you can give me a single apartment to myself."

"Oh, yes, easy enough—my house is large, and will not be crowded tonight."

"Have you any other guests?" I inquired, feeling, from some cause for which I could not account, strangely ill at ease.

"There is no one here yet," he replied, "and it is getting rather late for the drovers, who often stop with me."

It was a relief to think that drovers were in the habit of putting up at the house, for that implied a certain honesty in the landlord, and a consequent security for lonely travellers; and I really needed this reflection to counterbalance a strange sense of something wrong, if not absolutely wicked and dangerous.

I informed the host that I was very tired and hungry, and wished a good supper and a good bed, and he assured me that I should be provided with the best he had. He went out of the room, as he said, to give the necessary directions and get a light. He was gone some ten minutes, and returned with a candle in his hand, which he placed on the bar. I had taken a seat during his absence, and, being a little back in the shade, I now had a chance to scrutinize his features closely without being perceived in the act.

I did not like the appearance of his countenance. His face was long and angular, with black eyes and bushy brows, and the whole expression was cold, forbidding, and sinister.

He remarked that the night was very warm and sultry, and that it was likely to be showery, and then inquired if I had come far that day, and which direction? I informed him of my tedious walk over the by-road, and unguardedly added that I did not think my day's experience would incline me to travel through that region again in a hurry. He asked me where I was from, if I had seen many persons that day, if I was an entire stranger in that part of the country, and so forth, and so on—to all of which I gave correct answers.

Thus we conversed till a little bell announced supper, when he ushered me into a good-sized dining room, and did the honours of the table, trying to make himself very agreeable. That there was somebody else in the house I had good reason to believe—for I heard steps and the rattling of dishes in an adjoining room—but the landlord himself was the only person I saw during the evening, if I except a glance at a disappearing female dress as he was in the act of lighting me to my room.

My bedroom was small, but looked clean and neat, and contained an inviting bed, curtains of chintz at the single window, a chest of drawers, a looking-glass, a wash stand, a couple of chairs, and was really quite as well furnished as many an apartment in hotels of far greater pretension. With all this I was pleased, of course; and judging by the appearance that there was nothing wrong about an inn so properly conducted, I bolted my door, raised the window for a little fresh air, looked out and discovered the night was intensely dark, undressed, blew out my light, jumped into bed, and almost immediately fell asleep.

I was awakened by a crash of thunder that was rolling over and shaking the house to its foundation at the moment my senses returned to me; and being rather timid about lightning, and remembering to have heard that the electric fluid would follow a current of air, and also recollecting that I had left my window open, I sprang up hastily to close it. As I did so, my head barely touched some soft substance, just above me; but the fact produced no impression upon my excited mind at the moment. I reached the window, and for an instant stood and looked out to get a view of the approaching storm; but, as before, I could not see anything at all—all was as black as the darkness of a pit—and as before, too, the air was perfectly still—so much so, that I fancied I felt a stifling sensation. I was the more surprised at this that I thought I heard the roar of the wind, and the falling of rain; and certainly there was another clap of thunder, whose preceding flash of lighting I had not perceived.

Awed by the mystery, I hastily let down the sash, and returned to the bed in a state of some trepidation; but, as I put out my hand to feel my way in, it came into contact with a mattress nearly as high as my neck from the floor. Now really terrified by a sense of some unknown danger, and half believing that the room was haunted, I clutched the

mattress convulsively, and felt over and under it, and found it was separate from the bed on which I had been sleeping, and was slowly
descending!

Gracious heaven! how shall I attempt to describe that moment of
horror, when I first got a comprehension of the whole diabolical plot!
A plot to murder me in my sleep! I was walled up in a room prepared
with machinery for the express purpose of murdering the unsuspecting
traveller, and had been saved from the awful fate by the report of
heaven's thunder. The window of course was only a blind to deceive,
placed inside of a blank wall, which accounted for my seeing nothing
from it and getting no current of air when the sash was raised; and the
mattress I had hold of was arranged to be lowered by pulleys, and held
down by weights upon the sleeping traveller till life should be smothered out of him. All this I comprehended as by a sudden flash of
thought and as I stood trembling and almost paralyzed, there came a
quick rattling of cords and pulleys, and the upper bed dropped down
with a force that denoted the heavy weights placed upon it.

But though left out from under it—alive, as it were, by a miracle—
what was I now to do to preserve my life? As yet, all was dark, and no
one appeared; but I now heard voices speaking in low, hushed tones and
knew that soon the truth would be discovered, and in all probability my
life attempted in some other way. What was I to do? How defend
myself from the midnight murderers? I had no weapon but an ordinary
clasp-knife, and what would this avail against two or more? Still, I was
determined not to yield my life tamely; and as in all probability every
avenue of escape was barred against me, I resolved to crawl under the
bed and take my chance there. Mechanically, while considering, I had
felt for my clothes and drawn on my pantaloons; and now cautiously
trying the door, and finding it, as I had expected, fastened on the outside, I stealthily glided under the bed, and placed myself far back, close
against the wall. I had barely gained this position when a light shone
into the room from above; and looking up between the bed and the wall,
I saw an opening in the ceiling, about five feet by eight, through which

I suppose the upper mattress had descended; and, standing on the edge of this opening, looking down, was the landlord of the inn, and beside him a tall, thin, sinister virago, who looked wicked enough to be his wife, as undoubtedly she was.

"All right, Meg," he said, at length, "he is quiet enough now; and if not, I can soon finish him"—and with this he took the candle from her hand, and leapt down upon the bed, and then sprang off upon the floor. "Now hoist away," he continued, "and let us go through with this job as quick as possible."

Again I heard the noise of ropes and pulleys, and knew the upper bed was being raised, which in another moment would disclose to the human monster the fact that my dead body was not under it. What then? Merciful heaven! It must be a struggle of life and death between him and me!—and I was already nerving myself for the dreadful encounter, when I experienced a kind of transitory sensation of a crash and a shock.

The next thing I remember was finding myself exposed to the fury of the tempest—the wind howling past me, the rain beating upon me, the lightning flashing, and the thunder roaring. I was still in my room, but it was all open on one side of me, and it took my bewildered sense some time to comprehend the awful fate of heaven's peculiar providence.

The lightning had struck the portion of building I was in, and had thus given me life and freedom!

As soon as I fairly comprehended this, I leapt to the ground outside, escaping injury, and ran for my life. I took the main road, and ran on through the storm, as if pursued by a thousand fiends, as I sometimes fancied I was. I ran thus till daylight, when I met a stage-coach full of passengers, hailed the driver, and told him my wonderful story. He thought me mad, but persuaded me to mount his box and go back with him. On arriving at the inn, he found a confirmation of my fearful tale.

The house had not only been struck, but, strange to relate, both the landlord and his wife had been killed by the bolt of heaven, and were found dead among the ruins!

I subsequently had to appear before a magistrate, acting as coroner, and depose to the facts and the jury returned a verdict in accordance therewith.

I got away from that fearful region as soon as I could; but to this day I have never fully recovered from the effects of that night of horror at the inn!

Fire-Setter

TORONTO WORLD
NOVEMBER 7, 1891

This is a lively account of the disruptive activity of a poltergeist. Disturbances of this sort were commonly reported a century ago, less so during the last half-century. The focus of the forces is generally the daughter of a farming couple, a pubescent girl, unfulfilled in love, who is found to be associated with setting the fires. A century ago, the girl would be described as a victim of "spirit possession." Today, psychiatrists would speak about "disturbances of the self," about "ego-boundary disturbances," or more specifically about delusional states characterized by "thought insertion" and "thought broadcasting."

"Spooks, or What" appeared in 1891.

◆ ◆ ◆

Spooks, Or What
Mysterious Doings in a Thorah Farmer's House
An Incorporeal Firebug
Cats Take Fire, Towels Burn up and Wood Disappears
Queer Pranks in Broad Daylight
A Young Girl's Name Connected with the Mystery

Over Fifty Years in the House in One Day
The Ghost's Queer Pranks Astonishing All the Neighbours,
Who Are Visiting the Scene by Hundreds
What the Inmates Say
These Strange Phenomena
Have Now Been Going on for Over a Week.

Beaverton, Ontario, November 6—The residents of the sleepy township of Thorah have been for the past week considerably excited by the reports of curious antics rumoured to be performed by supernatural means, in a house owned and occupied by Robert Dawson, a reputable farmer on the first concession of Thorah, about three miles from this village. The story, told by neighbours arriving here, was that an adopted daughter of Mr. and Mrs. Dawson had been seriously ill with brain fever; that about a week ago she went into a trance and on awakening suddenly jumped up, exclaiming, "Look at that!" and pointing with her finger towards the ceiling of the house. The rest of the members on looking towards the point indicated by the girl were surprised to see the ceiling on fire. They immediately extinguished the fire and nothing more was thought of the matter until the following day, when the girl again startled the family with the same exclamation and the interior of the house broke out in flames. This performance, according to the rumour, was continued every day thereafter.

From an investigation by the *World*'s Ghost Exterminator, it is evident that the ghost sleeps just at present, but for a time it was fully as persistent as the one detailed for Banquo's special benefit.

The house is situated about one hundred yards from the road on lot 17, concession 1, Thorah—about seven miles from Cannington and three from Beaverton. It is a small and rather an ancient structure and is built of logs. There is a window in the front of the house, but no door; entrance to it being by a door in the rear through an old summer kitchen.

On arriving at the house Mrs. Dawson, the wife of the farmer, introduced the girl, whose name had been mentioned in connection with these mysteries. She was engaged in washing dishes. The girl was adopted by Mr. and Mrs. Dawson from an immigrant home in Belleville some time ago. She was originally from England, where she was known as Jennie B. Bramwell, but since coming to her present home she has adopted the name of Jennie B. Dawson. Miss Bramwell, or Miss Dawson, is a bright intelligent girl of about fourteen years of age. She is well educated and an excellent conversationalist.

After being shown over the premises, both upstairs and down, Mrs. Dawson tells this story of the girl's illness and the mysterious fires:

On Monday afternoon, October 25, she and her husband went to a neighbour's to spend a few hours, and on returning home in the evening Jennie informed them that the house had been on fire and pointed out the place—near the chimney. Mr. Dawson, thinking that there might still be some fire around the chimney, remained up all night to watch it, but nothing occurred during the night. After breakfast on Tuesday morning Mr. Dawson went out to the barn to load some grain to take to market, and Mrs. Dawson also went out into the yard. They had scarcely left the house when the girl, Jennie, came out shouting the house was again on fire. On entering the house they found that the west gable end was on fire. With the aid of water the fire upstairs was extinguished, but no sooner had that been accomplished than the fire broke out in several places on the wall in the room in the lower flat, and while extinguishing it there it again broke out on the wall in another room in the east end—there being no visible connection between any of the fires. They finally succeeded, with the assistance of some neighbours, in getting the fire extinguished. The next day the fire again broke out, and as on the former day, when it was extinguished in one place it would suddenly break out in some other place, several feet away.

On one occasion, while the fire was burning at the extreme west end of the house, a picture hanging on the wall at the opposite end of the house suddenly took fire and was consumed before their eyes. On examination it was found there was no fire near it. The family had now become thoroughly aroused, and after succeeding in extinguishing the fire, they removed the stove from the house as they had an idea that the fire was caused by it. But the removal of the stove had no effect, as on the following day—Thursday—the fire again broke out. While sitting looking at the wall fire would suddenly break out on it; a stick of wood lying in the old summer kitchen suddenly took fire and was partly consumed; a piece of paper pulled from the wall and thrown on the floor would immediately take fire and burn up. A towel which Mrs. Dawson had been using to wipe a table with on being thrown onto another table suddenly took fire and would have been consumed had not water been thrown over it, and a basket hanging in the woodshed also took fire.

The dress of the girl Jennie took fire and she narrowly escaped being burned to death. Mrs. Dawson also had her right hand burned while helping to extinguish the fire. Wherever the fire appeared it would char into the wood over half an inch in a second, and the other side of the board or log would instantly become so hot that a person could not place their hand on it. A peculiar thing connected with these fires was that as soon as any of the burning lumber, paper, cloth or wood (no matter how furiously they were burning in the house) was thrown outside the fire would immediately die out. After all the fires had been extinguished Mrs. Dawson pulled a piece of paper from the wall and rolled it up in a piece of old muslin dress and roped it on the centre of the floor and, accompanied by Mr. Dawson and the rest of the family, stepped outside to see the result. No sooner had they stepped out of the door than the muslin and the paper became ignited and burned furiously. Friday was no exception—in fact the fire was ten times as bad, there being nearly fifty fires in different parts of the house that day. But the climax was reached on Saturday when a kitten, which was lying in the centre of the floor of one of the rooms, became enwrapped in flames and rushed out into the orchard, where the flames, like that on the wood, paper, etc., immediately died out. On the kitten being examined it was found that the hair on its back was badly singed. The fires in the house also broke out twice that day.

Mrs. Dawson, to prove what she said, showed the towel, basket, kitten, etc., which had so mysteriously taken fire, and everything was as she had stated. The kitten, which was examined closely, was badly singed. Mr. John Shier, brother of Mrs. Dawson, was also present and corroborated what his sister had told, as did also the girl Jennie. Mr. Shier also added that when he was first told of the fires he just laughed, and so lightly did he treat it that he did not visit the place until Wednesday and saw the mysterious fires himself. He was there when the cat took fire and when the linen and towel were burned, but neither he nor Mrs. Dawson nor any other of the members of the family could in any way account for the origin of these fires. Neither can any of the neighbours who were at the fires.

On asking if it was true that the girl Jennie was ill or subject to fits, Mrs. Dawson said: "The girl was taken ill some weeks ago with whooping cough, but when she was recovering from that she was taken down with brain fever, but was now all right again. During the girl's illness the doctor in attendance injected into her arm morphine, and immediately after the girl went into convulsions and for some time after was subject to them. However, she could in no wise connect the girl's illness with the fires."

The house is still standing, but all the partitions have been removed from the top storey, and the furniture has been taken to a neighbour's. A peculiar feature was that no fires occurred at night—all being in daylight, and they appeared to be more numerous during the two days when the stove was outside.

Chemist Smith Thompson and Editor Robinson of the *Cannington Gleaner* have visited the scene and are unable to explain the phenomena. Everything has been suggested that reasoning minds could imagine as a natural cause for the phenomena, but they have in turn been rejected. Human agency and electricity have been mentioned, but at every fresh suggestion of cause the apparently angry author of the mysterious fires repelled the insinuation by blazing out in a new place and destroying all topographical calculations. If it be human agency the one who constructed the machinery must be an expert and a model of ingenuity. If it be electricity the house must be charged more powerfully than any building yet tested.

There is a great stir in the neighbourhood and the house is daily visited by scores. All are politely received and given every facility for inspecting the rooms, charred articles, etc. Both the girl and Mrs. Dawson tell their story in a plain, unvarnished manner, devoid of exaggeration and seemingly with a firm faith in the supernatural character of the manifestations. Mr. and Mrs. Dawson have lived in the place for a number of years and are well-to-do, kind and highly respected people. The neighbours speak in the highest terms of them and also of the girl Jennie. The neighbours are all deeply impressed with both what they saw and what they were told.

PART III
MORE CREEPY FARMHOUSES

In the previous section, the reader encountered stories and tales of hauntings that took place in the last half of the 19th century; specifically, between 1872 and 1891. There is more than a taste of the supernatural to the descriptions of these events and experiences. The supernatural begins to wane in the stories and accounts that appear in the present section. Here the reader will encounter ghostly visitations that took place between 1891 and 1915, from the late Victorian period to the Georgian and Edwardian periods. The descriptions become increasingly realistic, though there still lingers about them the whiff of sulphur and a wisp of brimstone. But by the end, we have definitely entered the modern period, which is at once willing to be persuaded yet expecting to be sceptical as well.

Ghostly Guide

OTTAWA FREE PRESS
JANUARY 15, 1891

Here is a readable tale about a helpful spirit. This one takes place in a lumber camp rather than on a farm. The story appeared as "My Ghostly Guide" in 1891.

◆ ◆ ◆

My Ghostly Guide
A Lumber Merchant's Story

In January 1853 I was engaged as assistant clerk in a large lumbering camp in the woods about a hundred miles north of the Ottawa River. Our main shanty was by the side of an outlet of Red Pine Lake about two miles from the south side of the lake itself, a sheet of water of oblong shape, about a mile and a half wide and five miles long. There was a fairly good road from the edge of the lake to the shanty, and from the north or opposite side of the lake, a road had been made for some miles through the forest, to a point where a smaller camp had been established, and where a number of our men were engaged in making timber. From the main shanty to the smaller one was probably twenty miles. One day my chief, Mr. Simpson, sent me off with some instructions to the foreman in charge of what we called the Crooked Creek camp. I started with my snowshoes on my back and moccasins on my feet, at a brisk pace. It was a bright clear day. The road to the lake had been well worn by teams, and as there had been a thaw covered with frost, the ice on the lake was hard and smooth. The road from the lake to the Crooked Creek camp was rather rough and narrow, and a stranger might have difficulty in following it. However, I knew the route well, and arrived at my destination in good time, just as the men were returning from their work, with axes on their shoulders. I spent the night in the camp, being asked innumerable questions, and hearing all the petty gossip the men had to relate. It must be remembered that these shanty men go into the woods in October or November and excepting in rare instances hear nothing whatever from the outside world until they come out in the spring. Next morning I executed my commission and about ten o'clock started back for the main camp. I had not travelled more than half the distance when a snowstorm set in. In the woods the flakes fell down steadily, and I had no difficulty in keeping the road. It was about sundown when I reached the edge of the lake. The snow had covered the track across the ice and there was nothing to guide me to the entrance to the road to our main camp on the opposite shore. Out on the lake the storm was blinding, but I did not doubt my ability to reach the other side and find the road. So I started across the lake. When less than half a mile from the edge of the woods the snow was so thick that I could see neither shore. Moreover it was getting dark and exceedingly cold. If I should lose my way on the lake and have to spend the night there I would certainly perish. What was to be done? I turned in my tracks and managed to reach the north shore again, stopping in the shelter of some bushes to recover my breath. Should I stay there all night? To tramp back to Crooked Lake camp was my first decision, but on reflection I remembered that any person travelling that road at night was liable to be attacked and eaten by wolves. Moreover, I was hungry and fatigued. While I was thus communing with myself, jumping up and down and slapping my hands to keep myself warm, I saw a man dressed in a grey suit with a toque on his head and a scarf around his waist, about two hundred yards out on the lake, beckoning to me to follow him. I at once jumped to the conclusion that Mr. Simpson had sent one of the axe-men to meet me and guide me across the lake. So I ran with all my might towards him, calling to him at the same time. When I came close to the spot where he had stood, I looked around. He was not there, but a lull in the drift showed him some distance farther on, still beckoning me to follow. No reply came to my calls to the man to wait for me, but every few moments he would appear some distance ahead beckoning me towards him. I could not tell what to make of the man's eccentric behaviour, but thought possibly he was angry over being sent to look me up, and was taking this method of evincing his displeasure. At last I saw him on the shore, pointing towards the woods, and reaching the spot where he had been standing I found myself at the point where the road to our camp left the lake. The road was easy to follow, and I hurried forward, still somewhat puzzled over the refusal of my guide to wait for me; and wondering also why he had not brought a horse, and sled. I reached the camp just as the men had finished their supper, and everybody was surprised at my return. Mr. Simpson said he supposed that even if I had started from Crooked Creep camp in the morning I would have turned back when the snow storm came on. Somewhat bewildered I asked which of the men it was that guided me across the lake and pointed out the road to the camp. "Why did he not wait for me?" I asked in a rather injured tone. The men looked at one another in amazement. Not a man had been out of the camp that evening. Every man had returned from work at the usual time and remained in camp until my arrival. We were nearly seventy miles from the nearest settlement and there was no camp nearer than the one at Crooked Creek. Every person in the camp became restless and nervous. That man who guided me across Red Pine Lake was not a being of flesh and blood, was the general conclusion of the shanty men and my description of his disappearances and reappearances tended to strengthen their theory. The experience was such an inexplicable one that very few of the inmates of our camp slept that night. I was grateful for my rescue, and it was evident that, whoever my guide was, it was not my destiny to be eaten by wolves or frozen to death in attempting to cross Red Pine Lake in a snow storm.

My Tower Ghosts

KING'S COUNTY NEWS (HAMPTON, NEW BRUNSWICK) JANUARY 3, 1895

This well-written account describes a demon that appears and reappears in a country setting. At the end, the narrator assures his readers that the devil he has described "really existed." The story appeared under the title above in 1895.

◆ ◆ ◆

At one corner of my house is a tall, wide tower, rising high above the trees which surround it. In one of the upper rooms of this tower I work and think, and here in the evening and early part of the night, I used to be quite alone except for the ghosts.

Before I had come to this house, I knew that the tower was haunted but I did not mind that. As the ghosts had never done anyone any harm, I thought I should really be glad of their company which must certainly be different from the company of ordinary people. So, when I had arranged an upper room in the tower so that I might pleasantly work and think therein, I expected the ghosts to come to me, and should have been very much disappointed if they had not.

I did not exactly understand these ghosts, of which I had heard nothing definite except that they haunted the tower, and I did not know in what way they would manifest themselves to me. It was not long, however, after I had begun to occupy the room before the ghosts came to me. One evening a little before Christmas, after everybody in the house but myself had gone to bed, and all was quiet outside and inside, I heard a knock and was on the point of saying "Come in!" when the knock was repeated and I found that it did not come from the door but from the wall. I smiled.

You cannot come in that way, I thought, unless there are secret doors in these walls, and even then you must open them for yourself.

I went on with my writing, but I soon looked up again, for I thought I heard a chair gently pushed back against the wall in a corner behind me, and almost immediately I heard a noise as if some little boy had dropped a number of marbles, or perhaps pennies, but there was no chair in the corner at which I looked, and there were no pennies nor marbles on the floor.

Night after night I heard my ghosts—for I had come to consider them as mine, which I had bought with the house—and although I could not see them, there were so many ways in which they let me know they existed that I felt for them a sort of companionship. When in the quiet hours of early night I heard their gentle knocks I knew they would have been glad to come in, and I did not feel lonely.

Now and then I thought I heard the voices of the ghosts, sometimes outside, under my window, and sometimes behind me in the distant corner of the room. Their tones were low and plaintive, and I could not distinguish words or phrases, but it often seemed as if they were really speaking to me, and that I ought to try to understand and answer them. But I soon discovered that these voice-like sounds were caused by the vagrant breezes going up and down the tall chimney of the tower, making aeolian tones, not of music, but of vague and indistinct speech.

The winter passed, and at last there came a time when I saw one of the ghosts. It was in the dusk of an evening, early in spring, and just outside of an open window, that it appeared to me. It was as plain to my sight as if it had been painted in delicate half-tones against a sombre background of tender foliage and evening sky.

It was clad from head to foot in softest grey, such as phantoms of the night are said to love, and over its shoulders and down its upright form were thrown the fleecy folds of a mantle so mistily grey that it seemed to blend into the dusky figure it partly shrouded. The moment I saw it I knew it saw me. Out of its cloudy greyness there shone two eyes, black, clear and sparkling, fixed upon me with questioning intensity. I sat gazing with checked breath at this ghost of the tower.

Suddenly I leaned forward—just a little—to get a better view of the apparition, when, like a bursting bubble, it was gone, and there was nothing before me but the background of foliage and evening sky.

Frequently after that I saw the ghost or it may have been one of the others, for it was difficult, with these grey visions, with which one must not speak or towards which it was hazardous to move even a hand, to become so well acquainted that I should know one from another. But there they were; not only did I hear them; not only, night after night, did my ears assure me of their existence, but in the shadows of the trees, as the summer came on, and on the lonelier stretches of the lawn I saw them and I knew that in good truth my home was haunted.

Late one afternoon, while walking in my grounds, I saw before me one of the spectres of my tower. It moved slowly over the lawn, scarcely seeming to touch the tips of the grass, and with no more sound than a cloud would make when settling on a hilltop. Suddenly it turned its bright watchful eyes upon me, and then with a start that seemed to send a thrill even through the grey mantle which lightly touched its shoulders it rose before my very eyes until it was nearly as high as the top of my tower.

Wings it had not nor did it float in the air; it ran like a streak of grey electricity along the lightning rod, only instead of flashing down in, as electricity would pass from the sky, it ran upward. I did not see this swiftly moving spirit reach the topmost point of the rod, for at a point where the thick wire approached the eaves it vanished.

By this time I had come to the conclusion, not altogether pleasant to my mind, that my ghosts were taking advantage of my forbearance, with their mystic knocks and signals in the night and their visits in the daylight, and that there must be too many of them in my tower. I must admit that they annoyed me very little and I was not in the least afraid of them, but there were others who came into my tower and slept in some of its rooms and to the minds of visitors and timorous maids there was something uncanny and terrifying in these midnight knocks and scratches.

So, having concluded from what I had seen that day that it was the very uppermost part of the tower which had become the resort of these grey sprites, and from which they came to disturb our quiet and repose, I determined to interfere with their passage from the earth to my tower top. If, like an electric current they used the lightning rod as a means of transit, I made a plan which would compel them to use it in the conventional and proper way. The rod was placed that the lightning might come down it, not that it might go up, so I set myself to put the rod in a condition that it would permit the ghosts to descend as the lightning did, but which would prevent them from going up.

Accordingly I thoroughly greased the rod for a considerable distance above the ground.

"No," said I to myself, "you may all come down, one after the other whenever you like. You will descend very quickly when you reach the greased part of the rod, but you will not go up it again. You are getting very bold, and if you continue your mad revels in my tower you will frighten people and give my house a bad name. You may become dryads if you like and shut yourself up in the hearts of the tall and solemn oaks. There you may haunt the blue jays and the woodpeckers, but they will not tell tales of ghostly visits, which may keep my friends away and make my servants give me warning.

After that there were no more grey flashes up my lighting rod, though how many came down it I know not, and the intramural revels in the tower ceased. But not for long. The ghosts came back again; perhaps not so many as before, but still enough for them to let me know that they were there.

How they ascended to their lofty haunts I could not tell, nor did I try to find out. I accepted the situation. I could not contend with these undaunted sprites.

One evening in the autumn, outside the same window from which I had seen the first ghost of the tower, I saw another apparition, but it was not one of the grey spectres to which I had become accustomed. It was a jet black demon. Its eyes, large, green and glaring, shone upon me, and it was as motionless and hard as a statue cut in coal.

For only an instant I saw it, and then in a flash, like the apparition I had first seen from that window, it disappeared. After that I saw the demon again and again and strange to say the ghosts in my tower became fewer and fewer, and at last disappeared altogether. The advent of the black spirit seemed to have exerted an evil influence over the spirits in grey, and like the Indian in the presence of the white man, they faded away and gradually became extinct.

The last time I saw one of my ghosts it appeared to me late on the November afternoon among the brown foliage of an aged oak, just as a dryad might have peeped forth from her leafy retreat wondering if the world were yet open to her for a ramble under the stars. The world was open to my grey ghost, but only in one direction. Between it and me could be seen among the shadows of the ground the dark form of the demon, trembling and waiting. Then away from the old oak, away from my house and tower, along the limbs of the trees which stood on the edge of the wood, slowly and silently, my ghost vanished from my view like a little grey cloud, gently moving over the sky, at least dissolving out of my sight.

Now, in the early hours of the night my tower is quiet and still. There are no more knocks, no more revels in the hidden passages in the walls. My ghosts are gone. All that I hear now are the voices in the chimney, but I know that these are only imaginary voices, and therefore they produce in me no feeling of companionship. But my ghosts really existed.

The Fire-Spook of Caledonia Mills

N. CARROLL MACINTYRE

Students of Canadian mysteries are familiar with what is known as the Fire-Spook of Caledonia Mills. Between 1899 and 1922, the MacDonald Homestead at Caledonia Mills, a small community of the Highland Scottish located south of Antigonish, Nova Scotia, was subjected to terrific, poltergeist-like effects: strange lights, peculiar noises, mysterious fires, unexplained movements of animals and house-hold articles, and so on.

During the winter of 1922, these effects were studied by the well-known detective P.O. Carroll from Pictou and Dr. Walter Franklin Prince, principal research officer of the American Society for Psychical Research. The Halifax Herald *bore Prince's travel expenses from New York in exchange for exclusive coverage of the investigation. Carroll and Prince, working independently, came to the same conclusion: The cause of the manifestations was the person of Mary Ellen MacDonald, the adopted daughter, who had no knowledge that she was the agency through which the effects were made manifest. In the parlance of psychical research, she was the "focus" of the poltergeist effects.*

Here is an account of a visit to the site made some fifty years after the events, as described by N. Carroll Macintyre, a native of Antigonish, in his fine publication, The Fire-Spook of Caledonia Mills.

◆ ◆ ◆

Growing up in the town of Antigonish, most people were always interested in the stories about the Spook Farm. It was in the fall of 1961 that I had my first opportunity to visit the MacDonald homestead. A friend of mine, Art Farrell from Glencoe (across the woods from Caledonia), promised me a trip to the historic site. In preparation for the occasion, I asked questions and read any material that was available in order that I might fortify myself for the adventure.

On a sunny Saturday afternoon, I was formally escorted to the Spook Farm by Art Farrell, Ed MacDonald from Salmon River, and our driver from Roman Valley, who was also to be our tour guide. Since Roman Valley is the next community to Caledonia Mills, we were assured that our guide was well familiar with the area. We boarded his old Jeep and made the trip through the woods to the home site. As we drew near the location, we were warned just to look about and not touch anything or take any souvenirs. He told us several stories about the farm, some of which I knew to be true, while others had the distinct flavour of local folklore. Being a "townie," I was subjected to more jibs and jabs than the others.

Upon arriving at the location of the farm, I was immediately disappointed. There was no haunted house, no barns—they had all fallen down years ago. There were just indentations in the ground where they once stood. As I wandered about the area, I tried to reconstruct the strange occurrences of the winter of 1922. I did not experience anything "eerie" (which I was well prepared for); it just appeared to be another old deserted plot of land that could be found in any rural area of Antigonish Country.

We were told by our guide, "Don't touch nothing." Having ventured to the area of mystery, it was my decision not to leave the old homestead without a souvenir, no matter how minuscule it might be. When no one was looking, I stuffed a piece of burnt shingle, which I had dug up from around the foundation, into my back pocket. We finally completed our investigation of the area and boarded the Jeep for the trip back to the main road.

As we approached the halfway point in our journey to the main road, our guide stopped the Jeep and asked if anyone had taken anything from the farm. Not wanting to give up my souvenir and hoping that it was just a whim on his part, I immediately answered no. We then proceeded. As we drew nearer to the main road, the Jeep was once again stopped, and the same question was asked. Our guide was not satisfied with the answer of no, and refused to move. Without warning, he turned towards me and said, "Macintyre, you took something." Of course I remembered the shingle in my back pocket, and produced it. The Jeep was turned around, and we returned to the farm, where I was asked to replace it, which I did.

Many would pass this off as normal, but to me it was a touch of the abnormal. I was pleased with the experience; at least I had something to tell about when I returned home. It was several years later, when I mentioned the occurrence to the noted folklorist C.I.N. MacLeod, that he stated some people had the "Celtic feeling," and when certain people visited such a location, they were able to draw out of the area a type of extrasensory perception. It appeared that our man from Roman Valley had that feeling and caused the return of my souvenir.

Evidently I did not learn my lesson...

◆ ◆ ◆

It was probably the poltergeistic aspect of the Fire-Spook of Caledonia Mills, always in the back of my mind, that prompted me to chronicle the events that took place on the MacDonald homestead from 1899 to 1922. That aspect had to do with my last visit to the farm, the first week of May, 1971.

I was asked by one of the senior members of the Casket Printing and Publishing Company Ltd., Eileen Henry, to give her a tour of the Spook Farm. As it was ten years since I had visited the site, I was only too glad to oblige. Of course I wanted to see for myself the changes that had taken place in the area during the past decade.

On a sunny Saturday afternoon, we parked the car at the end of the lane heading up to the farm. It was considerably more difficult to find the actual site, as it had grown over. However, after some misses, we arrived at the precise location where the house once stood. I gave Mrs. Henry an impromptu tour of the area and reconstructed some of the events that had taken place some fifty years previous. Of course, I added a few stories that were well-laced with local folklore. I remember Eileen distinctly hanging on to my arm all the way back to the car.

I could not resist the temptation to dig about a bit in the area of the old foundation. To my surprise, I came across an old-fashioned, hand-painted egg cup that had resisted the test of years underneath a board.

I should have learned from my experience years earlier—the shingle episode—and left well enough alone, but for me the temptation was too great. I placed the egg cup carefully in my pocket, and took it away from the home site of Alexander "Black John" MacDonald. That evening, after returning to Antigonish, I drove down to our summer farmhouse at Frog Hollow. When I arrived I realized that I still had the egg cup in my pocket. I decided that a small shelf in the kitchen would be the proper resting place for my new-found treasure. I knew that it would be a good conversation piece, and on many occasions late at night would lend itself to a good ghost story. However, this was not to be.

On the Victoria Day weekend, a few Saturdays later, I held the first gathering of the summer season at the farmhouse. The Saturday night affair was enlivened by the addition of the egg cup. The result was that numerous stories were told of Mary Ellen the Spook. Of course, as the evening wore on (as well as the refreshments), the stories got better and spookier. It seemed that the egg cup was the centre of attraction that evening.

Around 1:30 a.m., my guests began to leave, and by 2:00 a.m. there remained myself and two friends to help clean up. It would have been about 2:45 a.m. when we finished—dishes were done, ashtrays emptied, fires put out, et al. A suggestion was made by Dubie that rather than go back to town we stay the night at the house, as it was quite late (early) and we were all well "under the weather." I remember that I was quite adamant about the fact that the beds would be damp and we would "catch our death" if we stayed the night. As I had the only transportation back to town, my friends had to concede and return to town with me. Was it some premonition on my part that we did not stay in the house that night, or was it that I was just plain scared that we would "catch our death"?

Three and a half hours later, at 6:15 a.m., I returned to Frog Hollow, as Antigonish Harbour was popularly known. The only thing left standing of the once-lovely old farmhouse was the chimney. It had burnt to the ground! Would we have "caught our death" if we had stayed the night?

The Haunted Axe

TORONTO WORLD
JANUARY 12, 1908

The pioneers and settlers who occupied the land, who felled the trees, who furrowed the earth, who erected the farmhouses, the churches, the courthouses, the jailhouses—who built this country from scratch—held many strange beliefs. What they believed or half-believed about cursed objects and jinxed sailing ships, about devils in the woods and angels in the clouds, came with them from the Old Country, particularly Scotland, Ireland, and Wales, where supernatural customs were honoured and such traditions went unquestioned. A few of these practices may have been influenced by the traditions of the indigenous population.

Here is an engrossing tale that need not necessarily be taken with the utmost seriousness. It is a cautionary tale, and it is told with some

of the poise and polish of a born storyteller. "The Haunted Axe"
appeared in Toronto World *in 1908, although apparently it had origi-*
nally appeared in the columns of the Chicago Tribune.

♦ ♦ ♦

Ste. Lucia, a tiny hamlet, set deep in the woods of Canada, in the wild, beautiful country inhabited by the French and Scotch loggers and the She-She-Genge Indians, has set out to the world one of the strangest and uncanniest stories ever told.

Ste. Lucia declares, and the people of all that wonderful district between the Brokenhead Lake, where Read River flows down to the great lakes, believe that Felix Jorgelet's great two-edged axe is haunted. Furthermore, none dares touch the axe, for already, they say, Felix Jorgelet's axe has killed five men, and they whisper in awed tones that it will kill any one who claims it as his own, or attempts to use it.

Neither do the people of the Whitemouth Lake neighbourhood, nor even those at Ste. Lucia, where there are a trading post, a store and a saloon, theorize much or attempt to explain things away on scientific lines. They care not for explanations—all they know is that Felix Jorgelet's great axe has killed five men—and *sacre*, will theories bring back men after Felix Jorgelet's axe has split their heads and spilled their brains?

So it is left for the outside world to theorize over the mysterious and awesome happenings—and meantime Felix Jorgelet's axe remains in the cabin of his foster brother, Angus Ferguson. Nor will Angus carry it into the woods that he may throw it into the wild rushing waters of the Whitemouth lest it split his head, nor will any of the She-She-Genges approach even the cabin where Ferguson lives, nor are the French less fearful.

There is hardly a spot in all the north woods so wildly beautiful as that country through which the Whitemouth flows northward, and near where it skirts the She-She-Genge reservation is its most beautiful spot—rushing rivers, which boil over stones, wooded hills, cataracts, leaping trout, majestic pines. In summer it is a glorious mass of greens; in fall, the green of the pines, the rich yellow of the birch, the vivid colours of the hardwoods, make it even more beautiful and when the snow piles higher and higher in winter, when the great trees bend under the weight of dazzling whiteness, then the woodsmen declare it is wonderful.

In this country Felix Jorgelet and Angus Ferguson lived together, hunted and guided those who came to capture the great speckled trout in the Whitemouth and the Brokenhead. In their little clearing, with no neighbours nearer than twelve miles except the She-She that had wandered from the reservation, they were known as great men, and in the woods, when the crews worked at getting out the timber, they were leaders of all.

It was hard to tell which was the better, the strange, quiet, strong Scot, or the tall, lithe, panther-like, equally taciturn Frenchman. They were foster brothers, for both had lost their parents when young and both had been adopted by Manato, the half-breed, who had been the wife of John McDiarmid. She was of the She-Shes, and it was said her father was an English soldier; but in the great north woods these things counted for little. She was a good wife to McDiarmid, and when no children came to them they adopted the two motherless little ones and took them to the cabin.

They were strong men in the woods, great hunters and trappers and acknowledged leaders in the lumber gangs, but generally the Frenchman was acknowledged the superior, because he was faster. And Felix Jorgelet's chief pride was his huge axe, which he had made for himself. When he worked hewing a giant tree the blade of his double-edged axe looked like a circle of fire around his head, and when he "roughed" a timber his axe filled the air with chips and he planed the side as if his axe were some great whirling saw.

But one day, about a year ago, Felix Jorgelet went into the woods, with his axe, to cut a timber and hew it square for use in building a lean-to. He did not return at supper time, but Angus paid no attention. People are not worried in the north woods when others fail to return, even for days, but somehow Angus worried that evening and went to bed with the impression that something was wrong.

The next morning he found Felix Jorgelet with his head split open and the bloody axe beside him. First he buried Felix, then carried the word to the settlement. In other places he might have been accused of murder, but the north woods understands a man's character, and they knew Angus had not killed Felix. Other communities might have suspected that some one else had murdered the Frenchman, but Angus and the others knew that no man could have killed Felix with his own axe. Therefore, it was an accident.

Angus Ferguson continued to live alone, but strangely, he refused to touch Felix's axe after carrying it from the dead tree.

Within a few weeks George Forseille, a big man and a noted axeman, sought to buy Felix's famous axe. At first Angus refused and told him that the axe was dangerous, but as George was not afraid, Angus' Scotch thrift overpowered his feelings and he sold the [text obscured] where "The Breed" had met his death. It was stolen by John Longarm, an Indian from the reservation, and he was found dead in the clearing not far from Forty-Mile Landing, on the Whitemouth, with his head split open.

From that time on almost everybody in the woods was afraid of the axe, and its reputation spread until none would touch it, until late in the fall Ed Dines, a reckless lumberman from Michigan, hooting at the idea that an axe could be bewitched, claimed it as his own, with none to dispute his possession of it. Dines was killed while chopping in the woods on the opposite side of a tree from a fellow workman. The axe, according to the lone witness of the tragedy, seemed to sink into the wood, twist, bound back and strike viciously upon Dines' head, killing him instantly.

People who live in cities may explain and give reasonable causes for the succession of tragedies, but the people who live in the north woods, and are either too simple or too broad to doubt anything, say it is haunted. So it stands in Angus Ferguson's cabin, where he carried it lest it might kill others.

The Snoring Ghost

MARGERY WIGHTON

This anecdotal account of a haunting was written by Margery Wighton. All I know about her is that she was a Vancouver-based journalist. Her account appeared under the title "The Case of the Haunted House and Snoring Ghost" in the Vancouver Sun *on December 27, 1952. No doubt the editors decided that a "snoring ghost" would make delightful reading between Christmas and New Year's—Marley's ghost and all that!*

The suggestion is made that the haunted shack in the story was erected over an old Native burial ground. In the 1960s, whenever anyone reported "mystery lights," it was commonplace to suggest that the cause was "swamp gas." Nowadays, whenever a house in Canada is haunted, someone suggests that it was erected on an old Native burial ground.

◆ ◆ ◆

It was the early summer of 1912. I was fifteen and living in British Columbia with my parents. Quite unexpectedly, my father had a very good offer for our fruit farm in the Okanagan Valley, and we moved to Vancouver Island, where he intended to start a poultry farm. We bought twelve acres of uncleared bush and arranged for the delivery of a sectional bungalow.

The problem was to find somewhere to live for about eight weeks while the bungalow was under construction. This matter was soon solved by the offer of a shack, belonging to a farmer, standing on the other side of a deep ravine, amid giant fir trees and thick undergrowth.

For the first few days, things were normal enough, and tired with helping my father unravel the plans of our bungalow, we came home each evening, and after supper were only too pleased to go to bed.

The third night, I went upstairs about nine o'clock and, while undressing, my mother sat on my bed talking to me. We had left my father reading in the little sitting-room. In the middle of her conversation, my mother stopped abruptly and laughed. My father was snoring downstairs!

"Daddy must be tired," she said. We both listened to a comfortable, monotonous snore, so distinct one would have imagined the sleeper to be in the room.

My mother rose and walked downstairs and I followed in my dressing gown. "I thought you were asleep," she said. "We heard you snoring."

My father was indignant. "You must both be mad," he said. "I'm reading a good book."

We came upstairs again, and no sooner had I taken off my dressing gown than we realized the snore was continuing. "Really," my mother said, "Daddy must be teasing us."

We laughed to relieve the tension, took off our shoes, and crept downstairs again, thinking to find my father pretending to snore. To our astonishment, we found him, as before, busy reading.

He looked annoyed and took off his glasses. "If you two think this is awfully amusing, I don't," he said.

The laughter died from our lips. We told him about the snoring. He said we were still crazy and reluctantly followed us upstairs. And there it was again! Just a quiet, peaceful human snore.

"There's someone in here," my father exclaimed, getting up impatiently. "But where?" he asked, looking around the bare walls, where there wasn't even a cupboard.

We banged about, thumping the walls, hitting the wooden ceiling. We moved the bed and table around but the snoring continued. We ransacked the second bedroom, but as we passed through the doorway we could not hear it any more.

My father went to the little kitchen, at the foot of the stairs, while my mother and I stood at the top. We said "there" each time the snore came. He could not hear anything downstairs at all.

We then decided it must be something outside. But as we stood together outside the little shack, there was not a sound to be heard but the faraway cry of a night bird in the bush.

My father then stood under my low bedroom window, while my mother and I went back to my room. The snoring went on unabated but my father could hear nothing whatever.

Completely nonplussed, my mother and I went to bed in the second bedroom. My father determined not to sleep till he had "laid the ghost."

The moon shone through the windows and I found myself unable to sleep. At 2:00 a.m., my father came into the room. "I'm damned if I can stand it," he said. "I've tried everything to stop that snore. I thought I'd found one of you two snoring now."

Next day he and the owner raked the roof from end to end. That was really all they could do, since there was no loft and the place had no foundations. We could see under the flooring boards and there was absolutely nothing.

When evening came, the owner returned to see if he could near the snoring, and sure enough it started again most punctually. Night after night our "snorer" enjoyed his slumbers while we had little rest.

People suggested owls, deer, chipmunks, spiders, and Indian tom-toms. But outside suggestions were disposed of, since once you left my bedroom you could hear nothing.

My father couldn't stand it and slept downstairs, while mother and I nervously occupied the second bedroom.

And we stood this for six weeks, with no hope of solving the mystery. Then our architect friend, Clem Webb, arrived. We told him all about our snoring ghost.

We congregated in the little bedroom once more, as we had done so often. Nine o'clock came, nine-thirty, ten. Nothing happened, for the first time for six weeks!

Clem Webb never did hear it. He completely laid the ghost, and we never heard it again. We moved into our own bungalow about three weeks after his arrival, and almost forgot all about it.

But a year later, the owner of the shack wrote to a Vancouver firm for a new car. When it arrived, driven by a man from the garage, he decided he must have a few lessons before allowing the man to return to Vancouver. Having no room for him in the house, he put the driver to sleep in the haunted shack.

At midnight there was a wild knocking on his door and there stood the driver, trembling from head to foot.

"The place is haunted," the man kept repeating. "I heard someone come in, although I locked the door, walk upstairs and throw his boots off. Then the next thing I knew he was snoring loudly. Yet there's not a soul there, I went all round with a lamp."

He refused to return and left next morning.

The shack was still standing in its lonely setting among the tall dark pines when I visited the place in 1937. It was empty and had been for some years, people said.

I wandered once more through the deep gulley, along the trail over the dried pine needles. The maple leaves had turned a burnished gold, and no one standing in that quiet spot would ever dream that such a disturbing mystery haunted the little shack.

Perhaps the Indians are nearest the truth. They say it's built over an old Indian burial ground.

Who knows?

Not That I Believe in Ghost Stories

WAYNE MACDONALD

Wayne MacDonald was a reporter for the Calgary Albertan *who had an interest in offbeat subjects. One day he wrote an account of two nights spent in a haunted house in Calgary and the story was published on February 3, 1962. The account was so popular with the editor and readers that he wrote a sequel, which was published two days later. Both accounts are included here.*

◆ ◆ ◆

1.

HALFWAY HOUSE, Banff National Park—Dozens of skiers have fled from this country ski lodge late at night. They believe it is haunted. I wanted to run on the first night of my visit here to check their stories. Not that I believe in ghost stories, but strange things happen in Halfway.

Frightening things happen, especially at night, but despite my imagination, they can all be explained—so far—by using common sense.

That's the hardest thing up here—common sense.

I skied into Halfway with guide-companion Glenn Cowan late Wednesday afternoon. The cabin itself is one-roomed, log, and situated high on a knoll in a wind-swept valley. Immediately to the east the blank cliffs of Redoubt Mountain tower high in the frosty air.

To the south, Mount Temple reaches for the gods and beyond that the Valley of the Ten Peaks nestles on the horizon.

The cabin has two bunk beds, a steel one and a wooden one. It has two stoves, one of which doesn't work.

There's a wooden table, a wooden bench, a wash stand, some cookware and plates, and that's all.

Glenn and I arrived in time for supper. After bacon, eggs and fried bread, he left.

The sun was lowering behind the peaks as he started; the evening was still.

My mind was working overtime. I heard new noises—creaks and groans. The crackling fire startled me, and I imagined a broom in the corner had moved.

I told myself that ghosts don't exist.

As night came on, it worried me that the sky was black. There were no stars; the moon was hidden.

A wind was starting to wheeze in the pines and even this sound was unfriendly.

I tried to read. I placed three candles on the table and huddled close to the book. Each new sound jerked me from the pages. I found myself stepping to the window, fighting the reflection of the candles in the glass, peering into the blackness.

I finally admitted that no matter what, I was in Halfway for the night. I could never find the trail to Temple Chalet without moonlight.

I returned to my reading. Suddenly, without warning, two candles blew out.

I lit them again and sat, almost fearing to move. When I did I found an eight-inch crack in the log by the window. The wind had extinguished the candles.

I decided, shortly after 7:00 p.m., that the best place would be bed. The fire was burning low; I had been warned not to burn too many candles. I felt sleep would drown my fears.

In bed the noises magnified. I heard a low creaking and something banging on the door, but I had been warned of this. The wind often rocks an overhead sign on the cabin.

The fire was now dead, save for final glowing embers. I fell asleep. An hour later, I awakened in terror. Bright shadows were leaping across the room. My immediate reaction was that the moon had risen. But this light was too bright.

I silently reached for my glasses. The fire was raging.

A full, orange blaze was crackling in the stove, hot and bright and loud. I was terrified.

After ageless minutes I rationalized. There must have been an unburned log in the stove. It must have caught fire after I fell asleep.

The night went without further event. I wakened in the morning to a cry of "Anybody home!" A park warden stepped in, tripping on the bench I had placed against the door. He was on his way to Skoki and stopped to check how I was.

How was I?

Oh, Halfway's fine—in daylight.

2.

Lake Louise: A grey-haired man turned to me in the coffee shop of the Post Hotel. "So you spent two nights in Halfway House?" he asked.

I replied I had.

"Son," he said, "you're mighty lucky to be alive."

The man was Ray LeGace, manager of the hotel and a twenty-year veteran of the Rockies. He's like most residents of Lake Louise; he honestly believes there are ghosts in Halfway House.

"I'd never stay there alone," he said. "In fact, I don't think I'd stay there at all. Especially at night."

Ray believes the tiny skiers' cabin halfway between Lake Louise and Skoki Lodge is occupied by the ghost of a Calgary painter who died there several years ago.

The painter and his dog lived in Halfway for several months. He refused to come out in even the bitterest weather because he was waiting for a perfect mountain sunset.

He wanted to see a "perfect" sun dip behind Redoubt Mountain—but it never happened. The painter was never satisfied with the colours of the sky.

He starved to death in the lonely lodge.

Others in Lake Louise believe the ghost to be a woman, an attractive girl killed in an avalanche. Or two brothers buried in snow in the '30s. Or a mountain-born skier killed on Mount Ptarmigan.

Everyone you talk to has a different tale to tell. Only a handful will say there's no ghost.

My second night in Halfway was much like the first. An over-imaginative mind was my greatest foe.

I had busied myself during the day, melting snow, washing dishes, writing, preparing food. There were no fears in daylight, but as darkness fell, uneasiness returned.

The loneliness was hardest; the knowledge that no matter what, I couldn't get out. I had never skied before my journey in, and I could never find my way to Temple Chalet without a guide.

The darkness on the second night brought with it a storm. It snowed heavily, and the wind came up, whistling through the pines, pounding on the lodge, banging at the windows, sniffing at the candles.

But at the same time, it was melting.

Water dripped throughout the night from the roof, splattering on the snow around the cabin. The dripping sounded—in my mind—like footsteps in the snow.

Drip, drip, drip. Step, step, step.

Was someone out there?

I buried my head in my pillow and tried to sleep.

The wind again banged the sign above the cabin door. It crashed against the logs, fell back, crashed, fell back, crashed.

The sign is suspended from three links of chain. The chain, when the sign wasn't banging, grated against the metal hook, creaking and groaning. It was a horrible sound.

And the crackling of the fire bothered me. I started every time a chunk of wood "popped" in the heat. It would seem the fire was finally dead, and suddenly, "Crack."

But the ghost—or ghosts—didn't come.

I wakened in the morning to a voice—a distant yodel. By the time I dressed, Glenn Cowan was at the door to guide me back to Temple.

He seemed partly disappointed, partly relieved, that the ghost who visited him hadn't visited me. When he stayed at Halfway a fortnight ago, he was startled when his fire suddenly went out. He turned to see a plate on the middle of the table move to the edge and crash to the floor. A cup in its saucer on the table tipped.

As he hurried to get his skies on to escape the "thing," he suddenly smelled a woman's perfume. "It was as if I was helping a woman on with her coat," he said, "and I suddenly smelled the perfume in her hair."

Is there a ghost in Halfway? A ghost that has haunted Cowan and skiers by the score? A ghost that keeps Ray LeGace away?

I don't know.

The people who have fled Halfway cannot be swayed. They're convinced the ghost is there.

On the other hand, skiers have stayed in the cabin for weeks, for months, and more. One stayed throughout a winter.

I doubt the ghost is there—but can I say? A prime minister of Canada believed in them, and writers have told of them through the years.

We scoff at their beliefs, but who can tell?

PART IV
OTHER GHOSTLY PLACES

G host stories are ageless in the sense that they have frightened listeners around campfires and fires in hearths and fireplaces from the beginning of recorded history to our own time. The reader will find in this section modern ghosts; that is, spirits who have put in appearances from the 1960s to the 2000s. The ghosts remain much the same, but the observers of them are inclined to be more critical, more sceptical, and often more thoughtful. The assumption has always been that places are haunted. Perhaps people are haunted too—by ghosts or by lack of ghosts.

Granny's Cottage

JEANETTE EARP

Some things take time to come to fruition.

It took two years for a suggestion of mine to flower. I wrote a letter to Mrs. A.J. Earp, a resident of Niagara-on-the-Lake, Ontario. I had learned from a friend of a friend, who resides in this picturesque community on the Niagara River, that Mrs. Earp had a story to tell about her years living in "Granny's Cottage."

So I sent the letter to her. The letter was delivered, but, as happens from time to time, it was misplaced in a drawer and lay there, only to be discovered two years later. Mrs. Earp phoned me, somewhat abashed, and inquired if I was still interested in receiving information about the haunting of "Granny's Cottage." I assured her I was, so she wrote the letter that appears here.

It is an extremely well-organized description of a series of peculiar experiences. In her letter, Mrs. Earp mentions Ray and Eileen Sonin. Ray was a radio broadcaster with a booming voice that could be heard on Calling All Britons!, *his weekly early evening program, carried by Toronto's CFRB. At the time, his wife, Eileen, was the city's best-known sensitive (or medium) and the author of two popular books based on her ghosthunting experiences:* Ghosts I Have Known: The Psychic Experiences of a Natural Medium *(1968) and* ESPecially Ghosts: Some True Experiences of the Supernatural in North America *(1970).*

It seems there was a poltergeist in "Granny's Cottage." It was worth waiting two years for this letter!

◆ ◆ ◆

August 18, 1998

Dear Mr. Colombo,

As promised, the long overdue response to your April 1996 letter.

The few unexplained occurrences which I experienced while living alone in "Granny's Cottage," 240 Gate Street in Niagara-on-the-Lake, certainly puzzled me but I never felt or heard any sinister or other presence in the house during my seven years there. The house was built circa 1818 with extensive alterations made in the late 1960s, a few years before I moved in. I should mention that at this time I worked in St. Catharines, returning home in the late afternoon or early evening.

The unexplained events, as I remember them:

(a) Books turned upside down

There was a long, two-shelf bookcase under a window in the living room which contained, among other books, my 16-year collection of hardcover *Horizon* magazines, filed chronologically by issue number and year. I noticed one evening that all, or almost all, of the *Horizons* were upside down on the shelves; one would have to stand on one's head to read the spines. They were still in chronological order, aligned neatly at the shelf edge. None of the other books were disturbed.

(b) The moving vase

While watering houseplants one morning before leaving for work, I topped up a vase of roses in my bedroom. Noticing that I had overfilled it, I placed the vase on the rear windowsill while I mopped up the spill on the dresser. Running short of time, I left the vase on the sill rather than return it to the still-damp dresser top.

When in my room that evening, I noticed to my surprise that the vase was not on the windowsill but on the floor beneath it, the water level still at the vase rim and the roses undisturbed in their arrangement. I know for certain I had not placed the vase on the floor.

(c) Rearranged curtains

My little cottage had crisp, tie-back curtains on every window. Returning home from work one evening I discovered all the curtains on the garden side of the house had been drawn, the tie-backs and their securing pins laid neatly on the table or chest nearest each window.

(d) A curious cat

My cat, Theo (black, partly Siamese), liked to stretch out on top of the sofa back when I sat there evenings, reading or listening to music. The sofa sat in the middle of the room facing the fireplace. A number of times Theo would suddenly sit up straight and seem to follow with his eyes something descending the stairs behind and to the right of the sofa. He would then lean back as though avoiding whatever was passing behind the sofa, then crane his neck as he seemingly followed with his eyes that something as it passed through the doorway into the room beyond.

Did Theo have repeated bouts of indigestion or was he actually "seeing" something? As I understand it, the stairs were new with the recent renovations, the original stairs being not much more than a ladder rising from the kitchen area at the back of the house.

(e) An uncomfortable Eileen Sonin

Mrs. Sonin may have been known to you. She wrote one or more books on ghosts, spirits or things that go bump in the night. I knew her and her husband through a mutual friend in broadcasting.

One evening I met friends for dinner at the Oban Inn. Ray and Eileen Sonin were at the next table with friends and we had a jolly time. I invited everyone back to the house for coffee and more conversation. Mrs. Sonin had been lively and cheerful through dinner, but once seated in the living room it wasn't long before she began complaining of a headache and was clearly feeling some distress. The Sonins left shortly after.

I learned from our mutual friends a few years later, after I had married and moved to a new address, that Mrs. Sonin had not been physically ill but had experienced such distress from something in the house that she had had to leave. Apparently the next day she called my friends, asking them to urge me to find new accommodation: Something very disturbing was in the house.

(f) More uncomfortable friends

Those friends to whom Eileen Sonin had expressed her unsettling feelings were occasionally overnight guests in the cottage. The husband stayed only once, but his wife visited frequently, leaving mid-morning the next day. (I would have left for work an hour or two earlier.)

Again, kindly, nothing was said at the time, but apparently she felt most uncomfortable during those few hours alone in the house.

Even more remarkable was the husband's experience the one and only time he stayed the night. His wife and I went to a concert in St. Catharines after dinner. He planned to have a leisurely bath and settle down to watch a game on TV. We came back rather late and were surprised to find him sitting in the car in the driveway. He said he had changed his mind and had gone to the Oban to watch the game in the bar, had not been able to get back into the house, so had waited for us in the car.

We thought his story strange, not least because of his appearance.

What I learned subsequently was that while relaxing in the bathtub, he suddenly felt such dread; the room became chilled and he sensed such an overwhelmingly evil atmosphere that it was almost palpable. He fled the bathroom, threw on some clothes, and hurried from the house to his car. He felt foolish, frightened and distressed that he had not picked up Theo, the cat, and saved him from whatever evil was in the house. And this was a sensible, no-nonsense, successful businessman.

I don't believe he felt anything untowards when we three joined Theo in the living room a little later, chatting over tea and cinnamon toast.

Fortunately, none of these weird sensations troubled me during those seven years in the cottage. Whether the two subsequent tenants experienced anything I do not know. I doubt it, for surely they would have mentioned something to me—we are friends.

The house has once again undergone major alterations. I don't know the current residents.

A wordy account, I fear, but I hope I have described the unexplained occurrences satisfactorily.

Sincerely,
Jeanette Earp
(Mrs. A.J. Earp)

The Whole House Was Haunted

EILEEN M. WILLIAMSON

Newfoundlanders refer to small isolated communities as outports. Such outports were—and in a marginal way continue to be—the backbone of life in Newfoundland, and the source of much of the charm and culture of the "Great Island." Successive Smallwood administrations reduced the number of these communities, however, so that by the 1990s the conditions of outport life were closer to memory than to present-day experience.

Eileen M. Williamson, the author of a memoir of life in such a small community, was born and raised in Regina, Saskatchewan. While living in Springdale, Newfoundland, she founded and edited a biweekly newspaper that eventually enjoyed a readership of seven thousand subscribers. Eileen did all her work on a portable typewriter. Later she employed a company in the closest city, Grand Falls, for her offset printing, and she taught a business course to the young people in the community.

Her vigorously written book is called Outport: A Newfoundland Journal *(1980) and it tells about life in the outport of Badger. Most interestingly, the memoir includes this matter-of-fact account of the acceptance of the poltergeist-like disturbances that occurred in a new house that was built close to the old cemetery.*

The reader will meet John, Eileen's husband, and her good friend Debbie. There is no indication of the year of this account, other than the fact that Joey Smallwood was the Premier of Newfoundland and Lester B. Pearson was the Prime Minister of Canada, and the Trans-Canada Highway was formally opened in 1962.

◆ ◆ ◆

I didn't mind working on into the night when Betty was with me, but night after night was spent in my recreation-office room in the basement while John was at organization, club and town council meetings. I hated being alone. Although the house was newly built, it was across the road from the cemetery; there was something very strong about the basement, and indeed I began to think the whole house was haunted. You can't prove ghosts to anyone who has never experienced them and doesn't want to believe in them. You can lead a full, happy and useful life without believing in ghosts—but the people who do give credence to the existence of ghosts are equally intelligent, normal people, many of whom have seen something of the supernatural.

It was one of my pupils who made me realize that I wasn't the only one who sensed something unnatural about the house. He said, "I can't come for any more lessons."

"Why not? You've practically finished the course and you're doing so well."

"I don't like coming here," he answered flatly. "You're too close to the cemetery, and it's dark when I finish my lesson."

I told him that no one in the cemetery would hurt him—and he could come in at the front door, which wasn't so close to the cemetery.

"No," he said. "There's something spooky about the house."

I was beginning to think he was right. I'd be trying to write up some event or an article, and all of a sudden I'd have the horrible feeling that I wasn't alone. There was someone or some thing watching me, hiding in the shadows of the big room, or in the rest of the dark basement, perhaps behind the furnace. I'd stop typing to listen. There was a complete stillness—then perhaps I'd hear what sounded like a door quietly closing (although I knew all the doors upstairs were open) or I'd have the illusion that someone was moving about stealthily, a rustle on the floor. Then there would be a horrifying chill in the air. It was a dead, flat cold with sharply defined boundaries, so that if I moved over towards the blazing fire in the fireplace, I was out of it.

I always thought I didn't mind Gremlins—they aren't too frightening, just annoying. I would set up an advertisement, reach for the glue, and find that the illustration I'd been working on and going to stick on the paper wouldn't be there. I'd search on the floor, under papers, and then, not having moved out of my chair, I'd see it on the coffee table across the room. Gremlins seemed just mischievous—but this other thing was really frightening. When that dreadful chill crept over me, I felt I almost had to push my way out of my chair, and run upstairs. And nothing would induce me to go downstairs again to finish my work.

"Don't work down there when you're on your own or if you're nervous. But of course there aren't any ghosts!" John said, and dashed out to his meeting.

On Monday and Thursday nights when my pupils came, their presence seemed to prevent the ghosts romping around.

However, the ghosts didn't altogether confine their activities to the basement.

One evening about nine-thirty, although there'd been no sign of them for several days, again there was the start of that chill in the air, and the strange atmosphere. I dropped everything and fled upstairs. I grabbed my book, raced for my bedroom and went to bed. And then there was an extraordinary sound—it seemed like a rocking chair, squeakily rocking back and forth, back and forth, occasionally stopping, and then going on again. I sat bolt upright, my hair standing on end, paralyzed with fear, until about midnight John came home.

The next day I told Debbie. Of course she roared with laughter. Then she said, "Why didn't you phone us—we'd have come over!"

"How could I get to the phone," I answered, "with the hall full of ghosts, and that rocking chair?"

We had a guest staying with us for a few days.

"Did you sleep well last night?" I asked her the next morning, as I handed her a plate of bacon and eggs.

"Not too bad," she said, "but did you hear anything in the night?"

"No, what was it?"

"It was the most extraordinary thing. I read for a while after going to bed, then turned out the light. I wakened with the feeling there was someone in the room, and then all of a sudden the light beside my bed blazed on, but no one was there!"

"Oh—how awful." We stared at one another. "I'm quite sure this house is haunted, but no one believes me, and I didn't think the ghosts would come when you were here. They don't usually when there are strangers around."

"Well, I think the house is haunted. One of the houses we lived in in England was haunted, and there's a definite feeling. I thought this one was as soon as I came in, but I didn't like to say anything to you in case you hadn't noticed anything."

A few weeks later we were sound asleep one night when, about three in the morning, we heard the most awful crash, which literally lifted us out of bed.

John looked over the entire house, even down in the basement, although nothing would have induced me to go down there.

"I can't find anything," he said. "Can't imagine what it was."

The next morning I went into the dining room to put the breakfast on the table.

"There's something missing—oh, there's no picture on the wall."

John came in and we looked behind the buffet. There we discovered the picture, quite a large one, about sixteen by twenty, had fallen. The nail was still in the wall, the glass wasn't broken, although it was quite a drop to the floor for such a large picture, the wire was still intact.

"But surely," I said to John, "that picture falling wouldn't have made such a thunderous noise!"

Debbie had acted as editor for the paper two or three times when we were on holidays. Usually I took everything that I thought she'd need over to her house, so that she could work there, but of course I always left her the key to our place in case she found she needed something I'd forgotten, or in case she wanted to look up something kept in the basement, where copies of the old newspapers were stored.

The day after we returned from England, she raced over and said, "You know, you're right—this house really is haunted!"

"What happened?"

"We came over one evening to look up something, and were in the basement when we heard the most tremendous crash upstairs. We tore upstairs and looked in all the rooms, but couldn't find a thing that could have fallen—there was nothing! So we went down to the basement again to pick up our things and turn the lights off—and there was the most awful, icy, appalling chill. It was really quite frightening. We sure didn't linger there!"

The climax came one winter afternoon. A howling blizzard was blowing outside, but every light was on in the recreation-office room, a lovely big fire was blazing away in the fireplace, no ghosts had appeared for several weeks, and I was working happily and busily—when I was hit in the face with a snowball!

I jumped at least seven feet straight up. I put my hand on my face—it was wet! On a smaller desk which was used by my typing pupils, and about three feet from my own desk where I was sitting, there was a fairly good-sized snowball, beginning to melt!

I was too petrified to get up and run out of the room, but I had to speak to someone in a hurry—some human voice. I reached for the phone, dialed Debbie's number, and breathed a sigh of relief when she answered immediately.

"The ghosts have just thrown a snowball at me," I said.

There was a roar of laughter, and I joined her a bit shakily. She said, "Did they hit you?"

"Yes—my face is still wet!"

"Did it come through the window—there's an awful wind blowing."

I said, "Even if it did come through the window, I'm not sitting under it—and there's the snowball melting on the typist's desk. And that's about three or four feet away!"

"Well, feel if the windowsill is wet."

I got up, and reaching up to the high basement window, I felt all along the still. It was bone dry.

Just then, to my great relief, I heard a couple of my typing pupils coming up the path to the back door, chatting merrily, so we rang off.

I rushed upstairs to let them in. "I'm so glad to see you," I said. "Come on in. You can both bear witness to the fact that my ghosts have been throwing snowballs at me!"

Somewhat reluctantly, they came downstairs. Both stared at the small lump of snow sitting in a puddle of water.

Their eyes like saucers, one of them breathed, "Lard Jaysus—let's go 'ome!"

"Of course you can't go home—you can't leave me now. Let's go to work."

Briskly I mopped up the snow, and they proceeded with their "hunt and punch" method of thumping the typewriters.

I Wish I Had Listened More

A.B.

A.B. are the initials chosen by a correspondent from Chipman, New Brunswick, who wrote to me about her family tradition and a scary experience that happened a number of years ago on farmland not far from there. The tradition and experience are described in A.B.'s letter to me, which I received on May 28, 1990. I have edited it slightly for presentation here, and have agreed to disguise the correspondent's name for family reasons.

◆ ◆ ◆

May 28, 1990

I lived most of my young life with my grandparents, whom I adored. They lived on a small farm in the country. I was the oldest child of a large family. No member of the family had ever seen a ghost, but we had experiences that were very mysterious and similar to ghost stories.

My great-grandparents also lived there, and they told me that many years before, a big giant of a man had a stone house in the apple orchard facing the shore. He lived there alone and was said to have money and valuable antiques. He was also supposed to have his own grave dug, and had buried some of his treasures there. In later years the stone house tumbled down, and I think to this day the stone pile is probably still there. I very often ran down and looked at the stones.

My grandparents also told me that often in the night there were lights to be seen going through the field. I often saw the trails where someone came and went through the fields to the grave where the giant of a man was buried. I often sat by the grave and imagined I was talking to this man. My grandparents said he was a very quiet person.

Then, many years later, as a married woman, I took my children to vacation there. I had always loved it there, as I had been born there, as had my mother, grandfather, and great-grandfather. My younger brothers and sisters were a bit jealous of me because I had spent so much time there. While I was visiting, my youngest sister came to visit too.

By this time my great-grandparents and my grandparents had passed away, but my mother was still living there. So I told my sister the story that was told to me when I was young. She would not believe it. So the first night we spent there, there were peculiar sounds and the children could not sleep. We all huddled in one room and we actually saw the doorknob turn. The children were crying and we were trying to keep them quiet. It was a terrible night.

Finally, daylight came, and we ventured out but could not see anything. But there was a room which was called the storeroom which had a large trap door that led to the cellar. It was used in the winter. In the summer an outside entrance was used to go to the cellar, and a large heavy rug was used to cover over the trap door.

In the storeroom we found the rug pushed away and the trap door raised. No one had been near that room. So I said to my sister, "Perhaps you will believe some of these stories now. You come with me and I'll show you the stones that once were a house and this man's grave."

The stones were there, all right, but what a shock when we went over to the grave! It was mostly dug up, with a big gaping hole there, and a few stones that looked like the ones on the pile. Needless to say, we went back to the house in a hurry. But to this day no one has ever found out what went on that night.

I just wish I had listened more to my great-grandparents and grandparents. I could have learned much more. But I do know that the man in the house was real. His first name was Stone, and my uncle's middle name was also Stone. I loved my grandparents very much and they went back quite a few generations and the house is still there, although it is rundown a lot.

My grandfather was an only child. When he would see my uncle coming up through the field, he would often say:

Brothers and sisters have I none;
But that man's father is my father's son.

On Old Road

KHERU

One of the enthusiastic readers of my book Mysterious Canada *is a young man who wishes to be identified as "Kheru." About nine months after the book's appearance, he phoned me out of the blue and asked if I would like to hear his ghost story, which was set outside a city not far from Toronto. I said no, but politely added that I did not want him to tell it to me; I wanted him to write it out for me. He did so in a very clear script, using a ballpoint pen on lined paper. I received his account on August 20, 1997, and read it with genuine interest. It sounded like fiction to me, so some days later, when he phoned me again about the account, I asked him for further details about himself and his experience. He supplied these.*

Kheru is the pen name of a thirty-year-old croupier, or card dealer. The experience he describes in this account took place at a farmhouse in Orono, Ontario. "The house is located on Highway 35/115, just before the town's main exit. Heading north from Oshawa, it is on one's left, past the gas station and across from the motel." I am assured that every word here is true.

♦ ♦ ♦

In June of '94 I first heard the story of the haunted house "on Old Road." During a casual conversation the subject turned to ghosts. One of the other persons then spoke of an old farmhouse that he knew was haunted. He had been there and maintained that it was a place to be avoided. He was quite serious and sincere. I questioned him further and was told the tale of a murdering madman who one day went about slaughtering his wife and children in the house before taking his own life out in the barn. The date of this occurrence is unknown to me, but the house is over a hundred years old. I inquired as to the present situation and was informed that the aging house and barn still stood and were vacant. The most recent tenants were in some way involved in the occult and they lived there for three months, after which they left abruptly. The person who told me all this had grown up in the area and still visited there periodically. I had my informant show me the location on a map. He earnestly warned me not to go there, but I was too excited to listen, for I had always wanted to go to a "true" haunted house; in fact, I've had vivid and memorable nightmares of doing just that. I called for bus information and found that there was one bus in the early morning going in to the town and one bus to return in the late afternoon. The next morning I caught the bus going in. I brought provisions to stay the night.

The property was about four kilometres from the "downtown" area where I was dropped off. I had passed what seemed to be the house on the highway coming in, so I had a general idea of the direction to go. Down the quiet street, through some woods and over a creek I went to get back to the highway. I walked along the shoulder. There was trash and broken bottles; it felt like walking on an icy sponge. The sky was grey and overcast. Everything seemed damp. I felt a looming ahead and soon came into view of the ancient two-storey farmhouse. I stopped to look and saw that the side screen door swung freely open in the slight breeze. Glancing down before continuing, I saw a fat skunk belly up in the gutter. There was no smell. I approached the house and went to the back of its outside. I had brought a disposable camera and there I took the first picture. The foundation was crumbling and it felt as if at any moment the house would topple over onto me. This was an excellent photo op. Unfortunately, when I had the film developed, none of the pictures of the house came back.

I entered through the side screen door into the enormous kitchen. What a mess! Garbage was everywhere. Empty beer cases and bottles, broken dishes and clothes were on the floor. A huge musty couch sat right in the centre of the room, facing the door. There were also many cans of food still in the open cupboards. A vandal had spray-painted "SATAN LIVES IN THIS HOUSE" in big red letters upon the wall. The walls themselves were a gloomy yellow colour. There were drippings of red candle wax on the floor and counters. I went into an uncomfortably small room with a tiny stone fireplace. This was the fireplace the killer had smashed his infant's body to death on, as the story goes. Just then I noticed the sun was coming out, as rays brightened up the room.

Suddenly, a small yellow bird began flying into the window over and over. After about six thuds, I made a move to get up out of the chair and it was gone. I went into the front entrance next. The front door was nailed shut. The stairs going up were wide and wonderfully crafted from wood. Next, I went into the front parlour. It was furnished with a couch and a chair. There were boxes of dirty clothes and an old 1940s radio that was vandalized. I sat down on the couch with my back to the window, listening to the cars zooming by outside. There was thick, tangled growth obscuring any view out. I was about to lie down for some sleep, when I saw the carcass of a small black bird just inside the door against the wall. There was more red candle wax. It looked ritually prepared. Just as I was falling asleep, I heard a loud bang that woke me. Then I heard voices. Shaken, I stepped out into the hall to see a gang of school kids walking in. We met and I told them I was staying there until I could catch a bus out of town. The one kid who seemed to be the leader of the gang began telling me the story of the house; it was almost exact as to what I'd already been told. I was given a tour. There was a small opening inside the ceiling of the closet that led into the blackness of the attic where "childlike cries" have been heard. All the upstairs rooms were small and cramped. One had a mattress. The other had a chest of drawers and a desk upon which were children's books on astrology. We went back down to the main floor via the back stairway. It was unusually narrow. At the bottom to the left was a small bathroom that was disgustingly filthy. More dead black birds and candle wax were there also. We went into the basement next, with its earthen floor. The only light came through small apertures in the floor above. Looking up, I noticed the massive floorboards, at least four times the width of a railway tie and running the length of the structure. I had heard they were from an old ship. We didn't stay down there too long. It was dark and clammy and just didn't feel right. Soon after, the boys left to go back to school. I went back upstairs to look into the attic with my flashlight, which I didn't have on my first trip. Before I could climb up, I heard what sounded like chains softly rattling. I silently crept into the hall to search for the sound. I discovered it was only bare hangers being blown in the increasing wind that came through the broken windows. Then the hairs on the back of my neck stood up.

Next, I went outside to investigate the barn—the place where the murders/suicide ended with the killer's self-termination. I saw a thick, old, greasy rope still hanging high from a rafter. It ended with a well-made noose about twelve feet from the floor.

I then went back into the house and quietly wandered around looking for the secret room I had heard about. I never found it. I felt uneasy about staying the night. The place was depressing enough during the day; I wondered what the night would bring. I wished I had a companion. I left.

The sky was overcast and it seemed too dark for that time of the day. It also seemed too cool for early June. I caught the bus just in time. Passing the house on the highway, I saw the side screen door swing open in the wind.

The Yorkton Child

LORRAINE MOTH

The following letter speaks for itself. But I will not allow it to speak for itself, because I would be neglectful of my duties as the compiler of this collection if I did not comment on the letter, adding a few details of my own, including information on the setting of this ghostly folk tradition.

I have long been fascinated with the tale that is known as "The Girl at the Crossroads." It is a common enough piece of folklore: A little girl is last seen at a rural crossroads; her mother sees her simply disappear; the mother despairs; the spirit of the little girl reappears on the anniversaries of her disappearance, to the amazement and puzzlement of all.

The motif is known around the world, and in Canada it has been localized to the prairies, specifically to the small town of Yorkton, Saskatchewan. I first heard the tale from a CBC Television host in Calgary in the early 1970s, and I included it in Mysterious Canada, *which appeared in 1979, and reprinted it in* True Canadian Ghost Stories *in 2003. Some other references to the tale set in the prairies have turned up, but they add nothing to the motif.*

Segue to Lorraine Moth's self-explanatory email. Ms. Moth is as intrigued with the story as I am; indeed, more so, as she has conducted oral research and collected a couple of accounts of appearances of the girl. She is the first person to my knowledge to refer to the tale as "The Yorkton Child," a reasonable enough title and name.

Here is her letter. I wrote to her, offering to share any information I might find, and she wrote to thank me for replying to her query. I am only sorry I could not offer in exchange details as substantial as the ones included in Ms. Moth's letter.

◆ ◆ ◆

March 20, 2004

Dear Mr. Colombo:

I recently bought a book written by you called *True Canadian Ghost Stories* that gave your email address and I am writing now because of curiosity in regard to a local ghost story.

While in Ontario, I read, in two books, one of which was *Canadian Ghosts*, about the Yorkton Child.

I returned to Yorkton, Saskatchewan, six years ago and have been trying to find out more about this child.

The story is that this is the ghost of a small child who stands at the side of the road, near a crossroads and not far from a cemetery and that, when motorists stop to talk to the child, she vanishes.

I don't remember the story being told when I was growing up here, so I kept asking around to see if anyone knew about it.

A woman I work with mentioned that she had been driving eastward from a place called Burgess Beach, about twenty miles north of Yorkton, to get onto the main highway north to go home. As she was driving, she spotted a young girl in a white dress with long red hair, standing at the side of the road. Thinking that she recognized the girl from a family she knew, she didn't give any thought to it as she drove by, but then it occurred to her that the child had on a rather fancy dress, considering where she was, but when she looked back through the rear-view mirror, the child had disappeared. There was only grass on the side of the road and no trees to hide in and there had been no time even to hide. As it turns out, this is near a crossroad and not far from a cemetery. (In this area, years ago, young unmarried girls and women who died were usually buried in white and sometimes even in wedding gowns.) Could this have been the "Yorkton Child"?

Have you heard anything about this story? I certainly would like to hear more about this.

Lorraine Moth

My First Recognizable Supernatural Experience

TED CURRIE

Ted Currie is a freelance writer and researcher who lives in Gravenhurst, Ontario and contributes regular columns to the Muskoka Advance *and* Muskoka Sun. *One of his current projects is a re-examination of the mystery of Tom Thomson's death and burial.*

In the 1970s and early 1980s, shortly after graduating from York University, Currie lived in a local Bracebridge landmark, the historic McGibbon House—a three-storey brick dwelling at 115 Manitoba Street that had once housed a local physician and member of Parliament, Peter McGibbon. Rumour has it that in the 1920s Prime Minister Sir Arthur Meighen was a guest at McGibbon House. In the 1970s, the building was converted from a single-family dwelling into a mixed residential-commercial property. Finally, it was entirely demolished and replaced by a new mixed-use development identified as 111 Manitoba Street.

On February 16, 1996, Currie kindly sent me an account the many experiences he had had while a resident of McGibbon House.

◆ ◆ ◆

February, 16 1996

M y first and most profound experience of a spiritful nature while residing in the McGibbon house was in February 1978. I was in the habit, that winter, of working in the attic. I had a typewriter set up by the huge attic window looking down on Manitoba Street, Bracebridge's main street, across from Memorial Park. It was writer's heaven and the perfect solitude for lengthy writing campaigns.

On this particular evening, just past midnight, I decided to shut down business and make my way downstairs to my main-floor apartment. At the time there was no one living in the abutting second-floor apartment, so I had left the connecting door open, and the hall light in this unit on to assist me coming down. At the top of the stairs, on the landing, I shut off the main overhead attic light (the switch was on the wall) and stepped slowly down the steep stairs towards the apartment light. When I reached this next level, I went into the doorway and clicked off this light. The only light on then was shining from my kitchen on the ground floor, a zigzag and twenty steps from the second-floor landing.

Shortly after stepping out from the apartment doorway, in the black stairway (at that point), I walked into what appeared a chilled, floor-to-head fog/mist, which momentarily blinded me, and I recall being worried I was about to fall down the stairs. I stopped and felt the coldness pass, like a push of air you often feel when shutting a door. It was subtle and the entire occasion—encounter—lasted for only several seconds. I can clearly recall thinking, at that precise moment, I had just experienced a ghost—had the peculiar pleasure of walking though one. I must admit feeling frozen to that spot where we had crossed paths.

I regained my composure, after a few seconds more, and headed back down the stairway towards the light. When I finally arrived at the bottom, I stopped and looked back as far as I could around the corner. At that point I was pretty sure I had participated in my first recognizable supernatural experience. Then came denial. I sat down on the bottom step, scratched my head as if to enhance rational thought, and tried to settle my heart rate, which the chance encounter had stimulated.

It was then I felt the chill again, a definite air current of cold air coming down the staircase, enough to move the hair on the top of my head. I turned and faced up the stairs, and I could feel it against my face. It continued for several minutes until I ended the encounter by backing away. This wind current should have been impossible, based on the rise of furnace-warmed air in the apartment pushing upward—as hot air indeed rises—and in fact there were no devious areas in that concealed stairway (excluding the sealed-tight upper window) where the draft might have entered. I was, after two particular incidents, wise to the notion a ghostly presence had been rightfully encountered.

Two days later, in the afternoon, I was tending the antique shop when I entertained a group of visitors. They were dressed formally and I assumed they had just attended a funeral next door at the Reynold's Funeral Home. These people seemed more interested in the house than in shopping for antiques. In fact, one woman asked if she could look around the house, past the limits of the shop. I offered to show them the upper apartment (but not the attic). One lady in the group told me voluntarily that her uncle had died several days earlier. The deceased had once lived in the house. She even took me to his favourite room, on the ground floor, where she claimed he used to sit and rock in a chair while gandering out the large park-side vertical window. The uncle had passed away shortly before the time of my encounter on the back stairway. I didn't make any comment about this, as it didn't seem an appropriate moment to be discussing the possibility that her uncle had made a final visitation to, I guess you could say, an old haunt.

Of many strange bumps in the night to keep me company in that historic Bracebridge house over a period of six rather comfortable and inspiring years, I never again experienced anything like what had passed—rather, crossed my path—that February night when the very thought of ghosts was well down the list of hopeful encounters.

To this day, I do have recurring dreams about the staircase and attic—about four times each year—and unfortunately they have painted the attic as the hot spot for the powerful entity... if indeed the entity could be considered one that challenged trespassers. I never felt that way while I was living there, and some of my most prolific periods at the typewriter came in that attic studio. The dreams became prominent long after I had moved away and the building was torn down to make way for a new office and apartment block. In each dream, I push my way up the stairway, against the cold wind blowing downward, and prepare to challenge the entity lodging in the attic. I always fail before the top stair is reached, but I'm close enough to see the glow of the apparent nasty spirit, just beyond the blackened doorway. I wake shivering.

PART V
SUMMONING THE SPIRITS

G hosts and spirits flit across the pages of history, mysteriously appearing and disappearing before the incredulous gaze of the living. They come and go during times of crisis, and they seem to cluster around historic sites.

Spirits certainly prefer some sites to others. Edinburgh Castle has been a favoured haunt over the centuries, and so was Borley Rectory in Essex, England, for more than a century, before it mysteriously burned to the ground in 1939. In Canada, the spirits favour a few special sites.

Having made that blanket statement, I must qualify it. There are no regularly haunted sites in Canada where you can go with the expectation that you will behold a ghost or a spirit, but there are some places that are well and truly described as haunted, for instance, Fort George at Niagara Falls, Mackenzie House in Toronto, and Oak Bay in Victoria.

There are also places of visions. For the last two centuries, the Roman Catholic church has sponsored pilgrimages to the shrine of Sainte-Anne-de-Beaupré, outside Quebec City, where reports emanated of Marian visions—apparitions of the Blessed Virgin Mary—as well as attestations of "miracle cures." The same is true of the Martyrs' Shrine at Sainte-Marie-among-the-Hurons, in Midland, Ontario. The spirits visit as they see fit.

Is it possible to summon a spirit? In the past, witches and warlocks were reputed to possess a special power, including the ability to command the denizens of the spirit world and force them to do their bidding. The possession of this power over the spirits was based on family history (being the seventh son of a seventh son, for example), initiation by a witch or warlock (in a traditional coven), study and discipline (there are lots of books about magic and magick), or simply being chosen (nobody knows what the spirits may elect to do). Self-styled necromancers, self-proclaimed Wiccans, and so-called black magicians all maintain they have such powers, commonly known as the Black Arts.

Is it possible to exorcise a spirit? The power to banish spirits has been claimed by witches and warlocks, and also by priests and ministers of the Christian denominations, who call upon the power of the Holy Spirit by using the Holy Writ. The Rite of Exorcism may be found in the last pages of the Anglican *Book of Common Prayer.* When such powers are evoked or invoked, they are to be used sparingly by senior clergy, under the special dispensation of the bishop of the diocese. The rite of exorcism is performed from time to time but hardly ever in public or in the presence of members of the press.

Before the middle of the 19th century, communication with the spirit world was non-recurrent, sporadic, indirect, and one-way, with the ghost or spirit putting in an appearance and standing, floating, gliding, passing through closed doors or walls but saying nothing or at least nothing more than an admonition to the living. When confronted with human beings, most ghosts are notably mute. The mere presence of the spirit of the deceased is the message, it seems.

The modern spiritualist movement was born on the evening of March 31, 1848, in the Fox family cottage in Hydesville, New York. Members of the Fox family had been resident in Hydesville for about three months, having arrived there from Consecon, Canada West. Two young girls, Maggie and Katie Fox, proceeded to knock on a table and the raps were "heard around the world." Claiming to be in contact with the spirit of the dead, they set the parameters of the modern spiritualistic experience.

The defining characteristic of spiritualism is that during the séance, the spiritualist, or medium, offers the spectators present the opportunity to witness the exchange of information between the world of the living and the world of the dead. In contrast with the one-way communication that takes place during a ghostly visitation, this is two-way communication. Spiritualists claim the power to contact specific spirits of the dead during their séances: fathers, mothers, sons, daughter, grandfathers, grandmothers, aunts, uncles, nieces, nephews—"discarnate entities" all. Contact is sometimes hampered by the obstreperous presence of "lying spirits"—discombobulated entities, mindless entities—who interfere with the transmission. They simply get in the way, like static that interferes with long-distance radio reception. Spiritualism as a movement may well be a thing of the past, but it is wise to remember that spiritualists' churches with active congregations are to be found in all major cities. Their services are open to the public.

The practice of communication with spirits underwent a sea change in the 1960s, when it was renamed "channelling." The old-fashioned spirit medium was now the new-fashioned channeller. The word "séance" was replaced by "session," though it still meant summoning a spirit, which might be that of a two-hundred-thousand-year-old entity that might (or might not) answer the petitioner's questions or offer bewildering accounts of what life was like in the distant past. This used to be called "direct-voice mediumship." Now it is known as "channelling."

Most fortune tellers are women, but unlike the image of movie star and New Age channeller Shirley MacLaine, the neighbourhood fortune teller is not necessarily a glamorous woman. She may or may not be a gypsy; she might read palms, crystal balls, Tarot cards, or auras. She may meet her clients in the parlour of her house or in her storefront office. Rates are posted but negotiable. Satisfaction is guaranteed. All questions about Love, Life, Health, and Money are answered. Guaranteed, 100% accuracy. If the spirits are willing…

In the modern period, throughtout the Western world, the world of the spirits has become democratic. Spiritualism is undergoing globalization. The ghosts and spirits of old are being put to contemporary use.

These days, the spirits of the dead and intelligences of entities never born may now be summoned and questioned at will—to the satisfaction of all.

Here are the accounts of fortune tellers, psychics, clairvoyants, mediums, and "sensitives," largely from Canada's past.

I Have Been More or Less Clairvoyant

MRS. JOHN HENDERSON

Mrs. John Henderson is identified as a "Trance Medium, Toronto" in B.F. Austin's collection What Converted Me to Spiritualism: One Hundred Testimonies *(1901). The photograph of her in the book shows her to be a stout, grandmotherly sort of person. In the account that follows, she sounds like she knows what she's thinking and doing.*

◆ ◆ ◆

I was born April 16th, 1824, and am, therefore, in my seventy-eighth year. Since childhood I have been more or less clairvoyant, clairaudient and deeply impressional. I have lived in Toronto since I was eight years old, and have had the great joy of giving my services as Trance Medium to our own house circle of friends and enquirers—generally several times per week—for over forty years. During that time hundreds of teachers, clergymen, professional and business men have visited our home and professed to find instruction, encouragement, inspiration, in the messages that came through my lips, from unseen friends. A large number have thus become firm believers in spirit return. Latterly my life has been lived seemingly in two realms, and rather more in the spiritual than in the earth realm. My friends in spirit life come to me at all hours of the day and night. I meet them in my house as I pass from one room to another, up and down the stairs, hear their voices and often sense their presence when I do not see or hear them. Frequently when unaware of their presence they join in conversation by answering some remark I have made.

When one's life is so constantly in touch with spirit realms, it seems difficult to select any particular experience for recital. I will, however, at Dr. Austin's request, mention a few of my experiences which will serve as fair samples of the rest.

About 1850, my husband, who has always been in deepest sympathy and kindest co-operation with my spiritual development and mediumship, was in London, England. One evening I was sitting on our verandah in the presence of Mr. Boswick, his business partner, when I saw an immense glass-covered building and crowds of people thronging the avenues. I mentioned this to Mr. B. and he asked me if I recognized anyone. Almost instantly, upon looking down the aisle I recognized my husband, and he was walking up the aisle with a lady on his arm. We took note of day and hour, and allowing for the difference in time, found my vision was absolutely correct. I also saw him at the day and hour his ship arrived in port. This was also verified.

About twenty-one years ago my eldest daughter lived in Port Arthur, Ontario. I had visited her, but afterwards she had moved to a new house. One bitter winter night I had a desire to visit her, and did so in spirit, as I have frequently done in "soul flight," as it is called. I had a sensation of travelling, and at last arrived at her dwelling—all the surroundings being entirely new to me. I remember the sensation of extreme cold which I felt, and how I suffered from it. I did not enter the dwelling, but seemed to stand outside the window looking in. I saw her reading by the table—her husband lying on the sofa. Basil, the boy, was playing with his dog in the corner. He made the dog stand up, and placed his cap upon his head. Everything was so real and life-like, we took a note of time, &c., and on corresponding with our daughter found we were able to verify all the chief features of the vision.

On another occasion when my husband was on the sea, coming in with my wraps on I lay down on the bed and was soon lost to all around me. The doctor was called in next morning and I was restored to consciousness. Meanwhile I had followed my husband, was with him on the ship, and distinctly saw him by my side as we walked the deck. So real was it all to me I grew sea-sick. I appeared to myself, I remember, not larger than a child by his side.

At another time when my son Tom was in England, I distinctly heard him call me "Mother," three times, and I realized he was very ill at the time specified, and still unwell, and, as a consequence, Tom came home while my husband remained in his place.

While walking down the street in this city one day, I felt an instinctive desire to go over to James Street—a street I had seldom walked on. While walking down James Street, I began to perceive a peculiar atmosphere about me. It was full of the smell of woods and flowers. Suddenly something grey passed over my shoulder and with it such a thrill of emotion and deep impression that I said, "I have met with death." On entering the store shortly afterwards, my husband and his partner both asked me what ailed me, as I looked so ill. I said, "I have met with death." It was twelve o'clock, and at that hour, my husband's brother, as we afterwards learned by letter, died in the west.

In my teens I was engaged to a young man, but felt and told him I should marry another. He was leaving for England and required a certain paper. I told him to go to a certain store and a young man, John Henderson, would give him the paper, and I remarked casually, "I shall be married to him before you get back from England." I was then but slightly acquainted with Mr. Henderson, but had on another occasion pointed him out to my uncle through the window of the store we were passing, with the remark—"I shall marry that young man some day."

I have witnessed, under circumstances precluding the possibility of fraud on the part of the medium, the phenomena of materialization and held delightful intercourse with my friends and loved ones. To me spirit intercourse is as real as the communion we hold with friends in the body.

I have also had many deep impressions, seemingly unaccountable at the time, which have proved prophetic.

A Power Over Which We Have No Control

ALFRED H. SMITH

All that is known of Alfred H. Smith, aside from the fact that he was an enthusiastic spiritualist, is that in the 1850s he was a resident of the small community of Laprairie, in Canada East. Today's La Prairie is no longer isolated, being on the south shore of the St. Lawrence River on the periphery of Metropolitan Montreal.

Smith was anxious to publicize the cause of Spiritualism, but when the local newspaper editors derided the notion of spirit communication, he took the bold step of writing for support to Emma Hardinge, also known as Mrs. Emma Hardinge Britten, one of England's leading spiritualists. He addressed her in her capacity as an editor of the influential journal Spiritual Telegraph.

Mrs. Hardinge Britten travelled around the world in the cause of spiritualism. When it came time to prepare an account of her travels in America, she reproduced Smith's commentary, which describes some of his strange experiences. The following account of the death of a friend and its aftermath is taken from Emma Hardinge's Modern American Spiritualism: A Twenty Years' Record of the Communion between Earth and the World of Spirits *(1869).*

◆ ◆ ◆

Editor of the *Spiritual Telegraph*:

The newspaper editors of Montreal having unanimously refused to insert a single word in favour of Spiritualism, while they open their columns to every idiot who may find anything to say against that doctrine, the friends of the cause have determined to apply to you, as your journal is devoted to the spread of Spiritualism, and if necessary to pay for the insertion of each communication.

It may be asked, why are we so anxious to publish our communications with spirits? Our answer is, we cannot tell. We are forced to it by a power over which we have no control, and in consequence we ask you, in the name of God and of truth, to give publicity to the following:

It is about three years since I heard the phenomenon of Spiritualism first spoken of in Canada. I then, as well as at several periods since, looked upon the thing as a monstrous imposition. I however continued at the request of several friends to attend "circles" of the believers in this new doctrine, but to no other effect than to confirm me in my scepticism; and all the arguments of my friends and all the alleged manifestations were insufficient to convince me. But Providence chooses its own time.

In July, 1853, I left Canada, in company with an estimable friend, W.F. Hawley, Esq., of the Ordnance Department, Canada East, on a tour through the Middle and Western States; and on Saturday, the 27th of August, we arrived in Louisville, Kentucky, where my friend was seized with yellow fever, and after an illness of nine days he expired.

It has never been my fortune to be acquainted with a more honest, upright, or learned man than Mr. Hawley. He, as well as myself, had investigated the subject of Spiritualism, but with a contrary result. He was a believer, while I, until the moment of his death, remained incredulous.

As I seldom left the bedside of my friend during his illness, I took frequent occasion to talk to him of the new faith, when he invariably expressed his entire belief in it; and in a few days I had the inexpressible delight of witnessing the reward of his faith and the realization of all his hopes. Oh, sir! I cannot find words to express the transporting emotions which filled my mind at the moment of his death. Although I was the only living being present, yet I distinctly saw hundreds of moving forms around his bed, and in every part of the chamber, but of such dazzling splendour that I could not distinguish their features; the room was filled with superhuman sounds, which appeared to come from the ceiling; and involuntarily looking up I distinctly saw the spirit hover over the body which it had just left, as if uncertain whither to direct its course. It remained thus during the space of a minute, them moving gently to one side it entered a body whose transcendent splendour the tongue of man cannot express.

At that moment I felt my mind, as it were, regenerated.

I shall now give a few out of the many manifestations which have been witnessed, and can be attested, by the most respectable citizens of this village.

On Saturday, the 27th of August, 1853, my friend, Mr. William Fox, invited me to meet a circle of friends at his house; accordingly I repaired thither at eight o'clock that evening, and met a highly respectable company, among them a clergyman who came to investigate the subject for his own satisfaction. We had not sat more than twenty minutes when Mrs. Fox became greatly agitated; she was lifted forcibly from her chair, and suspended about a foot from the earth for a minute and a half; she was then placed in her chair again, but still agitated and unable to speak. It was evident the spirit had not sufficient influence over her. After some moments Mr. James Macdonald approached, and made a few passes over her, when she immediately spoke as follows:

Friends, it is now five weeks since I left your society on earth, and when I tell you my name, you will not be surprised that I desire to return amongst you in spirit, confirming the glad anticipations of a bright existence in the spheres which I cherished on earth, desirous to instruct you in the glorious realities of my present exalted condition, and give you a foretaste of joys which await the good and true in these blissful regions. But as there is another spirit who wishes to communicate, I shall withdraw until tomorrow night.

Farewell; your friend,
W.F. Hawley

To me that communication was most convincing. The style, language, and certain words of the phraseology were essentially that of my friend. The influence then changed, when the medium said, addressing Mr. Macdonald:

Friend Macdonald, I know the thoughts that now occupy your
mind, and I come to tell you about your son, whom it was your
earnest desire to hear of when you came to this circle. I have
just left him where, in spirit, I visited him, in a very bad condition both of body and mind, lying in a hospital in New Orleans,
suffering from a severe attack of scrofula; but you need not feel
uneasy; he is surrounded by the spirits of his friends, and your
father, who occupies a higher sphere than that which I inhabit,
tells me that your son, although obstinate, is a chosen vessel,
destined to do incalculable good among the faithful...

Mr. Macdonald then asked: "How am I to know that you are speaking the truth? What proofs can you give me? What is your name? It was written: 'Your father, who is present, will answer these questions to your satisfaction.'"

At this moment the husband of the medium came into the room, and, from some cause, the communication ceased; however, after a conversation of about twenty minutes on general topics, it was written:

My Dear Son—Your questions to the spirit who has just left, I
shall answer to your satisfaction. As a proof that what he told
you is true, you shall receive a letter from New Orleans on
Thursday next, corroborating the statement of your son's illness,
and on Friday, the 28th of October, you shall receive a letter
from himself, requesting to be again admitted to your friendship.
The name of the spirit is Thomas Henry Caldwell, your son-in-
law, and the favour which he requests you to do him is to pay an
account which he owed Mr. John Charlton at the time of his

death. You can pay this account, as the whole of Caroline's fortune is still in your hands, and Caldwell has left no issue.

Goodnight,
William Macdonald

Of the numerous family circumstances contained in these communications, not a soul present but Mr. Macdonald himself had the least knowledge. Although the communications were of so delicate and personal a nature, however, he candidly informed the medium, as well as all present, in a few weeks subsequent, that the letters promised from his son had arrived. Every statement of the spirit was fully corroborated. "In a word," added Mr. Macdonald, "unless it was spirits, no power under heaven could have made those disclosures to me..."

I am, yours, faithfully,
Alfred H. Smith

Spirit Rappings

SILAS TERTIUS RAND

The writer of this article, Silas Tertius Rand (1810–89), was a Baptist missionary among the Mi'kmaq and author of monographs and texts on Maritime history. Here he shows himself to be an acute observer of "spirit rappers"; that is, spiritualists who claim to communicate with discarnate spirits through rappings or knocks on wooden tables.

"Spirit Rappings" appeared in The Islander, *Charlottetown, Prince Edward Island, on September 23, 1853, though the article seem to have*

originally appeared in the Halifax Christian Messenger. *Rand's approach applies to the séances that were staged by the spiritualists of his day and age; the approach is also valid for today's channellers who appear on the stage and on television and claim to be in communication with the spirits of the dead.*

◆ ◆ ◆

I have lately had an opportunity of witnessing those mysterious operations, which have made so much noise in the world, called "Spirit Rappings." I did not "go to see" them. I paid nothing for the sight, and as I ascertained several facts respecting the matter which may be of service to the public, in guarding them against imposition, I have considered it my duty to make them known.

I lately read what I considered a very good article upon the subject in the *Christian Visitor*. I became satisfied that to consult a "medium" as an oracle is decidedly wrong, and felt strongly inclined to attribute the whole thing to satanic agency. On the former point my views are fully confirmed. I have not ascertained beyond a question that not the slightest dependence can be placed upon those responses, beyond what is known by some of the parties in contact with the operators. It can tell you all that you know, and it can tell you nothing more. By innumerable experiments, made by an intelligent friend of mine, himself a powerful medium, he has ascertained that the responses are entirely controlled by those spirits in the room that still inhabit houses of clay. Many experiments illustrative of this important fact, I not only saw but participated in. Without being a medium, and being declared by the "spirit" incapable of that dignity, I have myself called him forth to do my biddings, and in spite of the mediums made him give just such answers as I chose. But I had better pursue something like method in my statement.

1. It is not deception, nor sleight of hand on the part of the operators. On this head I am perfectly satisfied. I was well acquainted with the

operators on the occasion referred to. My own brother and my own nieces composed the party. I know they would not attempt to impose upon me. Nor could they have succeeded had they been so disposed. I put questions to the table myself, and spoke in a language which no one in the room understood but myself. They knew nothing of the questions put, and consequently could not have known what answers to give. Yet were the answers at such times all appropriate and correct.

2. It is something very mysterious. Several persons sit around a table with their hands upon it. In a few minutes one asks, "Are there any spirits present? If there are, rap." A rap is distinctly heard. "Rap again," says another. The rap is repeated. "Rap three times." ["Rap, rap, rap," is distinctly heard. There is a peculiarity about the sound. It appeared more like the pattering of rain than anything else I could think of.]

"Now then," says one of the party, "will you answer a few questions. If you will, tip the table towards me." The obsequious table tips in the direction indicated. Is the spirit of King William III present? If he is, let the table rise up and stand upon two legs." The table rises—the laws of gravity being to all appearance completely set at defiance—and stands on two feet. "Now, then, will your majesty show us how your majesty's horse leaped upon the banks of the Boyne?" Instantly the table rises on its "hind legs" and leaps "upward and onward," giving no bad representation of the picture of the event, so commonly seen, and of which every individual at the table and in the room are thinking at the moment.

This dignified question and answer will give some idea of the mode of conversing with the supposed spirits of the departed. You may obtain names and numbers, and the answers, "yes" and "no," in several ways. "Tell me," said I, "my age." At the bidding of one of the mediums, the table rocked from side to side, striking the floor with its feet forty-three times. "Now spell the name of my wife." "Now," says the medium, "when I mention the first letter of aunt's name, tip towards me." She then began the right one, J, when the table tipped as ordered. The process was repeated, and the letters were indicated which correctly spelled the name "Jane."

The table would cut up all sorts of pranks and shines at the bidding of the "mediums." I saw it stamp and dash about as if in anger. I saw it "shake its head," for a decided "no!" I saw it rise up and balance momentarily on one leg, and all this simply at the bidding of the operators, whose hands were laid gently upon the top of it. I call this mysterious. I cannot explain it.

3. But if I am perfectly satisfied that there is no magic, nor "satanic agency" in the matter, I am just as confident that the "spirits of the departed" have nothing to do with it whatever. And I KNOW that it cannot be depended on as an oracle, to inform us what will happen hereafter, or what has happened already. What we know to be true it can tell us with wonderful precision. Beyond that boundary line it cannot conduct us. All is uncertainty, contradictory, bungling, guess-work. It may hit right, just as we may hit right in our surmises, and in the judgements which we may form on different subjects. But this is all. Its answers will turn out wrong in so many instances, that no dependence can be placed upon it.

I must advance proof of this point. If it be true then, the folly and wickedness of appealing to the "spirit rappings" for a knowledge of the other world, or the truth of religious doctrines, is manifest. In advancing this proof I shall mention facts which go at the same time to confirm the position that the whole thing is conducted and controlled by the minds and wills of the operators, and those other embodied spirits who are present at the time.

1. Argument first. I myself repeatedly received answers which I knew to be untrue. The following questions were put, my hands not on the table: "Have I any money about me?" The answer was correct, affirmatively. "Now, then, what is it? I have but one kind, is it silver, paper or gold?" I was first told that it was silver. But this was not true. So it had to be "guess again." Accordingly I was assured that it was paper. Wrong again. Try once more, for I had stated that it was not copper. So it very correctly informed me the third time that it was gold. But what fool could not have done that? Surely a "spirit," be he bad or be

he good, ought to have been able to get at my pocket and peep into my purse somehow, and find out that there were two sovereigns in it. Manifestly, if he had to guess three times between silver, paper and gold, in so plain a case as that, he could not be trusted in the matter of more intricacy. But it was evident that the operators were "guessing," and that the answer each time was just what they were thinking of.

2. I was informed—proof second—that questions of the following import are often proposed. "How many children have I?" Answer correct. "How many of them are sons?" Answer correct again. "Now, then, what will the next one be?" To this "important" question the "spirit" has only to guess between "two," and so occasionally hits right, but it just as often hits wrong.

I ask again of what manner of service can the "spirit rappings" be, as an "oracle," if I cannot be informed with absolute certainty respecting an event of that kind, which is upon the eve of accomplishment? But I was assured by the mediums themselves, that answers to such enquiries were as likely to prove false as true.

Here then are the facts of the case. The enquirer knows how many children he has. He knows too how many are boys and how many are girls. His mind is upon this, and his own mind controls the answer. Here is a mystery—he feels it to be so—and he is convinced that there is no deception on the part of the operators; and he naturally enough concludes that if the spirit can tell him so correctly what he knows, it can tell him what he does not know. But here he is mistaken, and my brother assured me that he invariably found the answers were in accordance with what was uppermost in the mind of the enquirer, or of the individual whose mind happened to control the table. Sometimes a majority seems to carry the point. For instance, if a majority of the minds present decide in favour of the Roman Catholics, or Universalists, the spirit is sure to say they are right. If they be Baptists, then the Baptists are said to be right. I heard this question put in a variety of forms, but the answer was invariably that the Baptists are in the right. Nor would the spirit admit that they were in an error, not even in the smallest matters. We happened to be, the most of us, Baptists in sentiment. But one of the mediums was a Methodist, and she assured us that when "they" had a majority present, the "spirits" would stand up as stoutly as the Methodists.

Now grant me, either that our religious controversies are continued as strenuously as ever in the other world, or that it is the work of "embodied" spirits, and not that of the "departed."

But, finally, I could control the "thing"—whatever it be—myself, and make it give just such answers as I choose, whether true or false. I did this repeatedly. On one occasion I set them to spell the name of a friend. While, with my own hands upon the table, I would fix my thoughts upon the proper letter, the table would rise very correctly as soon as the "medium" had, in going over the alphabet, reached that letter. In this way the first name was correctly obtained. "That will do," said I. But the curiosity of my young friends was now excited, and they wished to know the other name. And they said, "We will find out in spite of you." "Very well," said I, "go on." But I fixed my mind upon the wrong letter, and "rap" would go the table, as soon as this letter was reached. The result was, that they could not find out the name, any way they could fix it. So I was informed that it invariably occurred, when an individual enquired the number of his own age, or that of another, if we were labouring under a mistake at the time, the same mistake would be made by the "spirit" with whom he was conversing.

Now, I ask, is it not absurd to suppose that because I have made a mistake of ten years in the age of my grandmother at the time of her death, she herself too must have forgotten, and that she cannot rectify the mistake, until, by dint of reckoning and pencilling, I have myself ascertained the correct number? Verily, if we have got to cipher out their ages for the "rapping spirits," before they can tell us how old they are, they must be miserably qualified to instruct us. My brother assured me that just such an event as this he had known to occur.

So when stolen property is enquired after. "Did so-and-so steal my wheat?" asks a Frenchman. "Yes." "Well I thought so." "Count off the number of pecks he took." "Thump, thump, thump," goes the table. "Ah! just three pecks! Well I thought it was about that."

Some lady had lost her silver spoons, or some article of wearing apparel, and she very strongly suspected that one of the female servants had taken the article. The spirits were appealed to for information. The "medium" of course knew nothing of the affair. He therefore left the whole "control" to the lady. She enquired, "Have I lost anything?" The answer was in the affirmative. "What is it? When the article is mentioned let the table tip." Various articles were run over, and as soon as the "spoons" are mentioned, the table tips. "Have they been stolen?" The answer in the affirmative. "By one of the servants?" "Yes." "Now when the name of the servant is mentioned, let the table tip." Several names are mentioned, and as soon as the suspected person's name is uttered, the table moves as directed. Now it might so happen that the poor girl suspected of taking the spoons, &c., might have taken them; but if it be the fact that the answer comes, not according to what is true, in the case, but according to what the enquirer, or some other person present, supposes to be true, then it is certain that its answers are not to be confided in, and every one must see how wicked and cruel it would be to fix a crime upon any one upon such testimony. And yet how easily might an unprincipled "medium" use this power for evil purposes! This is not all. The mediums themselves may be deceived, and so be innocent "mediums of mischief." My brother assures me that it was not until after repeated experiments, and cool, careful investigation, that he became satisfied that the answers come out invariably in accordance with the knowledge or belief of some person or persons in connection with the table.

In conclusion I would just observe that I cannot offer any explanations respecting the really mysterious part of the affair. I cannot tell—I believe no one pretends to tell—how mind controls matter in any case. I know not why, nor how, my hand or foot rises at the bidding of my will, any more than I do know the table rises by being commanded. I have many a time explained to my friends the working of the "Electric Telegraph," so far as to convince them that it is not the work of the devil. But I believe no one yet pretends to know why electricity magnetises iron, nor what either electricity or magnetism is. The time, however, has gone by when intelligent men were wont to ascribe every new phenomenon to supernatural agency. Investigation, cool, continued, and extending to the collection of as many facts as possible, is now the course pursued. No doubt mischief has been done by the "rappings." But what has not been made an instrument of evil, one might ask. Eclipses, comets, earthquakes, and lightning have frightened people out of their wits. They are natural phenomenon notwithstanding. At all events, the epithet "religious," so far as I can see, may as properly be associated with the "Telegraph" as with the "raps."

The Keys of the Instrument Were Sounded

"R."

The identity of "R.," the writer of the letter that follows, is not known and will probably never be determined. The letter, on the occasion of its original appearance in the London journal Spiritual Telegraph, *bore the intriguing title "Wonderful Manifestations by a Piano."*

The editor of that journal, and the leading British spiritualist of her day, was Emma Hardinge, also known as Mrs. Emma Hardinge Britten, who published R.'s letter in the journal and reprinted it in her travel memoirs, Modern American Spiritualism: A Twenty Years' Record of the Communion between Earth and the World of Spirits *(1869). In this volume, she went on to make some general points about the Canadian cities she visited:*

> *Spiritualism has taken a firm and deep hold upon the inhabitants of this country, and in some parts exhibits a condition of progress little behind that of the States.*
>
> *In Toronto, Mrs. Swain, one of the most powerful physical mediums of the day, has for years been producing irresistible conviction of spirit communion upon the minds of hundreds who have attended her séances.*
>
> *In London, Canada West, a number of true-hearted believers have rallied round the lead of Mr. John Spetigue, who, himself a devoted Spiritualist, has for years laboured in the cause, engaging speakers and aiding in the development of media, until his efforts have resulted in procuring a respectful hearing for the one, and a very general growth for the other.*
>
> *In Ottawa may be found a brave and devoted little band of Spiritualists, who depend chiefly on the abundant medium power existing amongst their own ranks, the place being too remote to secure the services of travelling lecturers and media.*
>
> *At St. Catherine's [sic] there are a large number of Spiritualists, including several very excellent and successful healing mediums.*

In the letter reproduced below, R. comments on the remarkable abilities of Toronto's leading physical medium at the time, Mrs. Swain.

The account concluded with the following note: "The author of the above communication sends his full name, in attestation of the facts stated.—Ed., Telegraph.*"*

◆ ◆ ◆

Wonderful Manifestations by a Piano
Toronto, October 14, 1856

D ear Friends—For the benefit of your many readers, I give you an account of one of the numerous demonstrations that we occasionally receive through the mediumship of Mrs. Swain, a lady of this city, who, for the different phases of that wonderful power of spirit influence, is rarely equalled.

Happening in her house a few weeks since, four persons beside the medium and myself took our seats, around a piano that was in the room—myself locking it and placing the key in my pocket—with the usual lights burning in the room. Shortly after the company had taken their seats, the keys of the instrument were sounded, and answers given in that manner to questions asked. Among many inquiries made was the question "who it was that was communicating with us," when the name was spelled—by striking a key as the letter of the alphabet was pointed to—of an old friend of my own, one who had been many years at sea, and master of several ships. To prove his identity he, at my request, did several things, such as making the noise of a gale of wind rushing through the rigging and blocks of a vessel; the splash of the water along the side; breaking of the heavy seas on deck; creaking of the guards and blocks; and rolling the heavy instrument, just like a vessel tossed about on a heavy sea. At the time I, and most of the other persons present, were leaning all our weight on the instrument, it raised up and down, rolled about as if it were possessed with life, and became light as a feather, instead of weighing several hundred pounds! To make assurance doubly sure, I put the following questions, knowing that no other person present beside myself knew the meaning of what I asked: "Now, friend," said I, "we will call the end of the instrument towards my left the stern of your ship, and the opposite one the bow." I was sitting at the front with my arms leaning on it. "Now, I want you to give your ship, as you call it, a list to port"; when immediately over it went to the opposite side to the one I was leaning on, and perfectly correct in seaman's language. It rested in that position for some time, nor could all our bearing down bring it back. I then asked the spirit to give "lurch to starboard," when over came the piano to the same inclination on the opposite side. I then asked him to give me a sample of a ship riding at anchor in a heavy head sea. Immediately, up raised the instrument at the bow, and then the end representing the stern, and so on, first one and then the other, with an occasional roll to each side. After that was over, one of the party was influenced to sing a sea song, when a beautiful accompaniment was played on the strings to the tune; and one wonder is, that the person who sang, in his normal state could not sing at all, but at this time those who heard him said that he sang beautifully. Now all this was done in a lighted room, with the instrument locked and the key in my own pocket; and I know that one or more of the parties present never had their hands or arms from off the front board all the time...

Yours sincerely, for the truth,
"R."

With the Spooks

DAILY COLONIST (VICTORIA, BRITISH COLUMBIA) JULY 20 AND AUGUST 3, 1887

What follow are two articles devoted to the work of the spirit medium known as Dr. Peck. Neither account offers the reader any particulars about the man's life or details about his qualifications. Was he a doctor of medicine? Perhaps he held a "doctorate" in spiritualism.

"An Evening with the Spooks" appeared in the Victoria Daily Colonist *on July 20, 1887, and "A Second Evening with the Spooks" appeared on August 3, 1877.*

◆ ◆ ◆

An Evening with the Spooks

So-called spiritual demonstrations through Dr. Peck, an American medium, who recently arrived in town, are attracting a good deal of attention. Some very remarkable manifestations having been reported by visitors to one of the séances (which took place at the home of S. Duck, Esq.), the writer expressed a wish to be present and was cordially invited. Tuesday was selected as the evening.

On entering the parlour of the house he found seated therein sixteen or eighteen ladies and gentlemen. The medium, an intelligent-looking man of pleasant and agreeable manner, shook hands with the visitors as they entered the house. He wore an ordinary walking suit and carpet slippers—the latter loose-fitting and capable, it seemed to the writer, of being slipped off and on as occasion might require.

A wooden cabinet stood in the southeast corner of the room. It was made on the premises of the host; was some seven feet in height by five broad and, perhaps, two and half feet in depth. On the side facing the room was a door, in which was a curtained aperture about fifteen inches square, with a ledge or shelf such as is seen in front of the ticket offices of theatres for persons who buy tickets to lay their money on. On this ledge was laid a small blank book of soft paper and a sharpened lead pencil. Within were a chair taken from the parlour set, a small drum with sticks, a large tin trumpet, two guitars, a mouth harmonicum and two or three pieces of rope.

Before entering the cabinet the medium enjoined on those present to form a circle—that is, they were to join hands and sit in a circle in front of the cabinet; they were to avoid disquieting thoughts, and, above all, were to keep their hands locked, or the "circle would be broken and the magnetic current destroyed." He also explained that the magnetic current was created by the contact of hand with hand, and that only when the current was perfect could manifestations occur. The medium offered to be tied to the chair in the cabinet; but no one seemed disposed to tie him. The cabinet was carefully examined and was certainly devoid of springs or traps, or other auxiliaries to deception. He then entered the cabinet, the door was closed and the coal-oil lamp was turned low down and placed beneath a shade of tissue paper. The light cast was very dim, scarcely sufficient for the recognition of persons across the room. Perfect silence was maintained for a few moments when, at the request of the medium, those who could joined in singing in a low key, "Yes, We'll Gather at the River."

After the lapse of two or three minutes more a hand pushed the curtain aside and grasped the pencil that lay on the shelf. The hand could be seen in the dim light moving rapidly over the paper with the peculiar sound that accompanies writing on soft paper. After the lapse of half a minute the pencil was laid down as a signal that the communication was finished, and the host tore off the leaf and took it to the light. The message purported to be signed by one "Sedgwick."

"Colonel Sedgwick," suggested one of the circle. Three taps on the middle cabinet were accepted as evidence that the suggester was good at guessing. The message was addressed to "dear friends" (which we took to mean the circle), and stated that several spirits were present and would try and show themselves tonight. After that a hand frequently appeared at the aperture, grasped the pencil and wrote messages to members of the circle. All those who received messages were believers in Spiritualism. The messages were signed "Hugh," "Jimmy," "Phil S——," etc., and the ostensible writers promised to materialize themselves for the benefit of relatives present.

Presently what was called the spirit band began operations. A guitar was thrummed, the drum beaten and the mouth harmonicum played upon. The "time" kept was execrable. There are no professors of music among the spirits or the performers would have been better taught. After the music the door was opened and the medium found bound hand and foot to the chair in a way that would seem to prevent him leaving his seat, to say nothing of allowing him to play the instruments. The medium being in a state of profuse perspiration and in an apparently exhausted condition which was manifested by efforts to recover his breath, a glass of water was administered and revived him immediately.

Then the door was closed, the circle rejoined hands and resumed singing the selections "Sweet Bye and Bye" and "I Have a Father in the Promised Land." Presently the curtains were gently pushed aside and what appeared to be the outlines of a man's face and bust were seen. A military coat was buttoned tightly across the bust and one lady instantly exclaimed that the figure was that of Colonel Sedgwick, an American officer who was killed in the war of the rebellion. She had seen his portrait once, and now recognized the figure as his.

The curtain fell and another face appeared—that of a young man with hair and whiskers. A lady instantly recognized the face as that of her dead son; but this must have been a mistake, because some time afterwards a very different face appeared at the aperture, and the lady asked if it was that of her son. The Christian name of the son was whispered from the cabinet and a request being made to ——— (the dead man) to speak, a tremulous voice said, "Dear Mother, may God bless you!" The face then disappeared. The voice sounded feminine. At any rate it did not sound in the least like the voice of the person it purported to speak for, who had a remarkably handsome and robust physique and a deep, sonorous voice. The spiritualists present, however, accepted the test without question.

The next face at the aperture was recognized by a gentleman present as that of his brother. "Is that you, Jimmy?" he asked. "Yes," was heard from the cabinet. "Dear old fellow, I knew you at once," said the gentleman. This face faded away and was succeeded by features which a gentleman recognized as that of his brother, Major ———, late of the U.S. army. "Is that you, Simeon?" asked the gentleman. A nod. "Are you happy?" Another nod. "Are A——— and S——— with you?" No answer, and the face disappeared. Next came the head of an old man. It was not a large head, the features were not shown, the spirit being seemingly anxious to exhibit the crown of his head, which was thinly covered with grey hair. Some suggested one name and some another, but there were very decided raps in the negative. The writer named "Captain S——?" A thundering "No!" on the side of the cabinet destroyed the identity at once. A lady finally recognized the head as that of her father, a Mr. B——, who died not long ago.

After the faces a request came from the cabinet for some gentleman to approach and put his hand inside. A gentleman did so. He said he felt a hand—it was the hand of a brother who died about eighteen years ago. A short gentleman was next invited to put in his hand. As the aperture was rather high (for him), he stood on a chair. He reported that he had his hand on the medium's head, and that he felt a hand on his. "Oh! such a beautiful hand," said he. "Soft, smooth—delicate. It's my poor brother's. Ah! there's a small hand and another. Oh! what a beautiful hand," etc., etc.

This gentleman stepped down and a lady was called by name to the cabinet. She reported that she felt a great, heavy, clammy hand, entirely unlike the hand of any person she had ever known. She was told to stand aside. The door of the cabinet was shortly afterwards thrown open and the medium discovered bound as before to the chair—"the work of the spirits," it was remarked. He was borne, chair and all, into the centre of the room, where some of the gentlemen released him from his bonds.

After the lapse of a few minutes, "the dark circle" was formed. The circle sat as before with their hands clasped, and the musical instruments were taken from the cabinet and placed on the knees of members of the circle. The medium took his seat in the centre of the room. The lights were turned entirely out, and the circle, sitting in utter darkness, sang in well-modulated cadence "The Sweet Bye and Bye."

The medium's controlling spirit was stated to be an Indian named "Tommy." Almost instantly weird sparks of light ascended from the vicinity of the medium and floated away like fire-flies. Presently a lady said she felt a hand first on her knees and then patting her head. Next a gentleman said he felt a hand fumbling in his hair. Then one of the guitars was thrummed, the drum beaten, the tin horn blown. All the instruments were then raised simultaneously and, judging from the sounds, were carried swiftly through the air round and round the circle—so near the heads of the people sitting there and so fast that the cold rush of air disturbed by the rapid sweep was distinctly felt. The music—now near, now far—so close that the instrument rested on the writer's head, his shoulders, his knees, his hands—then whirled away by some unseen agency to another part of the room and sending forth melody all the time.

While this was going on the drum settled on the head of a lady and the reveille was beaten upon it. Startled, the lady withdrew her hand from the person next to her and knocked the drum from her head. It fell on the floor. Instantly all the instruments also fell, and the medium declared that the "current was broken." Hands were joined again, singing was resumed, and the musical instruments again floated through the room, emitting music. A lady who declared that a spirit whispered in her ear and frightened her, here rose in a state of great agitation and withdrew from the circle. The demonstrations continued until about eleven o'clock when the circle broke up, the lights were turned on, and thus ended the most extraordinary "spiritualistic" séance Victoria has ever known, and the writer's first "Evening with the Spooks."

A Second Evening with the Spooks

Last evening was set apart by Dr. Peck for a test séance. Eleven ladies and an equal number of gentlemen formed a circle at Mr. Duck's house. A pair of leathern muffs with lock-buckles, such as are used to confine the hands of dangerous lunatics, were produced from the Lunatic Asylum and fastened to the medium's wrists and arms and the lock sealed—the medium remarking that he had had similar articles on before at Stockton, California, as a test.

Over these was loosely laced a straight-jacket and the medium was placed in the cabinet which was described fully in a previous issue. Those present then formed a circle, a drum and two sticks, a guitar, an harmonicum, and a horn were placed near the medium, the light was turned down so as to throw a dim light on the cabinet, and vocal music was indulged in.

During the pauses in the music it was quite apparent that scuffling and struggling were going on inside the cabinet. An Indian voice in broken English mouthed some gibberish, and a drum-stick, which could have been easily held between a man's feet, rapped against the side of the cabinet, but these were all. There were no spirit hands at the aperture, no spirit faces, no writing, no drumming, no guitaring, no harmonicuming, no horning.

After being in the cabinet one hour the door was opened, and the medium found still securely bound and in comatose state for want of air. He was taken out, fanned and given to drink from a glass of water and slowly revived. Then some spirit made a short speech, using the medium's voice for the purpose, and stated that the spooks would not allow their medium to be tortured to prove the genuinity of spiritualism; but the unbelievers present were at a loss to account for the inability of the spirits, after having allowed their mouthpiece to get into a tight place, to free him from his bonds.

Subsequently a dark circle was formed. The spirits were sulky and would not play on the instruments; but two of their spirits were described by the medium as being present and walking about the room. About eleven o'clock the circle broke up—the unbelievers strengthened in their unbelief and more than ever satisfied that Dr. Peck is a humbug; while the spiritualists present were as positive that the spirits, who can slip through keyholes and crannies, undo handcuffs and cunningly contrived knots, yet could not liberate Dr. Peck, had not had fair play.

Spirit Land

FREE PRESS (WINNIPEG, MANITOBA)
AUGUST 12, 1879

There are so many descriptions of séances and transcripts of lectures on spiritualism in the newspapers of the 19th century that I have begun to wonder whether the Canadians of the day were an incredulous lot, were starved for information about spiritual matters, or simply craved exotic entertainment. Perhaps they were "closet spiritualists," like former prime minister Mackenzie King, eager for contact with the spirits of deceased loved ones, yearning for evidence that "death is not the end."

The following story, typical of such entertaining articles, appeared in the Winnipeg Free Press *in 1879.*

◆ ◆ ◆

Every available seat in the city hall was filled last evening—the occasion being Professor Cecil's widely advertised "Evening in Spirit Land"—a novel entertainment in this city.

The Professor, after making some explanations as to the nature of the exhibition, invited the audience to name a committee of three from amongst themselves to watch the proceedings on the platform, and Messrs. S.J. VanRensselaer, A.M. Brown and W.F. Luxton were selected for that purpose.

On stage was a mysterious-looking "cabinet," in which were tambourines, bells, horns and other instruments and two chairs. These, with the ropes to be used, were examined by the committee, and pronounced to be what they apparently were. The Professor and his assistant then entered the cabinet, and being seated on two chairs were tied hand and foot by the committee as securely as could possibly be done. Van was asked to close the cabinet doors, but before he could fasten one, he received a slap on the ear, and for a few minutes enjoyed a Fourth of July pyrotechnical display. Van sat down. Mr. Luxton's turn was next— same result. Mr. Brown, ditto.

However, the doors were finally closed, and immediately the bells began ringing, the horns tooting, the tambourine and triangle joining in the chorus, while hands appeared through apertures in the cabinet doors, and above the cabinet. The doors were opened, and the mediums were found tightly tied. The Professor had previously announced that perhaps the spirits would work and perhaps they wouldn't—but there didn't seem to be any "perhaps" about it.

The next thing on the programme was the Hindoo box trick—an apparently ordinary heavy chest was locked, tied with ropes and the knots sealed with wax, after having been carefully examined by the committee. This box was placed in the cabinet, and so was the Professor's assistant. The doors were closed, and on being opened one minute afterwards the box was still found there, but the man had disappeared. The box was opened and the man was found snugly ensconced inside. The spirits were evidently working well and the spirits of the audience were also high, as was evidenced by the loud applause which followed this trick-manifestation.

Then the Professor's hands were tied with a handkerchief, and a rope slipped through his tied hands, Mr. Brown holding the two ends of the rope, but the Professor slipped it off without untying the handkerchief or breaking the rope.

Professor Cecil then entered the cabinet alone with some ropes, and in a very few minutes was found tied apparently more securely than when the committee had undertaken the job—and he only took three-quarters of a minute to do it. The knots were sealed, the cabinet closed, and in a few seconds the Professor was discovered with his coat off. Mr. Luxton's coat was then placed in the cabinet—the Professor being assured that, being a temperance man, there were no "spirits" in the garment—but it didn't make any difference. In a few seconds the coat was on the Professor. Then they sewed it on him, and almost instantaneously it was thrown out of the cabinet, still sewed.

Mr. Brown went into the cabinet with the Professor, and shortly appeared crowned with a tambourine, although he had hold of the medium all the time. Then Van went in—apparently to stay—and firmly grasped hold of the hands of the Professor, who was still tied. Van's coat was thrown out first, then his vest—and on opening the cabinet it was seen that he had still a firm hold on the Professor. The cabinet was closed again, and the spirits commenced taking off Van's unmentionables—but stopped in time to save an awful scene. Van's watch was found in the Professor's pocket. The Professor's mouth was then filled with water, yet he played on a mouth organ and then he released himself from the ropes.

An officer was asked to come forward with handcuffs. Policeman Grady accepted the offer, and appeared with a set of bracelets belonging to the city. These he placed on the Professor, who retired to the cabinet, and shortly appeared entirely free—the handcuffs being found fastened to the handle of a pitcher and the rung of a chair, which were in the cabinet. The Professor was placed in a pillory, which was locked and sealed, but he easily and quickly escaped from his uncomfortable position. He was then tied and a gag placed in his mouth, but he pronounced distinctly any word required of him by the committee.

His young assistant was then mesmerized, and tied in the cabinet, and spirit hands wrote on a slate, a message to Mr. Brown from Katie King, reading, "You are a bad man." Spirit faces appeared about and around the cabinet—one being that of Captain Kidd, the pirate, and another of Van's grandmother. The hall being darkened, a ghost came out from the cabinet and sang a song—but his, her, or its voice wasn't much like a ghost's, at least any ghost we ever read about or talked to, the sepulchral tones being wanting entirely.

Then the tricks of the spiritualists were exposed, and an explanation given of how he slipped out of the rope in the handkerchief trick, which was very simple—after one knew how—and the entertainment concluded, the Professor promised to expose other tricks this evening.

During the evening, the audience were kept alternately completely mystified and roaring with laughter—as the incomprehensible or the ludicrous was presented. Mr. Ormande presided at the piano, and played some selections with great skill, contributing materially to the enjoyment of the evening. The Professor's entertainment gave unbounded satisfaction to the great majority of the audience, although there were some who expressed themselves that more expositions should have been given. Doubtless these will get all they want tonight.

PART VI
SPIRITS ALIVE!

S pirualism is one way that men and women have attempted to account for the enigmas of life and death and the possibility (vital in all the world's major religions) of the personality's survival after bodily death. Furthermore, even if the spirits contacted during séances held during the second half of the 19th century have long since departed for distant shores, the spirit of the spiritualist movement of the past is very much alive. It persists in the New Age movement, with its renewed interest in old-fashioned spirit mediumship, séances, meditation lessons, and the channelling of the dead. This section advances the progress of spiritualism in Canada from 1881 to 1990.

Slade the Spiritualist

MONTREAL STAR
APRIL 30, 1881

At the time of his death in 1905, Henry Slade was regarded as the best-known medium in North America. He travelled throughout the United States and Canada, as well as Great Britain and Western Europe, producing astonishing effects, including slate-writing, acts of levitation, materializations, and so on. Critics dismissed his claim to be in possession of special powers; they regarded him as a talented performer and prestidigitator. Medium or magician, he was a favourite of audiences everywhere. Yet he took to alcohol and died discredited and destitute.

By all accounts, his slate-writing effects were riveting. He produced words on previously blank slates—little blackboards—and these productions astonished his public. The words that appeared often answered a question posed by a member of the audience. In the account that appears here, "A Montrealer's Experience with Slade, the Spiritualist," reprinted from the correspondence column of the Montreal Star *of 1881, there is a specific Canadian reference: poet and patriot Thomas D'Arcy McGee, who was assassinated by a Fenian in Montreal in 1868.*

◆ ◆ ◆

A Montrealer's Experience with Slade, the Spiritualist

To the Editor of *The Star*:

Sir—I notice that two or three of your correspondents have been discussing spiritualism in your columns of late. I took some interest in the discussion, as I have had some strange experience of spiritualists, and

I do not know whether mediums are frauds or connecting links between man and the spirit land. But I will tell you what occurred to me in New York the other day.

I heard a good deal about Slade, the medium. He is said to be by far the best-known "slate-writing medium" in the world. Whether his power is due to hypnotic influences, or to what Dr. Hammond called "syggognicism," I do not know, but he certainly can perform some of the most remarkable things it has ever been my lot to witness. But I will tell you exactly all I saw.

I saw Slade at midday. The room was well furnished, and of course there was plenty of light. I was courteously received, and was then invited to take my seat at a walnut table. I asked permission to look under the table to see if there was any apparatus by which he could be assisted, and he replied "Certainly." I knocked on the table, turned it over and failed to see anything unusual.

Then I sat down and Slade sat opposite me. He took my hands and the raps commenced at once. He ordered them whenever he pleased and he was obeyed. I asked if he would allow me to put my foot on his and again he replied "Certainly," and then with both his hands in mine and both his feet under my feet the raps continued the same as ever. I was satisfied. I could not discover how the raps were produced, and I believed that Slade could produce raps whenever he pleased without detection.

Then I asked for the slate trick. But on this point I may tell you that I had brought my own slate. I could not be satisfied by allowing Slade to use one of his. It might be merely rubbed over with some chemical compound that by turning towards the light might cause words or phrases to reappear. So I brought my own and I am satisfied that Slade did not tamper with it. I had even provided the pencil and when I told Slade, he said "All right." I handed him the slate and he placed it on the table and I bent over and immediately heard a scratching sound inside. This continued for some time, when the slate was opened and the following message was written in a plain hand:

"Why will people doubt when the fountain of wisdom is open
and the truth of the new life made manifest to all. In a few years
all will see the truths of which we know, and those who see
them now are the heralds of the coming dawn.

"B. Franklin."

I was puzzled. I did not believe that the spirit of "B. Franklin" had
written these words, but I wondered if Slade had ever been under the
influence of syggognicism or hypnotics? I did not think so, for I experienced no sensation such as people feel in recovering from the trance.
I was the same then as I am now, writing this letter at home. But I must
tell you more.

I asked Slade if he could give me a message from some well-known
Canadian, and he replied, "I shall try." Once more the slate was closed,
and soon after opened again, and the following letter, in a different
handwriting, appeared on the slate:

"There are principles and forces in nature unknown to science,
and the ethics of spiritualism is their crowning glory.

"D'Arcy Mcgee."

It will be seen that the spelling of McGee was wrong, and on pointing this out to Slade he said that he could not account for these things.
Sometimes the spirits of the late illiterate made no mistakes, and sometimes the spirits of the late accomplished many.

But the marvellous was still before me. I saw a white hand and arm
pull my trousers. A slate I held in my hand was jerked out of it, and passing under the table was then placed upon it. What could have done it? It
was like shooting a rifle bullet around a corner. A hand patted me on the
cheek. I saw it, felt it, but could not grasp it. There was no mistake
unless indeed I was in a trance. The table was lifted until the four legs

were six inches from the ground and with all my force I could not press it down. There was some force at work, but what it was I do not know, and when the performance was over, I left more bewildered than ever.

Fortune-Telling

DAILY COLONIST (VICTORIA, BRITISH COLUMBIA)
SEPTEMBER 24, 1886

This newspaper article must be one of the liveliest pieces ever written on the subject of fortune-telling. These days, there are fortune tellers in the major cities of the world—the Western world, anyway—who promise to answer for a fee a curious person's questions about romance, health, wealth, work, and future prospects. Indeed, in every town and village there is someone who tells fortunes, who sells fortunes. "Sailing 'Round the Stars" amused readers of the Victoria Daily Colonist *in 1886.*

◆ ◆ ◆

Sailing 'Round the Stars
A Trip to the Planets
Fortune-Telling by Consultation with the Heavenly Bodies

There is a rare pathos and beauty in the mythological stories of the planets, although it is a branch of literature overlooked by a vast majority of people. The attraction has not been wanting, however, to many superstitious persons both in the United States and England who are today turning their limited knowledge to good account pecuniarily. It is estimated that there are a thousand fortune tellers who use the planets as a means of plying their calling. From a source so exalted the subjects expect to hear marvellous things about themselves, and despite the seeming absurdity of it, hundreds of people seek these supposed planetary agents for advice and a peep into the future. Hearing that a fortune teller received visitors here in Victoria, a gentleman lately from the east called to test her powers, and, according to his own story, the experience was a novel one. Being ushered into a cozy sitting room he met a pleasant lady, who hearing his errand became enthusiastic on the subject at once. Producing a pencil and a slip of paper she said:

"Write your name, date of birth, and the hour, if you are positive of it, on this slip of paper. That will do. So you were born on the third of January at two o'clock in the afternoon. I don't believe you are right about being born in the afternoon, it was in the morning about the time Jupiter first appeared above the horizon."

"Why? Were you present when I made my bow to the world, madam!"

"No, I was not."

"Well, I was, and ought to know when I first wrestled with life."

The planet reader paused, then continued: "It may be so, yet your planet is Jupiter, if my calculations are correct."

"Hardly Jupiter, madam, for had I been descendant from the ancient God of war Zeus, my natural instinct would have guided me to a more heroic life than that of a plumber, which I don't mind telling you is my occupation."

"A plumber! And with such soft hands," she exclaimed. I saw I was cornered.

"Madam!" I replied quickly, "I am a boss plumber; I plan the work, my men execute it."

"Ah! yes, I see; I thought you might be one of those abominable newspaper reporters. Well, Mr. ——"

"Smooth is my name, Eph. Smooth," I interrupted.

"Well, Mr. Smooth," she continued, "you are born under a lucky planet. According to the belief of the Romans, Jupiter determined the course of all earthly affairs, and revealed the future through signs in the heavens and the flight of birds. I refer to Jupiter Capitolinus, the mythological God known as Optimus Maximus."

"Excuse me, madam, but the God Jupiter of mythology has very little connection with the planet Jupiter."

"Yes, he has, but antiquity is not to be viewed and explained according to the ideas and customs of modern times. Has it never occurred to you that from the first matter containing the seeds of all future being a race was created through God able to comprehend the source from which the various forms of the material world were produced; and in contemplating these forms as they were distributed into abiding places they perceived that the same energy of emanation gave existence to living beings as well as the God who inhabit the heavenly bodies and various other parts? These first people looked upon every planet and star as a living, breathing thing. To them the vast space in which they floated was not too great for comprehension, and they moved about in familiar contact with the inhabitants of these various parts thrown off from the same matter and distributed throughout the universe. Would it be reasonable to believe that of all the bodies formed from chaos, that the earth, the smallest, should be the only one inhabited by human beings? Would it bespeak the infinite wisdom of the creature to suppose that from his effort only the minor part of matter was turned to account, and the major part left a worthless mass? If he had desired to produce the earth, from chaos, without creating other worlds, could he not have done so, without forming six other bodies of twice the magnitude and importance in the planetary world? Therefore I contend that as every planet emanated from the same matter, was formed by the same creator, they are all inhabited by a race of living, rational beings."

"That is all very well, madam; but how could a race of beings exist on Mercury, or even Jupiter, with their proximity to the sun?"

"I do not say people of the earth temperament could exist on these planets—they are endowed with temperaments suited to the planet upon which they live. I believe there is a constant interchange of souls or life sparks between the planets. To die is but to live again. Death is a change necessary to fit a soul for the climate of another planet. It is the reformation of matter and conducted by the same agency that first produced the planetary bodies and then caused them to be inhabited. Can you reasonably say that Jupiter, revolving around the sun at a mean distance of 475,000,000 miles, is uninhabitable? Here we have a planet 88,000 miles in diameter, or one-tenth of the sun, its volume 1,400 times that of the earth, revolving at the rate of five hundred miles per minute, to the earth's seventeen miles per minute. Was all this created for naught? I tell you there are living beings on that planet, and, young man, they are souls from this world prepared for existence there. They are transformed by death into beings who can live in a ten-hour day and years that are equal to travel of ours—comprising nearly 10,000 of our days."

"Then you believe in the immortality of the soul, madam?"

"Most assuredly I do; it seems to me any one of ordinary sense ought to be convinced on this point. As birds migrate from one zone to another, so I believe human souls migrate, through intervention of the supreme power that rules the universe, from one planet to another. Nothing dies but life is formed from that death, and the great work of progression goes steadily on. A horse dies, soon worms are created, they in turn are transformed into moths and thence into beautiful butterflies. Every tree and plant of nature is reproductive in this manner. Could a power so infinite that it watches these minute details to perfection create all the great planets and only perform these things on the smallest and most unimportant of them? I am as positive that the planets are inhabited as I am that the earth holds me, and, young man, when your work is finished on earth you will undergo the change that fits you for an existence on your proper planet, Jupiter. After that, in time I believe you will undergo another change and be transmitted to some other planet, for life is eternal in some shape or another."

"Tell me, madam, will I be a plumber on Jupiter, or is the climate so warm that there are no frozen water pipes?"

"What!" she exclaimed, and springing from her chair she grasped my wrist, and gazing into my eyes as if my whole soul was there laid bare for inspection, continued in a sort of Hamlet soliloquy whisper, "Would you like to go there now?" There was a bright glitter in her eye, she was inspired, the lines about the corners of her mouth twitched perceptibly with emotion. There was a dangerous vehemence in her manner. Instinctively I looked around for my hat and shifted uneasily on my chair. I thought over all the mean things I ever did, and wiped the perspiration from my brow with my coat sleeve.

Opening my hand she furtively traced the lines along the palm, and then in a sad voice said, "You have not long to stay on this earth; your hours are numbered."

I began to feel that something terrible was about to happen and involuntarily shuddered as I thought of my prospective migration.

At last in sheer desperation I drew my hand away and jumped to the door. It was locked.

"Wait," she said. "I am permitted through the influence of your planet to reveal much of your future. Listen! You are already under the spell of Proserpina, who presides over the death of mankind, and if you remain silent I will unveil to you the scenes through which you will pass in the transmission of your soul from earth to your planet, Jupiter."

Closing her eyes she was silent for a moment, and then in a low, plaintive voice began: "You will first perceive a number of terrible forms, disease, old age, terror, hunger, death, the avengers of guilt. On you go to the resort for departed spirits. Among them you mingle. There are those who suicided, victims of love and despair, and hundreds of the sad experiences known to life. Then you will pass into fields adorned with all the beauties of nature—a most delightful recreation to your mind. There are hills covered with fragrant shrubs, grand valleys, flowery plains, shady groves, lucid streams, gentle and unclouded sunshine. Being freed from the passions and prejudices of mortality, you enjoy the pleasures of contemplation, until at the command of Zeno you drink the fatal waters and the oblivious draught causes you to lose all remembrance of the past, so when again you assume the cares and sorrows of humanity on Jupiter, Elysium is forgotten, the past is obliterated, and amid the new scenes you find nothing strange, for that other life has faded forever from your memory."

"That's very smooth, madam," I managed to say.

"Very smooth, indeed; that's about the appreciation I might expect from a plumber. You have no more sentiment or imagination in your soul than a stick. However, I have told you all I can, and in closing my séance I conjure you by all means to be ready at any moment to die, for your life is short. One dollar and twenty-five cents, please. Thanks! Good night."

The Greater Spread of the Truth

A.W. SPARLING

A.W Sparling, with his handlebar moustache, looks alert and inquisitive in the portrait that appears in B.F. Austin's 1901 collection, What Converted Me to Spiritualism: One Hundred Testimonies, *where Sparling is identified as a resident of Toronto.*

The important role played by physical and trance mediums in spiritualist circles in the late 19th century is highlighted in his testimony. One of the most impressive mediums was Mrs. Etta Wreidt, a "direct-voice" medium who was popular enough to catch the eye of William Lyon Mackenzie King, the prime minister of Canada, who consulted her on a number of private occasions. Their meetings took place in secret in 1932 at the Fulford Mansion in Brockville, Ontario.

Incidentally, that mansion is now an historic site, and if you ask one of the guides whether it has a reputation as haunted, you will learn that is said to be visited on occasion by the spirit of the builder's wife.

Readers knowledgeable about parlour magic will be aware that the effect called "the envelope and slates" mentioned below is well known as a conjuror's trick—the stock-in-trade of magicians and a standard item for sale in shops that sell magic tricks and stage effects.

◆ ◆ ◆

My first experience in the spiritual phenomena carries me back to the year 1863, again to 1873 and 1875. Of course at that time I knew nothing of Spiritualism, and hence looked upon the strange happenings as supernatural occurrences. It was not till the winter of the year 1897 that I, through curiosity, and with much prejudice, was induced by a friend to attend some of the addresses and manifestations that were being given in this city. My first attendance was at a trumpet séance at 25 Walton Street, this city, my wife and another friend accompanying me. We were complete strangers to everyone present and had never seen, met, or heard about the medium, Mrs. Etta Wreidt, of Detroit, until she took her place in the circle. After the services were opened with singing of such hymns as "Shall We Gather at the River?" "Sweet Hour of Prayer," "There Are Angels Hovering Round," "Nearer My God to Thee," &c., I came to the conclusion that these spiritualists were not as godless and as closely leagued with the devil as they were represented to be. The medium suggested that we sing her guide's (Dr. Sharp) favourite piece, "God Save the Queen," so it appeared that in spirit life they still retained their loyalty to country and to Queen. This was sung, and during the singing of it another voice joined in, which seemed to be at different times in various parts of the room and above our heads, and on its conclusion a strong male voice bid the medium, "Good evening," and spoke to each one with great courtesy, stating that each one's friends were there and desirous of talking with them, also requesting that we act as ladies and gentlemen and exercise the same reverence as we would if we were in any church. The medium being seated next to me, I, as soon as the circle was formed and the light turned off, took hold of her address and placed my foot in front of her, so that if she should attempt to leave her seat I would be aware of it, and also if she should be a ventriloquist I could detect it. I may say that as far as the medium was concerned during the whole of the séance I had her under test conditions satisfactory to me, and the result proved that she was perfectly honest and took no part in the manifestations that occurred. Our children and friends came and gave their names and identified themselves so completely, telling of circumstances and things that were only known to ourselves, and bringing messages of love, comfort, cheer, hope and encouragement, proving their continuity of life and interest in us, and the fact of spirit return. This séance led to further investigation of the phenomena, and a private sitting was had with the same medium and others, and the evidence obtained through independent writing, in which blank paper was placed in a sealed envelope between two common school slates, securely fastened, and never leaving our sight or possession and held above the table in the air, was satisfactory. The envelope and slates being opened by ourselves and all precautions against fraudulent methods being taken, I am satisfied as to the genuineness of spirit communication in that way.

Again I have had the great pleasure of seeing my dear arisen mother twice this summer and talked face to face with her, and also have in my possession now a spirit portrait of her and two of my children; also that of my wife's mother, who have all entered the higher life. These portraits were obtained through the mediumship of the Bangs Sisters during their late visit in Toronto and were produced in from twenty to twenty-five minutes and witnessed by several, amongst whom was a thorough sceptic as to the phenomena and who was also a materialist, and who examined the canvasses that were brought there by my own son Wesley, and opened by him and placed in position in the front of the window in the light and saw the production of the portraits. The testimony under oath of the witnesses to the production of these pictures can be had by anyone doubting the facts, the witnesses being fifteen in number, the canvasses used being the common Steinback used by all artists and obtained at the Art Metropole on Yonge Street, a reliable firm. We will be pleased to have any of the readers of the Sermon or of this volume call and inspect them and each say it is beyond their power to produce such work, and place their value as works of art at from $75 to $100 each.

In conclusion let me say that the phenomena and fact of spirit return are demonstrated beyond the peradventure of a doubt and proven by the testimony of thousands. We as spiritualists do not ask the investigator to "Believe—believe or be damned," but simply say "Come and see," as the Samaritan woman did of old. Thus they will be led into fuller and diviner truth and enjoy a joyous liberty and find in our glorious phenomena and philosophy the key that unlocks that mysterious and so-called sacred book, the Bible. I trust that this simple story may add to the greater spread of the truth, especially among my old circle of friends in this and other places, and lead them to investigate and find the truth.

Resist Not the Spirit

C.F. BROADHURST

B.F. Austin included the testimony of C.F. Broadhurst, a resident of Arnprior, Ontario, in his collection What Converted Me to Spiritualism: One Hundred Testimonies *(1901). The photograph of Broadhurst shows a burly individual, conservatively dressed, with a full handlebar moustache and a receding hairline. It is easy to see that he is the son of a farmer from the north of England.*

Broadhurst's testimony covers a lot of ground, including a premonition, divine inspiration, a crisis apparition, the operation of a medium, and astral travel.

◆ ◆ ◆

At the age of 22 I was engaged in Christian work in Hereford, England. I left there and went to my home, my father being a farmer living near a village called Mamble in Worcestershire. I had been at home two weeks and each Sunday had attended the church at Clowstop, one mile away. The third Sunday morning when I came down I told my father that I had to take the service at Clowstop. He asked me how I knew. I told him I had seen myself three times in the night standing in the pulpit preaching to the people, and every time preaching from the same text. He said, "Go, my boy, and the Lord be with you, but if you are going to preach at Clowstop tonight you ought to prepare yourself." I asked him what preparation I needed, as the one who gave me the vision would speak through me. That night was stormy, but I started off by myself and sat by the door. The chapel was well filled. Each time the door opened people would look around for the minister, but none came. After waiting twenty minutes I walked up into the pulpit and began the service. All went well until I gave out the same text I had used in my dream (the conversion of St. Paul). That was all I remembered. I felt as though I was floating. When I came to myself I saw by my watch I had been speaking three-quarters of an hour, but knew nothing that was said. I went home greatly mystified. I have had the same experience many times since.

I came to Canada in '93. I had heard a great deal about Spiritualism in England, but it was supposed to be of the devil, so I steered clear of it.

On the night of February 3, 1900, we had retired for the night. I was awake, thinking, when I felt a strange feeling and heard a report as if a revolver had been fired. I looked, and standing at the foot of my bed was a man in shining light. The hair was dark, his eyes blue, and he was standing like a statue. He had purple pants, but the rest of the body was nude. I did not speak—I could not. He gradually passed away. I told my wife what I had seen and got up, lit the lamp, looked at the clock and found it was 12:30. We retired about 12:00. I met a friend, Mr. M——, a miner, who is a medium. I asked him to come up in the evening. He took up a slate and pencil. I then asked who it was I saw the night before. His hand began to move and wrote "Theodore Brown, West Bromich, England." He then spoke through the medium and said, "Mr. Broadhurst, you have seen me." I said I did not remember him and had only been through West Bromich once, and then on my wheel. He then asked, "How would you like to see my astral body?" I said I would like to see one. "What did you think of me last night when I came?" I asked him what he was in England. He said he was a minister of the Gospel. He also gave me good advice respecting my health and said he would come again. I asked my wife if she knew him. She said she was once introduced to a young lady who was to be married to him, but had not seen him. He came again the night of the third. I have not seen him since, but others have, and given his name in full. At a sitting with Mrs. Etta Wreidt, the trumpet medium, I had a long talk with Theodore Brown.

My first "soul flight" was early last winter, while staying in Victoria, BC. We retired about 9:30. I felt a great power pass over me. I wondered what it meant. The thought came to me: Resist not the spirit. I kept passive and felt a sensation of floating away. My eyes were open to a glorious sight, which I have longed many times to behold again. Under our feet were lovely flowers, on each side beautiful trees. I was in company with one whom I knew. We were floating over the country at a rapid rate. I could see myself. I looked the same as in my body. I said to my companion, "This is grand; let's keep on going." I was travelling on the right-hand side of him. At last we came to some great mountains. We seemed to be going at lightning speed. I heard the roar of rushing water, and in an instant I seemed crowded, and struck the great volume. I had the sensation of spitting it out of my mouth. I was afraid. My companion took my hand and said, "Be not afraid, though you pass through deep waters I will uphold you." We went on over a great lake. I could see for miles the sparkling water on my left and the great waterfall on my right, which must have been hundreds of feet high. In front was an opening between two mountains, where we tarried, standing upon flat rock. Behind us was the lake. Here we talked together. Every word of the conversation I can remember and never could forget. At last we started to go. The lovely sights passed from view. I lost consciousness and could feel I was gradually coming to myself. My wife asked me what was the matter, as she had been trying to make me hear her but could not, as I was like one dead. I have been away several times since.

He Wrote Many Things to Me

D.F.

The death of a child must be the greatest hardship of all. In this account, a mother recalls the way in which the grief she felt at the death of her oldest son was replaced by relief when she was able to establish communication with the child's spirit.

D.F.'s full name has not been preserved, but when she prepared this account, she was living in East Kildonan, Manitoba. Her account was published in Psychic Phenomena in Canada *(1967), compiled by Winifred G. Barton, an Ottawa-based "metaphysician."*

◆ ◆ ◆

I am a Canadian woman of Scotch and Irish descent, belonging to the United Church, am the mother of four, and was a registered nurse before marriage.

About two years ago we lost our oldest son, a teenager. Six months after this my father died very suddenly. The impact of these two events caused me to give a great deal of thought to the subject of life after death. I read several books on the matter which gave me a good deal of comfort, but no proof.

Then one evening, around September 30, 1964, I was amusing myself at the piano when I was startled by the sound of a roaring fire in the fireplace behind me. I swung around, and to my amazement there was no fire to be seen, just two charred sticks of wood which had lain there since the last time the fire had been lit. But the crackling and snapping of a fiercely burning fire continued.

I got up and went over to the grate, gingerly lifted out one of the sticks expecting it to be hot—but it was not. Then I cautiously touched the other stick and it too was cold. Yet the noise of a roaring fire continued for about four minutes longer.

I stood staring at the grate in amazement, knowing that this was the work of some unseen force.

Next morning I went down to the same basement room and sat pondering over this unusual happening. I started thinking about a letter I had received from my sister in which she said that it wouldn't surprise her in the least if my son made his presence known to me in some way or another—perhaps scrawl a message across a paper or something of that nature.

I was struck by a sudden urge to get up and get a pencil and paper. The idea seemed like pure fantasy, but I sat there quietly with closed eyes and resting my head back on a cushion. The tip of the pencil was lightly touching the paper.

After a while I imagined that I felt my fingers beginning to move in a spiral scrawl. "It must be your imagination, woman!" I thought sternly to myself... but before long the movement became too definite to possibly be my mind playing tricks.

I got up and found some fresh paper, then settled back again in the chair. In a few minutes a name was written across the paper.

Now I had been looking for my son's identity, yet to my astonishment the name was that of a woman friend who had passed over previously. The first name given was a nickname by which she was known to her friends and family. She wrote several lines. This was a painfully slow process as my hand had to be pushed to form each letter.

After a few days of steady effort I became must faster at this writing and the words became quite legible and easy to read. She then brought my son and he wrote many things to me that he alone would know about. I was also given a wonderful guide.

Although I was completely convinced, my husband remained sceptical. But I did manage to persuade him to pay one visit to the local spiritualist church and after a while I began to attend regularly. When attending this church on Mother's Day, the minister gave me a very nice message—a thing he very rarely does.

He said a young lad appeared beside me, and when he realized that the Rev. C. could see him, he said, "This is my mother." Then he laced a long-stemmed rose across my front from left shoulder to right waist. He then turned to the minister again and added, "My dad used to work for the Hydro."

This final sentence was the proof I needed to tell my husband. It was twenty years ago that my husband worked for the Hydro and I'm sure no one present could have possibly known this fact. I was so pleased.

The lad came again the next Sunday, showed the Rev. C. a long child's pencil, and then said something about "Atlantic." I immediately thought of the ocean. Then the minister told me he was saying 232 Atlantic. That's the exact address where we lived for two years at the time my son was born. Next the Rev. C. said, "He gives me a name now, Aikins—no—that's a street also, he says 485 Aikins..."

What a thrill for me, as that is where we moved to from the Atlantic address and where we lived for twelve years when my son was a boy...

Everything Was a Mystery to Me

JANICE GARDEN-MACDONALD

Here is an unusual childhood reminiscence about a séance. It was written by Janice Garden-Macdonald and published under the title "When I Was Ten..." in The Great Canadian Anecdote Contest *(1991), edited by George Woodcock. Although this recollection is circumstantial in the extreme, the air of delight that swirls about this memoir commands the reader's attention.*

◆ ◆ ◆

When I was ten, everything was a mystery to me. Life and death. Electricity. And simpler things too—like how a lazy, one-eyed cat was able to catch and swallow Joey. And if he was so smart, why did he leave those tell-tale feathers all over Anne's kitchen? The bird (and the cat) belonged to my next-door neighbour and best friend. So, naturally, when she suggested we have a séance in my basement to bring back the beloved budgie, I agreed.

We descended the stairs curiously, three girls taunting the unknown. "If you want this to work, it's gotta be dark." Anne spoke with authority, for she was the oldest.

I turned off the light—a single bulb that dangled above our old chrome table. We were swallowed by the blackness. "Join hands," Anne instructed. We did so, gladly. Her faceless voice became eerie in the pitch dark—my niece tightened her bony grip around my fingers. Anne began to chant a deep alto drone. "Joey... Speak to us, great bird-spirit." We were fraught with expectation. "Joey, oh Joey. E-e-e!" Suddenly, a chilling shriek! We broke apart, reaching and grasping in the so-thick air, searching for the swinging light chain. My niece, bound to her chair, sat pale and trembling.

"Did you see it?" she screamed. "Did you hear that awful flapping noise?" We pushed and grovelled up the stairway, three abreast. Breathless and gasping, we swore each other to secrecy.

Now, when I think about our basement, I remember mostly the windows, painted shut, and the cold concrete floor. And of course I remember my mother (who had never heard of Margaret Laurence), standing at the top of the stairs screeching in nervous excitement, "Bird in the house!" It wasn't a budgie, but a terrified blackbird who had answered our invitation. My parents never understood how it got in. No open windows, no fireplace flue.

But the explanation was simple enough for three girls—an incarnate budgie, born in the dark basement of a child's wish. And now that I am well away from being ten years old, I am resolute to find—that everything is a mystery to me.

PART VII
HAUNTED PEOPLE

In this section and the next, you will encounter people who are haunted. Places are haunted too, but no firm line can be drawn between the influence of a person and the influence of a place. Some people are more sensitive or intuitive than others, open to the world of the spirit perhaps, and some places seem a little odd, soaring like mountains or plunging like valleys. We instantly respond to the spirits of person and place, as these accounts demonstrate only too well!

More a "Sensitive"
than a Psychic

DOUG TURNER

"As you suggested a couple of weeks ago, I have written the story of my unusual experiences, and it is enclosed."

So wrote Doug Turner in a personal letter dated June 10, 1994. After reading one of my collections of unusual experiences, he wrote and offered to send me an account of some of his own. I wrote back and encouraged him to do so. The following text comes from one of his letters, the last, dated June 7, 1995.

Doug Turner was born in 1935 in the farming village of Henfryn, in Huron County, Ontario. His ancestry is English with a little admixture of Scottish and German. He grew up on a farm and loves farming life but has worked in a bank, as a bookkeeper, and with a luggage manufacturer. He lives with his wife in Stratford, Ontario, and they have four adult children. "I have always had an interest in the unexplained, and I think that the fact that I am a Pisces may have some bearing on that," he explained.

His account is interesting for a number of reasons. I like the distinction between being "sensitive" and being psychic, and how odd events and peculiar experiences are part of the warp and woof of his life. The reader has the opportunity to make of them what he or she will. For Doug Turner, they enrich his life and broaden his outlook.

◆ ◆ ◆

June 7, 1995

My first experience of a psychic nature took place when I was six to eight years old, during the early 1940s. At that time I slept upstairs in my own room, and alone. On a number of occasions, while I was going to sleep, I would "float" up out of my body, so that I was just above it, and about eight to twelve inches above the bed. When I wakened enough to realize that I was "floating," I would "fall" back on to the bed, with the definite feeling of falling and a distinct shock when I hit the bed. At the time I did not realize what was taking place, nor was I concerned about supernatural matters. I realized years later that these "floating" experiences had been out-of-the-body experiences, even though I had not gone as far out as many others.

At that time I also had many floating dreams, or at least I have considered them dreams for most of my life. The stairway that led downstairs when I was young had a door at the bottom which was usually latched. I often dreamed that I was floating down the stairs towards the door, and I recall that I always felt that I was going to hit the door and suffer physical injury. Yet that never happened. I always floated right through the door. On reflection I suppose that these may also have been out-of-the-body experiences.

Unfortunately such interesting adventures did not last. During my high school years, from 1948 to 1952, my experiences were limited to several incidents of déjà vu. In those cases, I would realize, during an incident in the classroom, that I had experienced these exact words and actions during a dream I had had during the past few days.

There were no more such incidents until almost twenty years later, in 1967. In June of that year my father took his own life for reasons unknown, though I think that depression caused by feelings of failure and alienation may have been the cause. For about three months prior to his death, I dreamed almost every night of fire, although it was not until after the event that I realized the significance of the dreams. After Dad's death my wife, Ann, and I stayed overnight with my mother at their home. After we had gone to bed we both felt the strong presence of my father's spirit. I did not find the experience at all frightening. Since my wife had mentioned this feeling first, I have often wondered if it was a real feeling on my part, or something I imagined because of her suggestion. In 1993, it was confirmed in dramatic fashion that the feeling had been real—but that comes later in the story.

Both I and my wife have considerable interest in the supernatural. In my case I have inherited a love of Scotland, as well as an interest in the unexplained, from my Scottish great-grandmother. My wife is even more Scottish than I and has a great psychic ability. Cecily, a friend in New Zealand, has suggested that I am more a "sensitive" than a psychic, and I am inclined to agree with her. My wife has her own story to tell, but she has been involved in some of my experiences, as indicated elsewhere.

In 1967, there were two deaths in my family in addition to that of my father. The first was the death of a nephew of mine less than a month after he was born. We did not experience anything unusual in that case. Prior to the death of my father, the second death in the year, as well as my own dreams, my wife had a dream which indicated that my father might die. She was with him in a church facing a large, round, stained-glass window. A bat was trying to break through the window and my wife said to my father, "If that bat gets in, one of us will die!" The bat did break part of the window and enter the church. My wife woke up then, and it was the next day that my father took his life. A couple of months later my wife and I came home to our apartment and found a bat in the hallway. She insisted that I get the bat out, which I was able to do after several minutes, but she said then, "That means someone is going to die!" It was only about an hour later that my sister phoned to say that my niece had died.

It was after these events of 1967 that I decided to learn all I could about supernatural events, and over the years I have read every book I could find about everything from UFOs to the near-death experience. That, along with my personal experiences, has convinced me that there is much more to life than the physical existence we lead every day. I feel certain that some form of reincarnation exists, though I'm not sure how it works. I also feel that I have what is usually called a Guardian Angel, though in my case I have not seen or felt anything directly. The feeling is based on a series of extraordinarily fortunate events throughout my life. For instance, while I have driven many thousands of miles during my life, I have only twice had a car quit on the road, and on those occasions I was close to home and help was at hand.

I have also had good fortune financially in cases where things could easily have turned out badly instead. I have not been given any lucky lottery numbers though! Guardian Angels don't seem to operate that way.

After the 1984 federal election, I had a strangely queasy feeling in my stomach, a feeling that the next few years would not be good. In retrospect, that seems to have been an accurate feeling. I do not intend that as political criticism, because I have had similar feelings at other times. It was at about that time that I began to realize that my feelings were becoming predominant.

In 1985, I had an experience which demonstrated that even more. When I was young, we lived on a farm outside a small village in Southwestern Ontario, and in the mid-1950s had moved into the village. In 1985, I went for a drive past that farm, something I had not done for many years. As I did so, I was overcome by an intense feeling of sadness and nostalgia. That feeling was so unusual and so strong that I made note of it in my diary, though I couldn't forget it in any case.

My next unusual experience was in 1989. I have for years enjoyed corresponding with people around the world. Of those, the friend I have known longest is Gwen, from Australia, whom I have been writing to for about forty years. In 1960–61, she and a friend travelled around the world and stayed six weeks with my family and me. She married in 1963 and after raising a family she and her husband, Leon, have visited us, and many other friends in various places, several times since 1986. As they were leaving after their visit in 1989, I hugged Gwen and gave her a goodbye kiss. A moment or two later, as they were driving away, I suddenly felt a tremendous sense of loss, and then a real, physical heartache! I had always thought "heartache" was a figure of speech, yet here I was experiencing the real thing. The ache continued for a couple of hours until I eventually fell asleep. I have never been able to explain that in physical terms, and I should point out, too, that I have never had a physical attraction to Gwen, even though she was beautiful when she was younger, and is still a lovely woman. I have had a feeling for years that Gwen is someone I knew in a previous life. That might explain the love I have for her, and also the appropriate circumstances would explain my lack of physical interest.

I have a similar love for my wife's sister-in-law, Marlene, and I feel that it is also because she is someone I knew in a previous life. In her case, there is a definite physical attraction, which would indicate to me that she is perhaps someone I was married to at one time. I should point out that I do not feel this attraction to everyone, and so far it has been limited to Gwen, Marlene and two other ladies, to whom I also felt a strong physical attraction. I feel that four is a number that I could easily have known. I'm not sure how to explain the attraction except to say that it is a strong feeling of attraction inside me which can at times leave me feeling weak.

In September of 1990, I had another very interesting experience. I had in the preceding years acquired an interest in my family tree. On this occasion I had driven to a rural area a few miles from my home in search of a cemetery where my mother's ancestors are buried. The cemetery is small and no longer used. I did not know the area, never having been there before, although I had general directions. I found the general area with no trouble, but came to a crossroads, and from there did not know which way to go. I could see no sign of any cemetery, and I was momentarily confused, with the question in my mind being, "Where is it?" I looked around, then saw a Canadian flag on a pole beside one of the roads about three-quarters of a mile away. The instant I saw that flag my question was answered. I knew that the cemetery was there near the flag, even though I could see nothing. When I drove down the road the cemetery was, of course, there, almost directly

across the road from the flag and pole. I had never experienced anything like that before and I still wonder where the information came
from. From my deceased ancestors, perhaps?

It was later in 1990, near the end of November, that another event
occurred which I find almost miraculous. I was then part of a group
which gathered in the cafeteria at my place of employment for a meeting which turned out to be fairly long. I sat near a lady with whom I was
friendly, but she is not a special friend. Near the conclusion of the meeting, I felt a special kind of love for this lady. It was not similar to the
love I have described which I have for Gwen and Marlene, and I have
never had any "special" feeling for the lady. This love was like a "cloud
of love" enveloping both of us, and the only appropriate description I
can think of is the Biblical "love that passeth all understanding." The
feeling only lasted for a few seconds, and I'm sure was only my own,
but it was something I will never forget. I feel very privileged to have
had such an experience, and to know, at least to some extent, the meaning of the phrase from the Bible. I also know now what people who have
had a near-death experience mean when they refer to such love.

The most interesting event of 1991 happened in May when I read in
our newspaper that a horse called Strike the Gold was going to run in
the Kentucky Derby. I felt that he would win, and I found out a couple
of hours later that he had in fact won. Since I didn't read the paper until
late in the day, it is possible that the race may have actually been run
before I read about it. If that was the case, as seems likely, it would
seem to be a case of clairvoyance rather than a psychic prediction.

In late 1992, I experienced a strong feeling of depression at work.
The reason became apparent next day when I learned that twelve people had been laid off effective just before Christmas. While I was not
affected myself, I did "pick up" apprehension and anger, which is, I'm
sure, what those laid off felt.

In February of 1993, I saw, on TV, a video of a UFO at Carp,
Ontario. Several days later I read an item in the paper in which someone claimed that this had been only a balloon. I felt then that I needed

to see the video again, and that same film was shown on another program a few days later. I don't think it was shown because I wanted to see it, but I do feel that I was perhaps able to sense in some manner that it would be shown again.

My final experience is also one of the most interesting and happened in April of 1993. I have always enjoyed correspondence with people around the world and in 1986 I was writing to a lady in London, England, called Grace. My wife wanted at that time to find some pen friends in Scotland, and, since Grace was the friend of a newspaper editor in Glasgow, she volunteered to help. My wife wrote a short letter which was published in the Glasgow paper, and she received about half a dozen replies. One of those was from a lady named Evelyn. It turned out that Evelyn, her husband, Walter, and their family had lived in Stratford, where we also live, for a number of years. Evelyn had worked at the hospital and knew the city well. She and her family had also lived directly across the road from where we lived at that time. Evelyn and her family had returned to Scotland before we moved there, so we had never met, but this geographical closeness was the main reason for her writing in the first place. She and my wife became very good friends, and we had also talked on the phone several times.

In the fall of 1992, Evelyn suffered stomach pains and was hospitalized for tests. These revealed stomach cancer, and she had an operation to remove half of her stomach, along with her spleen and gall bladder. She continued to suffer stomach pains, and in late March was back in hospital for another operation. When doctors opened her stomach they found widespread cancer, and all they could do was close her up again. On April 8, Evelyn died.

We did not learn of her death until April 19, when we received a letter from Walter. That evening I retired about 11:30 p.m., as usual, and my wife came to bed at about 2:00 a.m. I had been asleep, but woke when my wife came to bed, and I recall that I had been dreaming about souls, which is unusual in itself. My wife says that she said something to me but I don't recall that. I felt then the presence of a spirit and

I knew that it was Evelyn. The presence was very strong. Then I felt the spirit move through me, moving from my waist up through my chest and head, in a wave effect. The feeling was akin to what you get when your hair stands on end, but much stronger. There was also a very definite cold feeling. The spiritual wave happened a total of three times, taking a total of about twenty to thirty seconds. I was not afraid and in fact, knowing that it was Evelyn's spirit, I found the experience rather pleasant. The whole thing was very real, and there is no possibility that it was only my imagination. The only other time I have felt anything similar was after my father died.

The next day I learned from my wife that she had been with Evelyn's spirit in our living room, and that Evelyn had come to the bedroom with her. Because of Evelyn's strong connection with Stratford, as well as with my wife and me, it makes perfect sense that she would visit here before going on. It is also worth noting that she did not visit us until we knew of her death. That would also mean that she was aware of when we did know. If she had come before we were aware of her death, we would not have realized the significance.

Almost exactly two years later, in April of 1995, I had an experience very similar to the one that had happened after Evelyn died. In this case the person who died, also a lady, was Janny. She had been born in Holland before World War II and had spent the war years there, where her family had helped the Underground and sheltered some people. Jan is the Dutch equivalent of John, and it was because her father wanted boys that both Janny and a sister were given boys' names. We often called her Jenny, but her real name was Janny, and her family lived in the very same house where Evelyn and Walter had lived some years before. They were the across-the-street neighbours of ours for many years.

Early in 1994, after both of our families had moved to different locations, Janny was diagnosed as having cancer of a type that turned out to be incurable. She spent long hours taking treatments that proved to be of no value, and shortly before Easter of 1995 she ended up in hospital on a permanent basis. Both my wife and I had always liked Janny, and I talked to her from time to time during her illness, so that I had perhaps a special feeling of closeness to her. We visited her in the hospital and had hoped to see her again, but it was not to be.

On the night of April 19, I had a dream. Not just an ordinary dream, but a dream of fire, something I had not had since 1967, when three of my family died. I dreamed that I was in a large building, like a hospital or library. There was a fire in the upper part of the building, somewhere above me, but lots of smoke was coming down, rather than going up, for some reason. I went back into the building several times, but eventually got out. Many of my dreams are like will-o'-the-wisps and fade away when I wake up, but not this one. I woke up after the dream at about 4:00 a.m., but it stayed with me in a very clear way. I went to the bathroom then, and it was there that I continued to think of the dream, and got a very strong feeling of impending death. It was so strong that I wondered who was going to die. I thought of my own family, even myself, but at the time I didn't think of Janny. While I knew that she was seriously ill, there was no real indication that she wasn't going to live for some time, though I suppose I should have thought of the possibility of her imminent death. Even her husband was caught by surprise when she died. She was all right when he saw her about 8:00 a.m. At about 10:15 a.m., she was suddenly gone, only six hours after my dream.

Five days later, after her funeral had taken place, my wife stayed up later than I, as is her custom. She had a visit from Janny's spirit, very similar to the visit from Evelyn two years earlier. When she came to bed, Janny came with her. I partially wakened, and it was then that I had a definite spiritual contact with Janny. In fact, earlier I had asked her, silently in my mind, to visit us, and I was pleased when she did. The contact was not as long or as pronounced as the one with Evelyn, but it was contact nevertheless, and I have no doubt at all that it was Janny.

I look upon this dream and contact by Janny, as I do Evelyn's contact, as evidence of the reality of life after death. I feel that these experiences show that there is more to life than we normally think, and that there is a spiritual life after this one.

It Began to Do the Figure 8

DALI ROY

Dali Roy, of Malvern, Ontario, read an article about my interest in "the mysterious" that was printed in the North York News. *Ms. Roy shares my interest in "the mysterious," so she kindly sent me the following letter, which I am reproducing with a minimum of editing.*

In her account she refers to the "witchboard," or Ouija board. Such boards had a vogue in the late 19th century and are even more popular today. Someone once noted that, each year, North Americans purchase more Ouija boards than they do sets of the ever-popular Monopoly board game.

*The word "Ouija" is said to derive from the words for "yes" in French (*oui*) and German (*ja*). The name is certainly catchy. The Ouija board is sometimes referred to as a "witchboard" because some contemporary practitioners of witchcraft, or Wicca, make use of the board, along with the Tarot cards, in their probing of "the unknown."*

Whatever its name, the board has a tenuous Canadian connection. Daniel Fox has been credited with its invention, or at least with its present popularity. Like his better-known sisters, the spiritualists Katie and Maggie Fox, Daniel was born at Consecon, near Belleville, then Canada West, now Ontario. It was his sisters' "spirit rapping" that launched the modern movement called Spiritualism in 1848 in upstate New York. The spirits would rap once for yes, twice for no, and it took a lot of knocking to spell out a word, not to mention a message of any length. To help the sisters spell out words, Daniel developed the board, with its alphabet, numbers, and the words "Yes" and "No." Or so the story goes.

Opinion is divided on the mechanism that moves the planchette across the surface of the board to spell out messages. Spiritualists maintain that the board acts as a medium through which spirits from the beyond may communicate with the spirits that reside in the here and now. Psychologists point out that involuntary muscular movements of the participants, so-called ideomotor movements, responding to subconscious hopes and fears, animate the planchette. Practitioners and observers alike are ever amazed at how the planchette seems to "take on a life of its own." Whatever the mechanism, it really does move.

◆ ◆ ◆

May 23, 1990

Mr. Colombo:

I have just read your article in the *North York News* and I am interested in your book. My name is Dali and I am eighteen years old. I have had an experience with the supernatural. The witchboard—or, if you prefer, the Ouija board—is what I am writing to you about.

I will begin by telling you that I have always believed in the supernatural because my mother has out-of-body experiences and my grandmother is a psychic.

This is my story.

I was at my cousin's house last year around this time. We had a couple of our friends over and in the basement we decided to play with the witchboard while our friends watched. It began to do the figure 8 over and over again, really fast. I don't know if this is evil, but it sure is pretty scary! My cousin Diane began to speak to it, asking it questions like "Who are you?" "How old are you?" and "Is there a Heaven or a Hell?"

We ended up finding out that its name was George and he was only five years old. But he would not tell us if there was a Heaven or a Hell. Instead, he ignored us and continued with his figure 8s. We asked him to spell some words, but he could not. At first we were confused, but I asked if he could spell and he said no.

This is when I stared to feel really weird. He started to spell out words, without errors, like the f-word and all those horrible words. My friends started to get restless and were starting to move about. One of my friends stood up really quickly and said, "Screw this stuff! I don't even believe in the Ouija."

All of a sudden the planchette flew out from under our fingers and hit him in the head, drawing blood. Following this the lights in the basement flicked off and on, then finally went out. We were terrified. I wished to God that I had never dealt with the witchboard, and we all ran out of the basement away from Diane's house. To this day, my cousin has not been in her basement.

Hopefully, one of us will get the courage to go down there. But I don't feel that I will ever go down there again.

I hope this is something you can use. If not, please send me back this letter. Thank you.

Sincerely yours,
Dali Roy

I Was Scared and Very Curious

H. NAGY

I sometimes think I am a magnet for people who have peculiar experiences to share.

I received these two letters from Mrs. H. Nagy, of Welland, Ontario. The first arrived on June 1, 1990; the second was dated June 6 of the same year.

In the first letter, Mrs. Nagy described the nature of some peculiar events and experiences that had occurred six years earlier and had left an indelible mark on her memory. In that letter, she alluded to "a bizarre culmination of happenings" that she did not describe. So I wrote to her, asking for more information.

In the second letter, she elaborated. It must have been a hard letter to write, but it makes fascinating reading. Far from just "a whirlwind of memories," the account in the letter is a vivid description of the possession of the living by the dead.

Both letters are reproduced here in slightly edited form.

◆ ◆ ◆

1.

June 1, 1990

I am writing in response to your advertisement in our local newspaper, the *Welland Guardian.*

In 1984, my mother-in-law passed away because of cancer. It was a long, painful time for her and we were with her when she passed over.

About four months later, "occurrences" started happening to me. There are too many to list here, but in general they include shaking chairs, the presence of a "white cloud" (which was also witnessed by my two-year-old daughter), and what I called "the feeling." This was an unpleasant "smothering" of my body. I had trouble breathing, and felt very confined, almost like I was being hugged by a bear. This feeling would last only a minute and then the "apparition" would appear.

I documented every time an "occurrence" would happen to me, and there seemed to be no rhyme or reason as to when it would happen. I was scared and very curious as to who or what this was and why it was happening only to me and not to my husband. I talked to many people about this, and the ones who didn't think me crazy thought it was because I was a bit more "sensitive" than my husband. It was a very hard time for my family, and I was always on edge because I never knew when it would happen.

It all ended in a bizarre culmination of happenings that were truly unbelievable, and I hesitate even now to put them in writing. I have talked to many people who, I thought, would believe me, and even they thought I was crazy.

But to sum it up, I told the apparition to leave and it did. During this culmination, I was brought to believe that the spirit was that of my mother-in-law. I will go into details if you are interested.

Let it be known that during this time I was tested by psychiatrists and by medical doctors for epilepsy, and there was nothing wrong with me physically or mentally.

2.

June 6, 1990

Your letter asking me for more details has started a whirlwind of memories for me.

One of the major things I remember is that I was almost always alone whenever anything strange would happen. This makes it very difficult for people to believe in what you are saying.

I remember how my family and I had just begun our dinner, and while I was sitting in my chair, it began to shake. Hard. The shaking lasted only seconds, then stopped.

I said to my husband, "What was that?"

He said, "What was what?"

I asked him if he felt anything and he said no. I passed it off.

Moments later it happened again, and this time it was harder and longer. I jumped up and yelled, "There it is again!"

I went and sat on the couch, and looked at the window, and that is when I saw what looked to be a translucent white moon hanging above my window. Moments later it was gone. No one saw it but me.

Days later my daughter pointed to the wall above the hutch and said, "Look, Mommy, moon." It was the same thing I saw.

This went on for some time, and every time before it would happen and the "moon" would appear, I would get the feeling of being smothered. Finally... after months of it appearing only to me, in front of the TV, while drying my hair, and once right next to me on the chair where I was sitting... I had had enough. I called a friend and asked her what she thought I should do. She asked me if I had tried just telling it to go away. So simple, I had never thought of it.

The next time that it happened, I was, of course, alone. The feeling of a presence was the strongest it had ever been, and instead of getting scared, I got angry. I had had enough of all of this. I yelled, "Who are you?"

The moment I did, my right arm went completely numb. No feeling from the shoulder down. Now this was the arm my mother-in-law had had amputated, due to cancer, so I concluded it was her spirit.

I said, "Okay, now I know who you are, now tell me what you want." My arms flew up in the air, my head went back, and I couldn't move. Now I was terrified. I began to cry. I screamed, "Go away, you're ruining my life!"

Then it stopped. Just stopped. The feeling slowly disappeared, and I never saw the "moon" again.

To this day, I still don't know why it happened. I'm still not sure if it was my mother-in-law's spirit. But to console myself, I tell myself it was her, and she was trying to tell me, in the only way she could, that she's okay.

He Appeared to Be
a Silhouette

DEBORAH HOYLE

I received the following letter from Deborah Hoyle, of Victoria, British Columbia. Ms. Hoyle works in the area of medical imaging. Her father is a Mohawk and her mother is of Welsh, Irish, and Scottish descent. After reading my request for "ghost stories," she sent me this account of the three apparitions of a loved one. I am reproducing her account with a little editing.

Ms. Hoyle's story is a heart-wrenching one. It deals with a category of psychical experience known as the "crisis apparition." Loved ones report apparitions of the dying with surprising frequency. It is of some comfort to consider or even conclude that time and, in this instance, space are merely hurdles that the expression of love and the need for consolation are able to surmount.

◆ ◆ ◆

September 16, 1990

Dear Mr. Colombo:

The story I have to tell is the story of the man I have loved since I was fourteen years old.

Doug was my boyfriend and the man I wanted to marry. We never dated other teenagers during our years together. But during the latter years of our seven-year relationship, we started to drift apart.

From the age of fifteen, Doug was plagued with double vision and subject to falls. During his marriage, he became seriously ill. I didn't know about his condition until a mutual friend invited me to visit him in the hospital. Doug had been diagnosed as suffering from multiple sclerosis. His wife left him. I stopped in as "a friend," even though I was still in love with him.

I had three experiences with Doug's spirit. They occurred while he was hospitalized and I was at home in my room. I was in bed and it was dark. There is a ledge the length of the wall behind my bed. I suddenly felt cool. I turned in bed to fix my pillow when what I saw shocked me. I saw Doug's head, and only his head, on the ledge. His head looked pure white and it slid from one end of the ledge to the other. Curiously, I wasn't afraid. Soon after, I got a phone call from the hospital about his condition. He had had a heart attack. That was the first experience.

The second experience was of Doug looking at me. This time he was floating next to the bed, with just his upper body visible. Again he was white and he looked straight-faced. Then after a while he disappeared. I again got a telephone call. After this second heart attack, the doctors found a brain tumour. He had been getting the wrong treatment. That was the second experience.

The third and last experience was frightening. This time, Doug was standing at my door. He appeared to be a silhouette surrounded by a white aura. The sight scared me. I put my hands up to my chest and jumped out of bed to turn on the overhead light. I ran right into him and he held me for just a moment. I made it to the switch and turned the light on. There was no one with me. It still brings tears to my eyes thinking of this moment. Again, I was telephoned.

Unfortunately, the day Doug died, I knew nothing about his death. He died on March 5, 1983, two days before his twenty-seventh birthday. It was also the anniversary of our first date. I tell people that we were together twelve years because, unofficially, we were.

A lady once told me that what had happened those three times was Doug saying goodbye to me. The only peace I get from what happened occurred two years after Doug's death. A mutual friend told me that Doug had told him, a couple of days before he died, that he still loved me.

Please forgive me if I have carried on too long. My feelings in this matter are intense, and to this day I believe that Doug and I were soulmates. He was the only boyfriend I've had so far in my life.

I wish you luck with your book, Mr. Colombo. I hope that this will help you. I hope my letter makes sense. It's difficult to describe, but I thank you for the opportunity.

Sincerely,
Deborah Hoyle

The Weird One in the Family

MICHAEL J. BAKERPEARCE

Michael J. Bakerpearce boasts of his English, Welsh, and Irish ancestry. Born in England, he came to Canada in 1955, and from 1969 to his retirement in 1987, he worked as a histology technologist in the department of pathology at the University of Guelph. Today he lives in Damascus, a community near Kenilworth, Ontario, and enjoys engaging in historical research.

Mr. Bakerpearce sent me a letter on September 9, 1992, and included with it the brief memoir titled "How I Learned to Recognize Ghosts." The letter suggested that he was giving some thought to writing a book about all of his ghostly experiences. When he completes this memoir, he has a title handy. He wants to call it Growing Up Psychic— *or perhaps* Growing Up Weird.

In his letter, he also referred to a "strange thing" that had happened to him not long before:

*I had asked the University of British Columbia for a library
search for information on a Norman knight called de Bacquepuiz,
no relation to Bakerpearce. When the photocopies arrived, I was
surprised to find attached a "family tree" for Mary Queen of
Scots and various relatives. I contacted the library to find out if
the copy should have gone to someone else and, if not, why had it
been sent to me. There being almost four hundred years between
de Bacquepuiz and Mary, I could see no connection. The answer I
got was, "I thought you might be interested."*

*What do you suppose moved a library clerk whom I had never
met, who resided and worked in British Columbia, a place I'd
never visited, to look up and make a copy of information on
Mary Queen of Scots and send it to me? (Am I the reincarnation
of someone on that list? It gives me goose bumps to think about
it, and yet I've suspected something of the sort for some time.
Anthony Babbington, perhaps?)*

*The Celtic blood that courses through Mr. Bakerpearce's veins
would not let him rest. He sent me two further accounts under the general heading "The Weird One of the Family" on October 5, 1992.*

*All three accounts appear here. What they have in common is the tragic
life and death, as well as the reappearances, of Mary Queen of Scots.*

*Everyone who enjoys reading this memoir will undoubtedly also
enjoy reading Mr. Bakerpearce's earlier memoir, "Everywhere I Go I
See Ghosts," which I had the pleasure of including in my collection*
Mackenzie King's Ghost *(1991).*

◆ ◆ ◆

How I Learned to Recognize Ghosts

I never really knew what a ghost was until...

Well, until my mother admitted to me the following: "If anybody
tells me they've seen a ghost, it'll be you."

We were returning from an outing in the Derbyshire countryside. I must have been about four years old, because I remember my youngest sister, Mary, wasn't around. She hadn't been born yet. A friend had taken all of us, all the family except for Dad and my oldest brother, for a spin in her "spanking" Lanchester Tourer.

It was Whit Monday, I think. I remember that the day and the weather were perfect for a drive. I can still see it... the sort of May morning that Piers Ploughman described hundreds of years earlier.

By mid-afternoon, we had completed our tour of the local beauty spots and were on the way home, when it was decided that we should call in at Wingfield Manor. Inexplicably, I recall only two of the stops we made. One stop was a ghostly hilltop of limestone outcrops and gnarled pine trees, where we had our picnic lunch and where I swore I could hear the sounds of horses and wagons passing by, though no one would believe me. The other stop was Wingfield Manor.

We turned off the main road onto a gravelled driveway that led to the front of the mansion, where the driveway made a circle. The car came to a halt a little way from the main doorway. Dark green ivy covered the whole front of the building, but it had been clipped neatly round the outside of the windows, through which I could see white lace curtains. Red and pink hollyhocks stood by the doorway and climbing roses made a bower over it.

I remember hearing Mum say, "Wait here. I'll go and see if they'll let us in."

She got out of the car, alone, and walked to the doorway. It opened as she approached, and a man emerged and stood at the threshold, waiting for her. He wore a long black soutane-like gown. Straggling grey hair fell to his shoulders and accentuated his sharp features and sallow skin. I felt anger showing in his whole being. I heard him say, his voice harsh, imperious: "Visitors are not permitted. You cannot come in."

When Mum said she just wanted to look around, he became quite aggressive. He told her, "Leave! At once!"

While this altercation was under way, I looked across to the nearest window, where I saw a hand move the lace curtain to one side. I could see a pale lady with a high white forehead and long reddish wavy hair staring directly at me. A broad white lace collar covered her shoulders and chest. She looked so sad it made me sad to see her. I don't know how long we stared at each other.

Then Mum came back to the car and the pale lady turned away and let the curtain drop back into place. All this took place in total silence. Except for the old man's voice, high-pitched and authoritative, telling Mum repeatedly that visitors were not allowed, and no, we could not go in, there was not a sound to be heard—no sound from the others in the car, nor any birdsong. Nothing.

Mum came back to the car. She seemed quite annoyed that the old man had not let her go inside. She got into the car and I remember that all the sounds came back as the motor was started up. When we set off again, everyone was in high spirits, laughing and singing. But I couldn't get the pale lady out of my mind. (Nor have I to this day.)

We arrived home, and as soon as the car stopped, I had to get out and run down to the garden to the little back-house that was there for emergencies. Emergency over, I went into the kitchen, where Mum was preparing dinner. We expected Dad to come home from work any minute now. Mum asked me what all the hurry was about and I told her I'd wanted to go while we waited at the old mansion. She said, "Well, why didn't you come with me? You could've gone there."

I told her I wouldn't have gone at that place. "That old man frightened me and the pale lady with red hair made me sad." I can still see the way her mouth dropped open. She often let her mouth drop when I told her about somebody or something that I had seen or heard in my peregrinations round and about.

"What old man? And what lady?" she asked. Her eyebrows were knitted—in disbelief, I thought at the time.

I described the mansion as I had seen it. I told her how I had heard her say she was going to go to see if we could go inside and look around. I described the old man who met her at the door and how I had heard him angrily telling her to leave. I told her about the pale lady who looked out the window at me.

She listened until I stopped. Then she said, "I don't know how you could have heard me say that. All I said was, 'I'll just hide in there. Toot the horn if anyone comes,' or something like that, I can't really remember. But, anyway, that place is in ruins. There's just broken-down walls, that's all. And you couldn't have seen anyone in there. There are no windows, for a start, and no one has lived there for hundreds of years. I just went round behind that broken-down wall because I couldn't wait until we got home, that's all."

I insisted that there was no "broken-down wall" and that what I had seen I had seen. Then she said, in an abstract sort of way, gazing into the distance, "Mary Queen of Scots was imprisoned there a long time ago. Some people say they have seen her ghost there. I don't know... if anybody tells me that they saw a ghost, it would be you."

I remember that she seemed worried about me. After dinner, I heard her telling Dad about it. Years later, Dad told me that they decided not to mention the incident again, thinking I would soon forget all about the experience.

Some time later, I came across a picture of "the lady" in an encyclopedia. I showed it to Mum, saying, "That's the lady I saw in the window at that old house where the old man was cross at you."

She looked at me with a strange expression on her face. She replied, "That's Mary Queen of Scots. I suppose those folks who say that they have seen her ghost in the ruins of Wingfield Manor must be telling the truth after all."

Then she told me what she knew of the tragical history of Mary Stuart, Queen of Scots. Only then did I begin to realize that a lot of "the people" whom I had encountered in various places round and about were really the ghosts of the people who had lived there a long, long time ago.

I Meet Mary Stuart for the Second Time

Sometimes I feel a ghostly presence.

It's not like a physical touch. Nor is it like the sudden icy coldness that some people report. Rather, it's an empathy, an often violent sense that something is passing between the ghost and me that brings with it a feeling of sadness. Sometimes the feeling is close to overwhelming. I am never surprised by its coming. It doesn't really frighten me, although sometimes the hair at the nape of my neck stands up. That's how I feel in London, two days after Christmas, 1944.

I have a few hours to kill before I leave by BOAC (British Overseas Air Corporation) for India. A light grey fog shrouds the city, blurring the edges of the buildings, reducing everything to a misty sameness. The city is cold, dreary, and depressing—a winter's day punctuated by the occasional boom of a crashing buzz bomb. I find myself entering the main entrance of Westminster Abbey.

I can't remember that I consciously decided to come here. There are brighter places to be, though I don't fancy myself in a darkened cinema with the roof crashing in on me. Perhaps subconsciously I feel that being in the Abbey will give me a head start if the worst happens.

Anyway, I enjoy visiting old churches and castles, places where I can feel the impressions of history seeping upwards through the soles of my feet and into my body.

The fog seems to have infiltrated the Abbey. It feels as cold and as drear as the street outside... except that there is some warmth here, unmeasurable yet alive... a warmth that comes from these stones which have witnessed so many centuries of human life in all its glory and despair. What might account for it is the absorbed warmth of more than a thousand years of prayer.

At first glance the Abbey appears deserted. However, an occasional shuffling sound leads me to believe that I am not alone in this vast building. Someone else is here with me.

If I stand still long enough, I am bound to see that person. The light is bad. Not enough of the grey light outside comes through the windows to make the stained glass visible. Some windows have been boarded up. Anyone could saunter up the opposite aisle, crossing behind a pillar, so that there would always be two pillars between us.

Then I see her, across the nave, a well-dressed, middle-aged woman who had walked ahead of me as I had crossed the forecourt. She had disappeared when I had entered the Abbey.

I walk up the aisle, glad to have my rubber-soled dress boots on. I hate the clatter that studded army boots make on church flagstones. I come upon the tomb of Elizabeth I. I look all about it. Suddenly I feel compelled to cross the nave to the tomb of Mary Queen of Scots.

Someone has tossed a small bouquet of blue and white irises, tied with a blue and white ribbon, through the wrought-iron fence surrounding the tomb. It lies a bit awry, on the plinth, below the feet of the statue.

I have a vision of some person extending hands between the iron bars to drop these irises onto the tomb itself. An overpowering sadness envelops me. I burst into uncontrollable sobs. Tears stream down my face.

The woman I had only glimpsed earlier appears in the distance and approaches me. She stands near me. "Are you all right, Airman?" Her voice is soft, quiet, cultured. For some reason I expect a Scottish accent, but there is none.

Yet it's strange for a civilian to address me as an "Airman." Usually civilians don't know what to call us, members of "Other Ranks," who have no NCO stripes to give them a lead.

Between sobs I tell her that I am all right and that I can't understand why I am crying. She says she wondered if I had lost a relative or a friend in the bombing. I tell her no, nothing like that, that I was all right until I saw the blue and white irises.

She takes my arm and leads me away, saying, "Come away a little and see if your crying stops."

I allow her to lead me five or six pews away. We sit in one of the pews. My tears stop. She asks me where I am from and if I have somewhere to stay overnight. I have the feeling she would like to ask me to stay with her. I tell her where I'm from. I also tell her that, short of breaking many regulations, I am leaving for India in a few hours.

I feel quite comfortable sitting beside her in the gloom of the church. After a little while she says, "Now, let's go back and see what happens."

I decide to walk around the tomb first, then approach the flowers from the head of the tomb. She walks with me, holding my hand. Her hand is warm, soft, and dry.

As soon as I see the flowers, the tears again begin to flow. We stand together for some time. I am weeping and she is holding my hand.

It must be approaching the time for me to report back to my departure point, I ask her if she has a watch. For some reason she is unable to tell me the time. Through my sobs I tell her that I ought to go. As I turn away to leave, the tears abruptly stop. She holds on to my hand. She says how pleased she is to have met me. She looks into my face and says, "You must be a very sensitive person. May God go with you wherever you go."

She sits in a nearby pew as I make for the main entrance. At the door I turn to wave, but she has disappeared again.

Outside, an early night is beginning to darken the already dreary city. It's drizzling too. I stand for a moment by the Tomb of the Unknown Soldier to adjust my forage cap, button my greatcoat, and adjust my side pack, respirator, and steel helmet.

In that instant, I see the whole ceremony of the Interment of the Unknown Soldier. I hear the bugles, the drums, and the bands. I hear the noises of hundreds of troops, horses, and ordinary people. I hear the rustle of silk gowns. I smell the perfumes of the ladies present, mixed with the smells of people and horses. Then, just as suddenly, the vision passes.

When I arrive home again, almost three years later, I tell my mother about my experiences that afternoon. She notes with some scepticism: "I don't know how you could have seen that. You must have seen a film of it."

"Even if the interment ceremony was filmed, which I doubt, it would have been in black and white. I saw it in colour, and I heard the guns boom and the bugle calls and I detected the women's perfume and I heard the rustle of their dresses so close behind me that I felt I could reach around and touch them."

"I don't know what to make of you," she says, sighing. "Really, I don't. But you always were the weird one in the family."

I Meet Mary Stuart for the Third Time

A woman stands waiting for me at the bottom of the jetty. She is old, grey-haired, unkempt. Glowering fiercely, she accosts me and addresses me in the slovenly local speech: "Ah wu just abaht to coom t'see wot'd 'append t'thee."

I am on the way home after making the rounds of the country stores, picking up the weekly orders for cigarettes, candy, and chocolate. It is my first trip into this area. My car, a prewar model so maltreated over the years that it leaks smoke, labours up a small hill to a hamlet dominated by the remains of Tutbury Castle one sunny summer afternoon in 1953.

History books have it that Oliver Cromwell demolished the castle with gunpowder. Built when the surrounding land was a huge bog, local lore has it that the builders skimped on the building so that the castle was falling down long before the Roundheads decided to remove it as a threat to their safety.

I have never been here before. It is worth a visit. I park my car near a row of old houses constructed from stone from the castle. I walk up the steep, cobbled jetty that used to be the approach to the castle gate. Between the houses there is a sign, nailed to one house wall, that points: TO THE CASTLE. I wonder how many people have trod this jetty before me, from the Norman knight who built it to the Roundheads who destroyed it.

It's a short jetty. It extends no farther than the wall enclosing the backyards of the houses on either side. It's closed at the end by a wire gate, latched with a huge, wrought-iron latch, and armed with a primitive "automatic closer" made of scrap iron—an automobile brake drum and several worn plough coulters on a steel cable over a pulley. If you let go the open gate, the weight drops and the gate swings shut with a loud ringing of coulters on brake drum.

For all that, the gate can not be left open; fastened by wire to the gate was a warning sign, painted in dribbling, blood-red paint: "KEEP CLOSED!" In small letters beneath it said "sheep."

Once through the gate, I walk onto what was at one time the castle bailey. Now it is a level area of grass clipped like a bowling lawn by the sheep, although there is no sign of them.

Huge stone blocks, too big for the local people to carry away for their own building projects, lie scattered around, half buried, in no particular order. In the middle of this disorder, I notice a small open area. It is clear of stones and beyond it there is a tower about twenty feet high.

I walk towards the tower, wondering if it is safe to climb its steps. Half a dozen gulls sitting quietly on the grass lift themselves, crying, into the afternoon breeze and glide away out of sight. I stop and look around.

Overhead, white cirrus clouds streak a powder-blue sky. The grass is very green, and the stone blocks appear grey in the early afternoon light. With the disappearance of the gulls, it is now quiet. An uncanny hush has settled on the ruins. Silence. Not even the sibilant wheezing of the yellowhammer that I see rummaging in the gorse bushes on the edge of the bailey breaks the silence.

It is too quiet. Something is going to happen. I wonder what, this time. The hair at the nape of my neck begins to rise. I brush it down with my hand. And wait, quite still.

Then I hear it, quietly at first, but gaining strength, a woman's voice, praying: "*Ave Maria, gratia plena, Dominus te...*"

I walk a few steps towards the tower. The voice dies. Am I mistaken? Could it be just the gulls crying? But there is no other sound. I retrace my steps. The voice begins again, not where it ended as I walked away, but back at the beginning again: "*Ave Maria, gratia plena, Dominus te...*" My doubts disappear. I listen, trying to orient the voice amid the fallen masonry, trying to picture a castle room, before I realize that it would have been on the floor above. The voice trails off, as though the person praying was put off by my presence. For some reason I cannot understand, I feel I must respect her privacy.

I walk over towards the tower. For safety's sake, the tower has been wound round and round over the years with strands of barbed wire, mostly rusty but some gleaming. Wedged and tied between the layers of wire, over the doorway, there is a grey, weathered board with a legend, in the same blood-red paint that appeared on the board at the gate. It warns in big letters "DANGER" and underneath "KEEP OUT" and in small letters below, "stairs unsafe."

Peering in, I see it isn't a big tower at all. Its diameter is just wide enough to accommodate a circular stair with three- or four-foot-wide stone treads, worn hollow by who knows how many boots. The top of the tower, open to the sky, lets in enough light to show that the ascending stone steps are loose and crumbling. How far below ground level they go, I cannot tell. I walk round it to look at the view: the lush meadows of the Vale of Trent under the summer sky.

In the seconds it takes for me to walk beyond the tower, another landscape meets my eye. Instead of green meadows and fields of ripening grain, with woods and the large prosperous farms that I had expected, I see a monotonous landscape, grey with winter frost; scattered here and there, mean dwellings where thin streams of smoke blow horizontally from chimneys; and farther off, the denser smoke from a charcoal burner's kiln—a grey, ashen landscape under a leaden, sunless sky. I do not feel the bitter cold, though I sense it. How long I stand there surveying this scene I do not know. Time seems to have lost its meaning in the awful silence.

I turn back towards the centre of the bailey, and as I skirt the tower, the sun shines again in a summer-blue sky. I wonder if the voice is still there, and go to stand where I heard it before. "*Ave Maria, gratia plena...*" The voice becomes audible, but dies away again as I walk towards the edge of the bailey to look at the view to the south.

Across the vale, across emerald meadows and golden fields of grain, almost hidden in the haze, the dark towers of Lichfield Cathedral appear on a grey-blue horizon. A few feet below me, on the bank of the moat, the gulls are sunning themselves.

The yellowhammer, startled by my presence, wheezes its danger signal in the gorse nearby. The silence is broken. Reluctantly, I retrace my steps towards the gate with its sinister, blood-red message.

As the gate clangs shut behind me, a woman, grey-haired, coarse, aproned, comes round the house at the bottom of the jetty and stands there waiting for me. Something about the way she stands evokes an unconscious memory. I have seen her before, but I am unable to remember or imagine where or when that was.

She stops me with her words: "Ah wa jus abaht t'coom t'see wot 'appened t'thee."

I ask her why, and she replies, "Well, tha's bin oop there s'long. 'Ast bin asleep?"

I tell her no, I haven't been asleep, and was up there barely half an hour. She looks at me sideways, quizzically, disbelieving, and says, "Tha's bin aoop there ovver teow 'ours. Wot ast bin oop to? Tha's not bin tryin' t'climb th'tower, ast tha? Nay, tha woodna be s'daft as that." ·

I tell her I just walked about, looking at the view, and I certainly did not try to climb the tower. I'm sure I have not been more than half an hour.

Then she says something that really surprises me. "Tha's bin oop there sin' jus' after teow, for ah timed thee by me kitchen clock when ah eard th'gate clang, an it's nearly 'afe past fower now. That's ovver teow hours bi my reckoning. What didst see, eh?"

I have no intention of telling her what I saw, and I find myself answering her in her own slovenly dialect. "Ah saw nowt that'd int'rest thee, old woman, an' why dost thou want t'know?"

At that, her mouth drops open, but she gathers herself quickly and shouts after me as I walk away to my car: "Who dost think thou art, anyway. Thou'rt nubuddy! Nubuddy in my book, anyway!"

She stands on the curb and watches me as I drive off. In the rear-view mirror, I see her walk into the middle of the road and stand, arms akimbo, looking after me until I turn the corner out of sight.

I stop at the little store by the railway level crossing, barely one mile away. The proprietor answers my query about the old woman.

"Oh her! Thinks she owns the bloody castle. Says it was built by her ancestors and she has a lawful right to it. You know Mary Queen of Scotts was imprisoned there, before they took her to Fotheringay, don't you?"

If time allowed, I would tell him I do know. But I still have a long drive home, so I just say, "Yes, I think I was told that in a history lesson some years ago."

I know the proprietor knows I saw something. He's all agog for me to tell him what happened up there among the ruins. But I leave him standing behind his counter, scratching his ear.

I drive off to Burton-on-Trent and Derby and then to home.

Ghosts in My Life

MARGARET J. YOUNG

I have always invited the readers of my books to contact me and share with me their own experiences of ghosts and related matters. I issued just such an invitation in my book Ghost Stories of Ontario *(1995). It caught the eye of the following contributor.*

Margaret J. Young, of Barrie, Ontario, took the invitation seriously and phoned me. She mentioned that she is the mother of Jim Young, who had contributed a ghost story to an earlier book. She then began to relate some of the odd and eerie experiences that had happened to other members of her family. I urged her to write them out for me. She said that her son had a computer, so I encouraged her to write out her experiences as a narrative and ask the son to keyboard them and send them to me on computer disk (in ASCII). This she and he did.

When I receive an account like this one, I read it through, copy edit it, and print it out. Then I send the copy to the contributor for fact-checking. When both of us are satisfied that everything is as it should be, I add the account to the collection I am amassing for use in the next book of accounts of extraordinary experiences.

What I did not expect is that Mrs. Young would send me so long an account—one that involved so many people and so many incidents. I am not quite sure what to make of it. It is not that I doubt Mrs. Young's word. I accept the reality of what she says and the way she describes it. I am simply amazed at the "coincidences" and all the suffering (especially around Easter).

In her letter to me, Mrs. Young asked the following question: "I would be interested to know if you have had any experiences in your life, John. You write of other people's stories, but not of your own. As you are a relatively new author in my collection, perhaps you have written some that I have yet to discover. Understandably, I enjoy your writing, and the subject is definitely a fascinating one ... one that is much more acceptable now than it was a few years ago."

Mrs. Young is not the first reader and contributor to one of my books to ask me if I have ever had experiences like the ones described here. Let me answer that question. I have not had any experiences of ghosts or poltergeists, forerunners or premonitions. I am what Colin Wilson calls "ESP-dead." There is no tradition of extrasensory perception in my family. Nor does any Celtic blood flow through my veins! Indeed, although I respect people who have such experiences—and the courage to share them with others—I am not convinced that I would like to be

"ESP-alive." What I most enjoy is communicating with people with strange stories to share.

◆ ◆ ◆

June 4, 1997

Dear John:

Your invitation to share unusual experiences noted at the conclusion of "Acknowledgements" in your book *Ghost Stories of Ontario* was all I required to put my grey cells to work, pen to paper, and contact you. Boy, does my brain need exercise! Already I am at a loss as to how to proceed. Hopefully my son will compute this, and by the time it is ready to mail, it will be in order enough to understand.

First I feel some family background information may be of some interest. My parents are of Scottish background. Their parents (except my maternal grandfather, who was killed in World War I in France) were immigrants from Scotland. To my knowledge, Dad's ancestors were Scottish but Mom's maternal grandparents were Irish. That is quite a combination for the supernatural!

I didn't see as much of my father's family, so have no recollection of any "happenings" on that side. Any mention of grandmother or aunt will be to my mother's family of five children, the two youngest daughters being the only ones to emigrate to Canada with grandmother.

I was born in Toronto in 1928 and lived there until 1948, when I married George and moved to Stroud (just south of Barrie). By 1954 we had four children, Kathie, Leah, Jimmie, and Lennie (Lenore). In 1960 we built a home in Painswick, now a suburb of Barrie, where I still live. In 1963 and 1964 we had two more daughters, Gina and Lori. I now have eleven grandchildren. You are already acquainted with my son, Jim Young, as you used a story of his and his wife, Shirley, "A Ghost Named Matthew," in your Ontario book.

I believe my grandmother was very psychic. As a hobby she would read fortunes with cards and with tea leaves. She would also read fortunes in a way I have never seen before or since. She would break an egg white in a clear glass of water, leave it overnight, and "read" it the next day. Unique, huh? She would predict deaths, sickness, and accidents, and she had many visits from her dead husband and other relatives.

If "inherited" is the proper term, she passed this gift on to my mother and me. My mother has a unique type of prediction as well. If she dreams of seeing someone through a window, she will hear of that person's death within a short period of time. I have partially experienced this same thing. In the 1970s I dreamed of looking out of my window and seeing a large plane losing altitude. I didn't see it crash because at the time there was a row of trees on the horizon; there is a subdivision there now. Due to time change and the fact that Mom was away for a month visiting in Scotland, I lost track of the date of her flight home. During my first contact with her after her return, she told me that her plane ran into difficulty just off the coast of Ireland. The pilot had to dump their fuel and return to Ireland for repairs. On checking times and dates, we found this happened the night I had experienced my dream. I have often wondered if my mother would still be with us at age ninety if "my plane" had crashed.

That was only one of my experiences. I could write a complete book of them!

The paranormal does not normally frighten me. But on three occasions that I recall, and on one occasion when I was too young to recall, it did frighten me.

My mom and grandmother related this experience to me. It occurred when I was less than two years old. Mom, my baby sister, and I were visiting my grandmother. Mom sent me into the living room to get my coat as we were leaving. The lights were out but I had been in the room in the dark before, even earlier that evening. They heard me scream and run out of the room. Our dog, a huge Airedale, also ran out of the room, his hair raised, growling. They said I was trembling and badly frightened. It took them some time to get me to return to the room that night, but our dog would never set foot in it. What I saw I'll never know, as I stubbornly refused to talk about it at the time. Today I cannot recall the experience at all.

My second scare happened when I was about ten years old. We lived in North York on Cedric Avenue. I was in bed in my bedroom. One night I abruptly woke up to see a small lady (approximately two-and-one-half feet tall) coming towards me. She approached from the outside wall right up to the foot of my bed. She was in full view about halfway between the floor and the ceiling. She had long hair that was a light brown colour and coned in ringlets. She wore a pink dress with a tight bodice and a very full hooped skirt. Her dress and hairstyle were in the fashion of the 17th century.

I can still see her clearly, even after all these years. Her face was perfectly shaped, with fine features, and she was very beautiful. But she should not have been in my bedroom in the middle of the night! I screamed and Dad came in to comfort me, but she didn't go away. She would glide backwards and then come towards the bed again. I couldn't believe Dad didn't see her. Even with the light on she didn't disappear. I was pointing to her to indicate to Dad where she was, but to no avail. I also found it hard to believe that my sister, in bed beside me, could sleep through it all. Dad stayed with me until I fell asleep. When he left, he left the light on. I don't know who the small lady was or what she wanted. I never saw her again. On looking back, I believe she was a benign presence. If I saw her now, I think I would welcome her.

I had no more visions until I moved to Stroud in the mid-1950s. There we lived in an apartment above a store. I awakened one night to see five or six angels outside our bedroom window. They were perched in the branches of a tree, but there was no tree there! My first thought was, "Where do they come from?" and my second thought was, "What the heck do they want?" The angels looked exactly like those seen in Christmas illustrations. They had wings, heads with long wavy hair, and long flowing gowns.

I wakened my husband, George, so he could see the sight. Of course, my macho man laughed and turned on the light to prove to me there was nothing out there. The funny side of this story is that I had to go to the bathroom and was afraid to do so. George said he would not accompany me. Suffering some discomfort, I finally got up enough courage for what seemed to be a long trek. Actually, the bathroom was located immediately across the hall from our bedroom. As I flipped the switch, the bulb blew. George said I raced back to bed without my feet touching the floor! The angels? They were gone, no doubt laughing as hard as we were. The purpose of their visit? Once again, I don't know. Did I go to the bathroom that night? No, and I didn't wet the bed either!

The 1960s and 1970s, once we moved to our present house, turned out to be busy years for company, human and otherwise. Our home was a gathering place for our children and their friends. Many nights I would awaken and feel a presence in the room. I don't recall that I saw anyone or anything, but I just sensed someone there and I always had the feeling of serenity and peace. I never told the kids about these "visitors." There was no particular reason why I refrained from mentioning the "visitors," but it never happened. The unexplained was a topic that was talked about in our home.

As our first four children grew into mature teenagers, we often left them home to be with their friends, while George, Gina, Lori, and I went to our cottage in Muskoka. In 1966 or 1967, when we came home, Leah, who had slept in our bed, asked if I knew there was a ghost in our room. She had seen one. I told her yes and asked if she had been frightened. She assured me that she wasn't, and felt it was her paternal grandmother (who had died in 1962) who was watching over us. Leah and I were the only ones who felt or saw this "spirit." It was felt only in our bedroom.

Leah and I are also the only ones in our immediate family ever to experience a premonition when a bird hits our window. My premonition occurred at the cottage in 1968. A sparrow flew into my closed bedroom window and was killed. Two days later I heard of the death of an uncle. (Leah's incident will come later, as I am trying to keep these events in order by date.)

One night in 1969 I was lying awake and saw two clouds form on the wall. The top cloud was white and it had A29 imprinted in it. The bottom cloud was red and slightly smaller. There was a word in it, but I was only able to determine the initial B before it faded away. I felt that this was an omen or a message about something that would happen. I'm afraid I drove my family mad with my warnings about the dangers of April 29 and August 29! Nothing related to the initial B was allowed— boats, bikes, balconies, barbecues, etc.—and no associations with people whose names began with this letter. After a few years, when nothing untowards happened, my warnings were totally ignored. But I keep these warnings in mind for future use!

In 1979 two things happened that no one will ever convince me were not premonitions. Leah's husband, Wayne, was a constant visitor to our house for a few years previous to their marriage in 1971. So we were very close to him. One day I was working at the kitchen sink and saw a movement in the hall. When I looked up, I saw Wayne's image walk from our bedroom into the bathroom, not through the doorway but through the wall! Strange to say, due to the presence of a closet in the hall, the bathroom is not visible from the kitchen.

The 1980 Thanksgiving weekend brought the entire family together at the cottage for our traditional dinner. When Wayne, Leah, Greg, aged six, and Brad, aged three, came in, Wayne, who was not a physically demonstrative or emotionally expressive person, gave me an extra long, tight hug. I was a little surprised and thought it was because two days earlier we had been told Leah had a malignant growth in one breast. That weekend was the last time I saw Wayne. Three weeks later he was rushed to the Toronto General Hospital and the diagnosis was acute haemolytic anemia. Three weeks after being admitted, he died.

Leah literally moved into the hospital ward and was allowed the use of an adjacent room. I moved into their home to look after their boys. They lived in Ivy, an agricultural area near Barrie, quite isolated, with one house next door and one across the road. The night Wayne died I was sleeping on the couch in the family room off the kitchen. Beyond the couch there were patio doors, which I was facing, and their drapes were closed. I could see lights passing below the drapes. I got up and looked out the window. There were no cars passing, no one with a flashlight, and both neighbours' houses were in darkness. I went back to bed and soon after heard someone trying frantically to open the garage door, which led into the kitchen. I thought someone was trying to get in and was angry at finding it locked. Later, when I discussed this with my children, I told them I thought it was Wayne, and Lennie suggested that it was not anger he felt but frustration. This made sense to me, as I realized that six weeks earlier he had been a healthy, happy young man at home with his family. He had been given no time to say goodbye or to prepare for his death.

Leah had her operation shortly thereafter. I stayed on with her a few more weeks. One evening the boys and I were in the recreation room in the basement. I walked to the other end of the basement to get some firewood. When I reached the centre of the room to turn on the light, I broke into a cold sweat, and my hair stood on end. I backed out of the room and closed the door.

The other experience of 1979 was Leah's bird premonition, mentioned earlier. For that entire summer they were plagued by the presence of a crow or starling that persisted in pecking at their basement windows all day and well into the evening. Other than the annoyance, the bird didn't really upset or worry them, but they couldn't chase it away.

By 1984 Leah's cancer required her admission to Princess Margaret Hospital in Toronto. She was determined to spend Easter of that year at home with Greg and Brad, now nine and six years respectively. We got a weekend pass and an ambulance brought her home. However, she was only home a few hours before she had to be transferred to the Royal Victoria Hospital in Barrie because of a pathological broken hip. Leah died in Barrie on April 29. It was Gina who reminded me of my omen in 1969. Did Wayne's appearance in my hall and the blackbird in 1979 foreshadow the deaths of two health-conscious, physically fit young people? Both died in their thirty-fourth years. I know what I think.

In August of 1991, my husband George died. Approximately six months later, two things happened. Gina's youngest son, Jesse, had turned two in January and had recently learned to talk. One night he told his mother that he had seen Gramps and Gramps was on a star. The second incident concerned Lori's son, Zach, who had celebrated his third birthday in February of 1992. One night he insisted his mother close the drapes in his bedroom because he had seen Grampa's face looking through the window the night before. Lori explained that Gramps was only watching over us to make sure that we were safe and happy. Although Zach seemed to accept this explanation, he still wanted his drapes closed. The thing that has made me often wonder about these two happenings was the young age of our grandsons and the fact that the two incidents occurred on the same night in different parts of the town.

In the summer of 1992, Lennie and I were relaxing on the deck of our cottage. A favourite pastime of mine is enjoying the beauty of the clouds on a quiet day. As I lay back gazing at the sky, one cloud passed over the cottage and it had George's face clearly inset in it. The face was looking down. By the time Lennie looked up, the cloud was out of sight. We decided that her dad was saying goodbye; that he was moving on. I guess he must have done so, for as far as I am aware, no one has seen him since.

Many times have I experienced the beginnings of what I call "astral flights." They always take place when I am asleep. I fight to rise over telephone wires and over the tops of buildings. I feel I am holding myself back, afraid to completely leave my body. Two years ago I had a totally different astral flight. I was in a strange house and I could hear a family talking and laughing. I entered a room to encounter a family of ghosts: mother, father, young daughter, son. I visited with them until they left, drifting up through the ceiling. They were very happy and they always welcomed me. I had this dream three or four times before there was any change. The last time I visited the house, I entered the room they were always in but they weren't there. I could hear them beyond the ceiling. When I called out to them, they would stop talking and laughing, and when I waited for a reply, they would start conversing again. I finally called out to them that if they wouldn't join me I would join them. There was silence, as if they anticipated my arrival. I started rising from the floor, but when my hair lightly brushed the ceiling, I told them I was sorry but I was not ready to do this yet. Then I slowly descended to the floor.

That was the last experience I have had. Since then I have had no more ghosts, omens, premonitions, astral flights. I honestly miss them.

A couple of experiences follow. They are not mine, but they were related to me and are worth mentioning. A friend of Leah's, who was also a nurse in Toronto, called when Leah was in the Princess Margaret Hospital to say that I should go down because Leah was very upset. When I got there, Leah told me she had seen herself die the night before. We never discussed the incident at the time because there were friends visiting her and they got terribly upset and joked about it. The subject never came up between us again, but I wish now that I had insisted that she tell me about it.

Mom's sister was also "one of us." One day she, a friend of mine, and I visited Lennie. When we left, my aunt told me that she was worried about my friend, as she had seen a black cloud hovering over her. Less than a month later, on Easter weekend, my friend's nineteen-year-old son was drowned. Easter seems to be a bad date for our family.

I realize this is a very lengthy account. If you are inclined to use it in the future, you have my permission to omit and edit to suit your needs. I hope that you find at least some of it interesting. I am sure everyone feels his or her own tales are unique. I did, until I read your book.

Most sincerely,
Margaret J. Young

PART VIII
THE GHOSTS AMONG US

Like many people, I enjoy listening to ghost stories. In fact, when I meet someone for the first time, I will often ask the person, "Have you ever seen a ghost?"

He or she will look surprised. "A ghost? You mean a spirit?"

"Yes."

Ordinarily, there is a short pause when the answer is going to be no and a long one when the answer is going to be yes.

Four out of five times, the answer is, "No. I have never seen a ghost or spirit. Why do you ask?"

I explain that I collect stories of hauntings, so I encourage people to recall their experiences. I then publish them in my books. People find this curious, but I have a follow-up question for those who boast of not seeing spirits.

"Okay, you haven't seen a ghost or spirit. But do you know somebody who has? Say a family member or a good friend?"

Here, nine times out of ten, there is a pause, then, "Yes, I do, as a matter of fact."

Then I learn about an odd event or experience that was reported by a mother or father, a sister or brother, a daughter or son, an aunt or uncle, a niece or nephew, or a friend or acquaintance.

My feeling is that everyone has had some such experience, or has a relative or friend who has. Ask yourself, "Have I ever had a weird experience that might involve a ghost or spirit? Do I know of anyone I trust who has?"

Such experiences are private matters and usually told to family members and friends. No one wants to admit to "seeing ghosts" or "having visions." It is not the "done thing" in our Western society, though such things are quite common in traditional Eastern societies.

But many people have a healthy curiosity about hauntings and such matters, and they enjoy pondering them and their implications when they happen to themselves or other people. I collect as many of them as I can, and with the permission of the informants, I include them in my book-length collections of supernatural and paranormal experiences.

The accounts that appear in the present section cover episodes that occurred between 1952 and 2003. In some instances, I have spoken with the informants in person or on the telephone, and in almost all cases, I have continued to communicate with them by mail or email. I have no reason to doubt the sincerity of the informants. They admit they are as puzzled by the happenings as I am.

What does surprise me is how events and experiences like the ones reported here occur and pass so quickly... and yet become engraved in memory, and become the cornerstones of stories that will be repeated for years and decades to come. It is almost as if the episode has a meaning or significance that may some day be revealed.

So there are ghosts—or at least ghost stories—all around us....

Strange Happenings

KELLY KIRKLAND

I received an email on February 16, 1996, from a correspondent who signed her name "Kelly." I was fascinated with what I read, so I corresponded with her. It emerged that the correspondent's full name is Kelly Kirkland and that she is a resident of Chatham, Ontario. She eventually sent me the three ghost stories I am publishing here. The second one arrived on February 17, and the third on March 13, with some follow-up remarks on June 10. The correspondent finds odd occurrences wherever she goes. It seems people may be haunted along with places.

◆ ◆ ◆

1.

February 16, 1996

This is a true story that happened to me. I'm not sure what it was, but it was really weird! One day just before New Year's, 1996, I was going to see my dad by train to Toronto. My train was scheduled to leave by 3:27 p.m., and my boyfriend, Jon, was supposed to drive me to the station. He had gone to the store to pick something up and he was not home yet when I was supposed to be on my way to the station. I was looking out the front door to watch for him, and I was very upset that I was going to miss my train (I did!), and I finally saw him coming up the street. I turned around to get my suitcase and when I turned back around I expected him to be in the driveway but he wasn't.

By then I was furious and I started to flip out and wonder where the hell he went to. Did he drive by the house and keep going? Did he forget something at the store he went to? Anyway, he finally showed up about fifteen minutes after I saw him and I confronted him as he walked in the door. I asked him why he hadn't pulled in the driveway and he told me that he hadn't even been on the street! I said that I had seen him fifteen minutes ago and he still insisted that he hadn't been anywhere near the house!

I still can't figure out what happened that day. I swear up and down that I saw his car coming up the street with him driving it! His car is hard to mistake because it has white spots on the roof where the paint peeled off. It was a very strange experience and I won't forget it any time soon.

2.

February 17, 1996

My grandmother's house has been haunted for years. I definitely won't stay overnight there!

When I was a kid, I used to sleep over at her house. The address is King Street, in Chatham. I won't give the exact address for obvious reasons. It is a one-and-a-half-storey house with white siding. The house is approximately one hundred years old, and I've heard various stories over the years about people who have died there.

There are three rooms on the main floor. As you walk in the front door, you are in the front hall. To the left there is the dining room; to the right are the stairs to go up. If you walk straight from the front door, you will end up in the living room. If you keep going straight, you will find yourself in the kitchen. In the back of the small kitchen, there are the back steps to go outside. Just before you get to the outside door, there are a few more steps to go to the basement. In the basement there is my uncle's barbershop. Behind the shop is the back room of the basement, where the washer and dryer are.

Now to the second floor. At the top of the stairs, there is a small hallway with the main bedroom on the left, a small bedroom on the right, and farther down another small bedroom on the right with a bathroom at the end. In the first small bedroom on the right, there is a dark stain under the carpet. No matter how hard you scrub it, it won't come out. I was told that it only gets brighter.

I was also told that a child suffocated to death in the main bedroom upstairs. The spirit of that child is supposedly what is haunting the house. The entity likes to take things, break things, and play with the lights.

One day I was teasing my little brother, who was three years old at the time. I took his yo-yo and was running around the house with it and he was chasing me. I had just bought a pair of sunglasses and had them with me while I was running around. I had them hooked in the top of my shorts. I noticed later that I no longer had the glasses. I looked in every last nook and cranny of that house. I looked everywhere I had been and even in places I hadn't been! I couldn't find them anywhere.

That was about nine years ago and I still haven't found those sunglasses. Our joke is that the ghost is walking around wearing them.

My grandma told me about a ghost that they used to see on the second step from the top of the stairs. The ghost was that of a woman who was sitting there, rocking back and forth. My mom used to jump over that step every time.

Another story is one that only happened a couple of years ago. My older brother was living at my grandma's for a summer and he thought he saw a shadow at the top of the stairs. When he told my grandma about it, she believed him, but when my step-grandfather came home and was told about the incident, he said, "Ah, I don't believe in ghosts!" And at that moment the lights went out!

I hope you like these. I still have more!

3.

March 13, 1996

Hello again, I just thought I'd drop you a line to tell you about my "new" apartment. A few strange things have been happening since I moved in on July 1st.

It was about the third night in the new place and I went to bed with all the lights OFF... when I woke up the next morning the ceiling light was ON. I know I didn't turn it on in the night and I know that the cats couldn't have turned it on by accident because the switch is up over the stove and they never go up there.

The second thing that happened could probably be explained, but it was still strange to me. I fell asleep with the TV on one night and when I woke up in the morning it was off. I might have turned it off in the night and just don't remember. The radio turned on during another night, but that could have been the cat.

The day before yesterday, my older cat, Sneaker, was staring at the window and was spooked by something. My bed is situated under the window, and to see what she was afraid of, I picked her up and took her over to the bed and she struggled to get out of my arms and ran off in the opposite direction. She was like that for about an hour... I couldn't get her to stay on the bed for anything. She always ran back to the same spot and stared. Sneaker always comes to you when you call her, but this time I couldn't get her to come to me. It was pretty strange.

The house that my apartment is in is a Chatham heritage house. It is a Victorian house that was recently renovated and restored. The people who originally lived in the house were the Grays of Chatham. The maker of the Gray-Dort car, William Gray.

I haven't talked to the owners about any strange happenings yet. I'm waiting for other things to happen. I don't want to look foolish... I could just be letting my imagination run away with me.

Email me back and let me know what you think.

Thank you,
Kelly Kirkland

I Could See a Human Figure

VIVIAN HARTLEY

In late March of 1997, Tony Hawke, the editor at Hounslow Press, the company that published my book Ghost Stories of Ontario, *forwarded some letters that had been addressed to me care of the publisher. I have reproduced one of these letters below. It was handwritten on lined paper, and it makes quite engrossing reading! As they say, it speaks for itself.*

◆ ◆ ◆

Dear Mr. Colombo:

First off, let me tell you how much I enjoyed your book *Ghost Stories of Ontario*. Some of the stories really gave me the creeps! Now let me tell you about something creepy that happened to me.

I live in Toronto, and in July of 1996, I was on vacation in New Brunswick. My husband and I rented a small cottage in a tiny village called Barnesville. It's a tiny place, on the grounds of a huge mansion, but set back in trees so there is no view of the main house or the road. The cottage is constructed of stone and is over a hundred years old. We stayed there for a month.

The first incident occurred when we had been there for three days, and I almost discounted it as imagination, though it scared me.

I was taking a shower after a long day at the beach. The bathroom was filled with steam. After I pulled back the shower curtain and was drying myself, I saw something out of the corner of my eye. The steam was swirling around, too fast, and was forming a shape. I stood there in shock and I could see a human figure, even shorter than me and I'm only 5'1". It dissipated and the water in the shower that I had just turned off came back on.

Over the next few days nothing happened, but I felt constantly watched. Then I was lying on the couch one rainy afternoon. I was definitely not falling asleep. I was propped up reading, and suddenly all my energy drained away. I felt drowsy and hypnotized, and a paralysis came over me. Strangely, I was not afraid. I couldn't move a muscle. Then a boy walked out of the bedroom and sat down on the edge of the couch and stared intently at me. He was wearing suspenders; about his dress, that's all I can recall. He had dark hair and a pale complexion, and light grey eyes. He was perhaps ten or eleven years of age. He placed his hand on mine and it felt cool and dry. While I could not see through him exactly, he looked insubstantial. I felt like I was having an asthma attack and began to gasp for air, and panic, struggling to move. He faded slowly and looked pained that I was so afraid. When he was gone I found I could move again and promptly sat up and screamed my lungs out. My husband came running from the kitchen. For some reason I told him I had had a bad dream.

I decided that since we still had three weeks in the house, I was not going to be in it alone. I did not feel threatened but I did feel nervous and could feel a constant presence. I had a very vivid dream that I spoke to the boy and he was crying and trying to clutch at me. He was pathetic, but I woke up sobbing and terrified. I felt his name was Warden.

I went shopping for the day and when I returned to the cottage my husband was driving up the driveway towards the cottage and he saw a white face at the front window. The face had a shock of dark hair. It was only then I told him about what I had seen in the previous days.

On a Saturday night we invited another vacationing couple and their two daughters, aged nine and five. The five-year-old stayed in the house playing while we barbecued in the backyard. After she was out of sight for a while, her mother called out, "What are you doing in there?" The girl replied, "Playing with Warden." We had said nothing regarding the boy to these people!

For the remainder of our stay the only thing that happened was the taps would turn on. I felt depressed sometimes, and my husband felt sad for no reason as well. I feel that the boy is trapped there and was trying to communicate. We spoke to a Protestant minister in the village, and I think he thought we were nuts, but he agreed to go to the cottage and pray for the spirit to move on. I hope it worked.

Vivian Hartley

My Experiences with the Supernatural

ROSALIE SYBULKA

I received the following letter from Rosalie Sybulka, a correspondent otherwise unknown to me, who lives in Red Deer, Alberta. The letter was dated April 4, 2004. It was typewritten and was the first of many such letters that I received following the publication by Hounslow Press of a book called The Midnight Hour, *a collection of old newspaper accounts and first-hand stories of eerie events and experiences.*

In her letter, Mrs. Sybulka recalls growing up in a house that seemed to her and to others the focus of a series of peculiar happenings. There was never much agreement among witnesses about what was happening at the time, or in later years about what actually did happen back then, yet the witnesses generally agree that odd things occurred! The "other experiences" reported here are fascinating in that they involve the death of Princess Diana. They may be coincidences; then again, they may not.

Family pets have a special claim on peoples' affections. The beagle pup owned by Mrs. Sybulka, it seems, led a charmed life ... and maybe an afterlife as well.

The reader will wonder about the "other touches of the divine" felt by Mrs. Sybulka, all the while thanking her for sharing her experiences and wishing her well.

◆ ◆ ◆

April 4, 2004

Dear Mr. Colombo:

I just finished reading *The Midnight Hour*, which I purchased at Chapters. I am pleased that you have provided a forum for people who have these experiences. I also enjoyed *Mysterious Canada* and hope to acquire and read the remainder of your books on the paranormal.

I decided to write to you as I have no computer and need to share my experiences with the supernatural. I have had extraordinary experiences since I was a child. I grew up on a farm in the Red Deer area and lived in a haunted house. I also have had prophetic dreams and death premonitions throughout life.

Haunted House Experiences

My haunted house experiences began when I was seven years old. My parents were farmers and struggled financially. In 1952, my brother and sister were born—they are twins. Soon after, we needed more room in the old house, so my parents moved a two-room house from the city and attached it to the old house we were living in. That is when things started to become strange. I remember the moving men coming in for supper as the newer house sat on blocks beside the old one. All the crew were seated at the supper table when one fellow decided he had to check something outside; he came back in and asked everyone, "Who is that man standing on the deck of the truck?" No one knew, as everyone was inside. My parents were in wonderment as well, since whoever would visit would come in for coffee or a meal.

My sister and brother slept in the newer addition. My brother swears he was bothered by a beastly encounter on several occasions. He and my sister were apparently in bed one night when they heard a swoosh-ing sound. Crawling along the floor beside their bed was a cow-faced entity that rose up to try and tear the covers off them. They cried out and I think at that point our parents came into the bedroom and the thing disappeared. I remember my sister telling me the same story, but if I ask her to recall this today, she says she cannot remember. (She cannot remember a lot of childhood and past events for some reason.)

I very seldom slept in the new addition, but I had recurrent night-mares that some "thing" was compelling me to go in there. I would wake up in a fearful sweat and to this day am uncomfortable in the dark.

One night, in the midst of winter, I decided around suppertime to have a bath. I pulled the small square tub up to the kitchen stove for warmth and proceeded. I was in the middle of it all when I heard foot-steps coming from the haunted bedrooms into the living room, heading for our kitchen. Naked and wet, in the midst of winter, I ran outside to where my mother was, in the cream separator building.

My parents also heard footsteps in our living room one night when they were home by themselves. I remember my father as being a real sceptic about things of this nature, but he was most perplexed at this incident.

When I was a child my father was not a forgetful person, but on numerous occasions we would return from town and find the corral gate wide open and the cattle out. Strangely, the gate was never left open when we were home. As farm children, we knew never to leave a gate open; we climbed over the fence since that was easier than open-ing a heavy gate.

One night when I was about eleven years old, our hired man offered to drive my grandmother home. She had been staying with us and lived about seven miles north. He asked me to come along and he drove my dad's truck. We had a driveway to our house with two entrances. Coming home, we approached the south driveway and our headlights caught the figure of a man with a long black coat and wearing a hat. He emerged from our bushes and was crossing the road to the neighbour's bush. It was about ten o'clock at night and pitch-dark. Who could see to walk about in the bush at that time of night? He was nobody we knew from the neighbourhood. I often wonder if he was a phantom or a real person. As he crossed the road he never looked our way, only straight ahead. He resembled someone from the '30s, but some people still dressed in that style in the '50s.

The haunted part of the house still stands to this day. In 1963, we built a new house. The original old house was demolished and the haunted portion served as a chicken house for many years. My brother still lives on the farmstead and has not had any more strange experiences that I am aware of. Upon recalling the history of our moved-in house, I remember my parents saying a preacher had owned it. It was rumoured he had committed suicide.

Other Experiences

In 1996, my husband and I purchased an acreage to the west of Red Deer where we now live. This land was partly treed and had served as a cattle pasture. There were thistles and nettles growing on some parts and dead trees scattered about. We had a major cleanup and maintenance job as we now had two properties to maintain—our acreage and our house in town. We owned an old motor home that we drove to the acreage in summer. We slept in it and prepared meals as we worked all weekend clearing dead trees and weeds. We also cut the grass. On August 31, 1997, about one o'clock in the afternoon, we had finished lunch and my husband decided to continue cutting down some weeds some distance from the motor home. I was very tired and decided to go into the motor home and lie down. It was a sunny day, and after I closed the door, in front of my face a stream of smoke curled into the air, as from a cigarette or an extinguished candle. This only lasted a couple of seconds and then dissipated. Neither my husband nor I smoke, nor did we have a candle or fire going anywhere. There was no smell whatsoever to this smoke, which was even more baffling.

About five o'clock that afternoon, my daughter arrived and brought her battery radio. We turned it on to get some music and were shocked to hear that Princess Diana had been killed in a car crash. We listened for more details and discussed the tragedy at length. I never mentioned my previous weird experience at the time because I was so shocked and saddened at the news about Diana. After the smoke incident, I tried to find a rational explanation for this occurrence. Some time later I was to get another shock when Elton John released his song to Diana called "Candle in the Wind." It was then when I made a connection between the two incidents.

In 1999, we sold our property in town and moved into our present new house on the acreage property. About a year or two later, one day, towards five o'clock in the afternoon, my husband was preparing supper. I went into the basement for pickles for supper and was overwhelmed by the waxy smell of an extinguished candle. My immediate thought was that my husband had burned something on the stove. I ran back upstairs and checked everything. Nothing was burned, only a pleasant aroma of supper, but an overwhelming wax candle smell in the basement. I remember an ominous feeling at the time and said to my husband I suspected we might hear of someone's death in the near future. Sure enough, a week later my sister's husband's brother's son was tragically killed in a car crash. Both Diana's death and this boy's demise were both shocking and unexpected. The tragic death of Dodi Fayez and the chauffeur are being invested along with Diana's as being suspicious, with many unanswered questions.

There is something about the date of August 31. Last year on August 31, my husband and I were awakened by both our smoke detectors going off in the middle of the night. We have one detector upstairs near our bedroom and another in the basement. They are not battery-operated but wired in electrically. This is a very scary occurrence when both go off simultaneously. We did a thorough inspection and checked for a power outage. Our computerized clocks were all fine. This all still remains a mystery.

A Touch of the Divine

On Sunday, November 4, 1990, I purchased a darling beagle pup from a lady in a nearby town. The pup was predominately white with some light tan spots. We were living in the city at the time but had a big yard. It was a Sunday afternoon, about 4:00 p.m., when she became part of our family. She lived with us for eleven happy years from the day and hour that we got here to the day she died at approximately 4:00 p.m., Sunday, November 4, 2001. We had become so endeared to her that the grief was almost too much to bear.

Three days later, my husband assumed his regular bedtime routine and climbed into bed and shut out the light. Having gone to bed earlier, I was already sleeping with a pillow over my ear to obliterate his snoring and any other noise. No sooner had he shut out the light than he heard plain as day our old dog shaking herself three times as she always did when needing to go out. I guess she had come back to say a final goodbye and that she was okay and to comfort us. When my husband told me about this experience the next day, I knew he was truthful. He has always been a bit sceptical of paranormal events, but there was no way he could discount this experience. I could only conclude that what he heard was meant to convince him that there is a life in spirit. I continue to be grateful to God for this special little dog who in her own way brought untold joy and a renewed faith in our lives.

(I am at present suffering from a terminal illness. I need to share these stories with others who might understand and hopefully find some spiritual benefit in them.)

I have had many other touches of the divine. If you decide to publish this, I am not sure how my sister and brother would feel about it. I personally stand behind what I have written and am not ashamed to divulge my name, address, and phone number.

You can contact me by letter if you wish. I hope you enjoy this mininovelette.

Yours truly,
Rosalie Sybulka

My Story

JANET E.M. BROWN

I received this email from Janet Brown, a correspondent who was new to me. It was followed by four emails that told her story in some detail. She titled it "My Story," and that is what it is.

With minimal editing, here is Ms. Brown's account, as it occurred to her and as she recalled it many years later. The reader must wonder whether Vern is still saying, "Yes!"

◆ ◆ ◆

April 29, 2004

Hello Mr. Colombo,

My name is Janet Brown. I have a ghost story to tell. Please excuse my lack of professionalism. I am a person with little education and I cringe to think of the errors I've committed in writing "my story."

I am sending you this story in four parts. I've needed to tell this tale for many years. I hope you enjoy it.

My Story

Part 1

In the year 1968, I was fourteen years old. We (my mom and dad and three of my five siblings) were living in a rented house in Windsor, Ontario. The address was 962 Esdras Place, in the east end of the city. The house was haunted.

I do not know to this day who (or what) haunted this place I called home (for approximately two years). At the time I was fairly certain it was my recently deceased uncle, as he'd told me at one time that when he died he would return. I had only a faint recollection of this as I suppose at the time it didn't really have the wanted effect of scaring me. I was in fact a pretty down-to-earth kind of girl, not by nature fanciful.

So as not to get into a great deal of detail, as I'm not much of a writer and tend to ramble on, I will try to tell my story as briefly as possible. I have needed to tell it to someone who could hear it objectively for many years, so here goes.

My uncle (my mom's younger brother) also actually lived with us there and one evening when my parents were going out for the evening, leaving me to babysit my younger brother, Kevin, Kevin came excitedly into the kitchen where my parents and I were, saying that our uncle Vern needed a bucket because he was ill. To make a long event short, he died a few weeks later. He died of a rare blood disease he'd contracted in Korea. He was in his thirty-eighth year.

Very shortly after that, my mother's sister's husband died of a heart attack, leaving her with five small boys. He was also thirty-eight and had served in the Korean War at the same time as my uncle Vern.

My mother went to Edmundston, New Brunswick, to help her sister. Around this time my brother Gary joined the Air Force and went to boot camp.

This left in our house me, seven-year-old Kevin, and my twenty-one-year-old brother Doug, and of course my dad. My dad worked selling Kirby vacuum cleaners, and Doug worked the afternoon shift at one of the car plants. (I don't remember which one.)

Another character in my story is my best friend, Mary. Mary had moved to Canada from Poland with her mom and brother. She thought me sophisticated and I thought her rather silly at times. Despite that, I did love her as a good friend. As they say, opposites attract.

Now I will do my best to tell of our ordeal that lasted about two weeks. By now, the memories are thirty-six years old, so the order of events may not be right. But I will try to tell them all.

The house was a storey and a half. The main floor had a living room, dining room, kitchen, my bedroom, and my parent's bedroom, and also a bathroom. The upstairs had a bedroom (which was half the area) where my brothers slept, and the other half was an unfinished room. There was also a basement where the washer-dryer was, a wood storage room (for the fireplace), a storage room, and a sort of workshop area. This is also where my uncle's bed was.

One sunny bright afternoon, about 1:30 p.m., Mary and I were hanging out in my brother's upstairs room. We heard the front door open and slam shut. I yelled down, "Is someone there?"

The answer was a very clear *"Yes."*

At that point I ran to the window to see whose car was there, thinking it strange that either my dad or brother would be home at that hour. Doug's work shift was not over till 3:00 p.m., and Dad was on an appointment out in LaSalle and I didn't expect him home till much later.

I again yelled down, "Is someone there?" And got the same response once more, a very clear *"Yes!"*

I can still recall Mary and me looking at each other, rather puzzled. We did the next logical thing and went downstairs to investigate.

Part 2

When Mary and I got downstairs, to the main floor, we didn't see anyone. Again I called, "Is anyone here?" and although we couldn't see a living soul, we received the very same, clear answer *"Yes!"* It sounded as though the voice was coming from the same space in which we were standing. (This is the only way I can describe it.) We were very confused and began to search the main floor, believing someone must be hiding. The floor was laid out so that you could go from the front hall either into the living room or into the kitchen, then through the dining room and back out the opposite way (in other words, in a circle). This did not solve the mystery as we found no one at all.

For the remainder of this haunting, whenever I would ask, "Is anyone there?" I received the same chilling *"Yes!"* I was in quite a predicament, to say the least. I was scared out of my wits but equally afraid of my father's reaction. I was a proud person and didn't want to set myself up for the ridicule I was sure would come. I did confide in my brother Doug. He was great, he simply went about searching the house as best he could (the wood storage room we were afraid to enter) and so on, but to no avail. I should mention that one of my main fears was scaring my brother Kevin and getting in deep s—t for that (teenagers, eh!). Anyway, the best way I can describe the rest of this terrifying time is to simply relate one thing after another, as my storytelling is amateurish.

One thing that constantly happened through that time was the sound that came from the unfinished part of the upstairs, adjacent to the boys' bedroom. That was the sound of wood being thrown around. Don, Mary's on again, off again boyfriend, was the only person besides us to hear that, and I believe it truly scared him. We had asked him to come over and do a search for us after he'd suggested that there might be some kind of sound system hooked up in the large fireplace. Needless to say, he didn't hang around long after that.

Another incident regarding the wood scared us terribly. Doing some housework, I was emptying the kitchen garbage. Mary and I were standing just inside the kitchen door (the hallway side). She was holding the container as I was lifting the bag from it. Just then, the two of us saw a piece of unfinished trim (wood) appear in front of us, where it hovered for several seconds and then dropped to the floor. This wood was the same type that was strewn about the unfinished room.

Another truly terrifying incident happened one day as Mary was getting ready to go out somewhere. (I forgot to mention that she was staying with me, for company, while Mom was in Edmundston.) Anyway, she had to go to the basement to get her cords from the clothes dryer. That day had been an uneventful one, and although my nerves were raw, I thought I'd better do some vacuuming, as I was letting the housework go. Mary went down to the basement as I began to vacuum. Several seconds went by and I was totally on edge waiting for her to come back upstairs. I turned the vacuum off and yelled to her, "Is everything OK?"

She replied, "Yeah, I'm just shaking out my pants."

With that I breathed a sigh of relief and started the vacuum again. What happened next, I'll never forget.

Mary came running from the basement stairs (off the kitchen) with the most frightening expression I have ever seen! I went to her and led her to the living room couch. She was hysterical and babbling uncontrollably. I was trying to calm her, and at the same time I was looking towards the front door, wanting so badly just to run. She later told me that if not for my calm, she didn't think she would ever have come out of it.

What happened to her was, she explained, that the door to the wood room had opened, and a voice had said three words. To this day I can't remember what the words were, perhaps because of the severe trauma I experienced at the time.

However, the next incident I'll relay was not forgotten.

Part 3

I think that before I go on any further, I should point out that all these incidents happened in the middle of the day. This to me is a rather odd thing in itself. In the evening, when my dad and perhaps my brother were home, only one scary thing happened.

One evening my dad was in the dining room doing some paperwork. Mary and I were in the living room with a couple of male friends, socializing. At some point, someone had the idea to go to the corner store. Mary, of course, had to get her pants from the dryer. I'll point out that, at that time, dressing properly (even to go to the corner store) was important, and newly laundered cords fit tightly, as they were supposed to. (Again, teenagers, eh!)

Now, our friends knew of our predicament at that time. We were experiencing a haunting, but it was a rather hush-hush subject, since Dad was in the adjacent room and little brother Kevin was at home that evening. So when Mary brought the point up that she had to go to the basement to get her cords, she looked pleadingly to me to go with her. I wasn't too afraid, since, as I'd mentioned, nothing had happened so far in the evening. (I'd stopped asking, "Is someone there?" days earlier, as my nerves couldn't take any more of that disembodied voice.)

When we got to the halfway-down landing (where the back door was and you turned left to go down the rest of the steps, about six steps), I said to Mary, "You go first," as she was much taller than I and could easily reach the light cord that hung from the ceiling at the bottom of the stairs. A very clear and distinct voice said, "No, don't."

Well, as you can imagine, we flew up those stairs double time. When we got to the living room, one of our friends exclaimed that he had spoken through the furnace vent to scare us. When we got outside, he admitted that what he'd said wasn't true. We told him we knew that, as we'd tested that very theory. As I said, I was quite a down-to-earth person and at one time tested poor Mary, hoping she was to blame but knowing in my heart she wasn't. However, while alone in the house one day, she and I went to the basement to the workroom area (I can't recall why that particular area), and I spoke the dreaded, "Is anyone there?" as we looked at each other face to face. The answer, as always, was a clear *"Yes!"* I am amazed, in retrospect, why we, or at least one of us, didn't go completely off the deep end while all these terrifying things were happening. I suppose it's the resilience of youth. That's all that I can conclude.

The next odd happening had to do with a large-sized pill bottle. My brother Kevin had some turtles which were kept in the dining room on the buffet (oddly enough). He kept their food in a pill bottle. One day, while vacuuming the dining room, I'd noticed the empty pill bottle under the buffet but had neglected to pick it up, intending to at the end of the job. I forgot. I think it was either that same afternoon or the next that Mary and I were sitting watching TV in the living room when we heard a sound from the basement. It sounded like a cork popping. I ran down to find, at the bottom of the steps on the floor, the empty pill bottle. When I picked it up, I noticed a strange kind of print inside in the powder left by the turtle food.

While excitedly showing it to Mary, who came running several seconds behind me, I exclaimed, "Look!" as I showed it to her and in the same instant wiped the print off with my finger. I don't know why I did that, but I guess it was just an impulse reaction to my terror of seeing it.

In conclusion, I remember Mary and I, one stormy and dark evening, being at our wits' end, sitting out on the front step waiting for someone to come home. We saw a car pull in the driveway and at first thought it was the police. We soon realized it was a taxi cab, and my brother Gary got out. He had come home on leave from the Air Force. We were thrilled to see him, and I don't recall any incidents after that time.

We lived in that house for approximately another year and a half before moving back to PEI, from where we had originally moved in 1966.

Conclusion

As a curious footnote to this story, I will relay a couple of odd things relating to these events.

Firstly, years later, my mom's sister Eileen (from Edmundston) moved to Windsor. While looking for a house, she came upon the house at 962 Esdras Place. She later told my mom that she'd felt a presence there. I don't know whether this was in response to my mother's telling her my story or not. My mom was so strait-laced and down-to-earth, to this day I don't know if she ever believed me or told anyone of it. However, I do know that she did fully understand that I believed it. Which makes me feel somehow better.

The second odd thing happened in the early 1990s, while visiting home (PEI) from Peterborough, where I now live with my husband, Ron. My dad simply, out of the blue, asked me to tell the story. Now, up to this time I believed he took it all for hogwash, childish nonsense from the past, as we'd never seriously discussed it.

He hung his head and listened intently without interruption until I'd finished the tale. Many family members were there too and listened respectfully. Then, to my total shock, he told me this frightening fact.

It seems that while socializing at the neighbourhood Legion, those many years ago, he had mentioned to a fellow there that he had moved into the house on Esdras Place. The man, in return, had asked if there was anything strange happening there.

When my father replied, "Why?" the man answered that the house was known to be haunted!

I was dumbfounded! After all these years, to hear what he was telling me was, to say the least, shocking.

To backtrack a bit, I recall Mary saying several different times through the ordeal, "It's Vern!" and I would always reply, "Why would Vern want to scare us?"

Secretly, I believed it was Vern. I thought that it must have been, rationalizing that such a strong entity could have driven us off the deep end if it had chosen to show itself. It hadn't; therefore, I'd concluded, it had to be Vern, as he would never commit such a horror.

Now, at the age of fifty, I've finally put down on paper the events of those terrifying few weeks that have "haunted" me for these long years.

Since that time, I have had the odd little supernatural occurrence, as I believe most people do. One noteworthy one happened while living in a house we built in PEI in 1974.

The incident occurred about two years later. I was wide awake in bed with my husband one evening. It wasn't too late, but Ron was already asleep, as he is a hard worker so therefore a sound sleeper. While lying there, I heard three very loud knocks on the dresser, just inside the bedroom door and adjacent to the bed. It startled me but it never happened again.

In conclusion, I hope that whoever reads this account will be respectful in their judgement of my story. It is totally true and has not been embellished. If anything, I may have left some tidbits out, as it happened so long ago.

Sincerely
Janet E.M. Brown

Strange Things

SYLVIE LORANGER-JOURNEAU

I was quite pleased to receive this email on July 18, 2004.

It begins with an account of a UFO sighting that the correspondent, Sylvie Loranger-Journeau, a registered nurse, experienced in her youth. It continues with the details that she can recall of a most intriguing experience of "missing time" that occurred not to her but to her mother. It concludes with the correspondent stating that she would be willing to send me information about other "strange events" that have occurred to her.

Her letters are highly readable and full of interesting insights and asides, so I hastened to email her back and assure her of my continued interest. I also asked her to question her mother more closely about her otherworldly experience. She agreed, and her reply is printed here too. It arrived on July 19, 2004. Email is fast!

Even faster came the third email, later that day, with a series of coincidences or premonitions, whatever they are!

The fourth followed on July 20. Along with it came, by fax, photocopies of the relevant article on the la grande noirceur, *the great darkness, not that of Quebec Premier Maurice Duplessis, but what is known in English as a Dark Day.*

The fifth and last letter in the present series arrived on August 9, 2004. It concludes in a fitting manner, with a reference to the Quebec legend of la chasse-galerie—*the "flying canoe" that has the power to transport voyageurs back to their loved ones for half the night: perhaps a pre–technology age version of a flying saucer or UFO?*

Ms. Loranger-Journeau and members of her family seem to be the loci of "strange things."

What more can be said?

◆ ◆ ◆

1.

July 18, 2004

Hello,

I have just finished reading your book *True Canadian UFO Stories*, and although I must say that I find a few of the stories hard to believe, I do have some stories of my own.

I've been convinced of the existence of UFOs for most of my life, as it started with strange occurrences in my youth. I'm a French-Canadian woman of a family of nine, brought up on 4th Avenue in LaSalle on the Island of Montreal.

Interestingly, my first sighting was of a disc of light, exactly like the one on the cover of your book, in a summer of either 1968, 1969 or 1970 at the latest. It was a hot summer evening. I was eight or nine at the time, but was allowed to stay up late because we couldn't sleep in that humid heat. My brother, who is seven years older than I am, came back from the store with Coca-Colas, all excited about a UFO in the sky.

Everyone in the house at the time (except my dad, who refused to acknowledge such a possibility) followed him to Champlain Boulevard between 3rd and 2nd Avenues to watch this disc of light over the Aqueduct. Several people were already there watching. It would remain stationary at times and then would start circling. We watched it for a good thirty minutes, at least, probably longer, until our mother got bored watching it and ordered us back to the house.

There are stories my mom has told us, and I doubt that she was telling lies. One story in particular is extremely strange, and I will have to have her retell the story again to supply you with more details. As my memory goes, here it is.

My mother was born in 1921. During the Depression, her mother washed floors for people to make ends meet. They lived on Dennonville Street and one of her "customers" was a Lis Ryan in Verdun. Her mom, being sick one morning and having no phone of her own or any public phones in the neighbourhood, sent my mom to Lis Ryan's in Verdun to tell her she couldn't come. (I guess she was afraid of losing her job.) After delivering the message, as she was waiting for the train at the intersection of Church and Wellington, on the southeast corner, across from the church, she disappeared!

From one moment to the next, she wasn't there any more. Instead, she was standing in the middle of very tall grass. She says there was no sound whatsoever. No bird sounds, no insect sounds, nothing. Scared to death, she started walking, not comprehending what was going on. It was very hot. She ran and walked for a long time, hoping to get out of this high grass (above her head), to hear something or see someone. Finally, she first heard the noise of children playing in the distance. She homed in on that noise, and suddenly found herself on a street again. The children seemed surprised, she said, and looked at her in a strange way.

She got home. However, she got home about eight hours after disappearing from Church and Wellington and after crossing a continuous field of tall grass only, when in reality she would have had to cross the Aqueduct, thus a bridge. Not to mention streets with cars. I often wondered about this experience of hers because I worked as an ambulance technician and as a nurse. I worked on an ambulance in Montreal for twenty years, and one of our standby points used to be Wellington at Willibord, but we often parked at Church and Wellington, and still do. I continue to wonder about it.

She used to recall that her mother talked about *la grande noirceur* [the great darkness] in Montreal, but she never believed her. I thought it was folklore, but I bought a book once (I still have it, but I have to look for it) about the history of Montreal, and there was this event listed! It probably has a meteorological explanation though.

I have had another sighting in Montreal in 1990, and have many more oddities to relate to you, but I guess I'll have to write you a letter. I'm not inclined to tell people about these things; however, I see no reason to withhold my name if you decide to use these stories. I'm a registered nurse (RN) and a paramedic. I studied at McGill in anthropology. I know I'm not crazy and don't really care if people end up thinking that I am. Maybe all of it has an earthly explanation. I'm very open-minded.

Please let me know if you want me to write you about the other strange events I've lived through

Sylvie Loranger-Journeau

2.

July 19, 2004

Hello,

I will definitely get details from my mom. I have a week's vacation coming up in a week from now, which will allow me to visit her, and to find that history of Montreal book. I live in Les Coteaux, Quebec. My mother still lives on 4th Avenue in LaSalle, which is an hour's drive from my home now, so visiting is more difficult.

The house was built by my father, who bought the land in 1941. It's a one-and-a-half-storey house, with no attic, which made hot summer nights unbearable for sleeping. My brother and I, who slept in different rooms, have on several occasions had scary experiences, each of us on separate occasions. I will relate my experiences, which are identical to my brother's.

We both are people, like my mom, who take up to an hour sometimes to fall asleep. (The bedrooms are on the second floor.) I would be awake in bed, looking at the window, which was in front of my bed, when a flash, exactly like the flash of a camera, would appear in the window. It was definitely not lightning. I am not afraid of thunderstorms; as a matter of fact, I love them and gladly watch lightning flash in the skies. I have no idea how to explain these flashes. Maybe it's an optical illusion. But both my brother and I were quite afraid of them. Needless to say, after one occurred, we would be awake for a much longer time than usual, being afraid to fall asleep.

Something else occurred on a much more regular basis, and this was witnessed by the whole family. We would be awakened in the middle of the night by a constant, electrical-sounding, humming sound just above the house. The noise was quite loud, and would last up to one hour at a time. It had a sort of circular pattern to it. It's hard to explain a sound with words. Like the sound of a transformer which goes wavy on a regular basis, every second. We would talk to our parents and to each other from our rooms, wondering what it could be. No one had the courage to walk outside to see if there was anything to see, but there definitely was no light coming through the windows. But it scared everyone, except my father (or maybe he just didn't want to say he was afraid). There are no companies near that area, no airports or trains. Traffic of cars was minimal back in those days. My father would always get angry with the bunch of us, and tell us to just ignore it and go back to sleep. (Easier said than done!) At times he would tell us it was probably a passing ship on the St. Lawrence Seaway. But that made no sense, and we all knew it. The Seaway is much too far away, and at best, the only thing that could be heard from a ship was its horn, which we were very familiar with. Also, that sound would occur in any season, including January and February, when the Seaway was closed.

One peculiar thing happened after one such night when the noise was heard. It was in the summer of 1968. My younger sister was one or two months old. My mom had washed her little knitted wool socks, in Zero as usual, in the evening, and hung them up on the clothesline to dry overnight. There were absolutely no clouds in sight that evening. My mom always got up (and still does, at eighty-three) at four or five in the morning. (She washes her floors at 4:00 a.m.!) She went outside to get the socks. But they disintegrated in her hands. She showed us this in the morning. All the wool had come apart. I have no idea if there was acid rain back in those days and if that could cause such damage, but there was no sign that it had rained during the night.

Of all the oddities I've encountered, the year 1973 will never be erased from my memory, and I hope I never relive such occurrences.

I was twelve years old at the time. My parents owned a convenience store in Ville Emard, operated by my mom, and my dad worked, so I had to babysit my younger brother, age six, and sister, age five, for the summer. I had a very good friend, C.R., who was one year younger than me. She taught me English. Vacation had just started, and we were sitting in the living room with the children, talking girl stuff, when we heard a loud bang. C. was scared, but when you are born and raised in a house, you know all the noises of that house inside out. I knew it was the sound of the basement door being slammed shut, but harder than I had ever heard it. It's a two-inch-thick wooden door with a one-foot-square window at the top. What surprised me was that I had checked that door in the morning to make sure it was locked and, indeed, the hook was on. I told C. to stay with the kids and went downstairs to check the door, thinking someone had come in after breaking the window. The door was closed, but the window was intact and the hook was off! I checked the basement to make sure nothing had been stolen, and couldn't find anything amiss. I put the hook back on, and although I couldn't explain it, dismissed it as odd. I had very strict orders from my parents to make sure to keep the doors locked at all times, because I was alone at twelve years of age with the charge of two children, so I knew I had seen that door locked that morning.

After that incident, hardly a day would pass without an incident. The piano in the basement would play on its own. Things would disappear from their usual location, would be searched for for days, and then would be found one morning exactly where they were supposed to be. We would go outside, come back in, and find all the lights on in the house. Nothing spectacular, but very unsettling. I will relate to you a few of the most unsettling and strange occurrences.

One day, my father was on vacation but left me and the kids to go get some groceries. I made sure as usual that the doors were locked. We were sitting in a swing, C. and I, with the children. The dog, a female cross between a Samoyed and a husky, was in the house. The kitchen door was closed but not locked, as I had no keys. The dog inside started barking and kept on barking for several minutes. That was unusual, as she wasn't a barker, but I let it go. My brother and sister were extremely difficult children to handle, always fighting and such, and disobeying every time they could. My brother used to be a real brat. He started saying he had to go in the house to use the bathroom, but he often would say that, and then play some prank. I had just ordered them to sit down after breaking up one of their fights, so I suspected some foul play on the part of my brother. But he insisted he had to go, so I let him. He then called out to me from the door (and I had been watching him, so I knew he hadn't opened the kitchen door) saying the door was locked. I thought it was a prank again, but walked to the door to open it. To my amazement it was locked! Yet I could turn the door handle. There were and still are two ways of locking that door. One way is by pushing the doorknob lock button, in which case the doorknob turned just a bit. The other way is from the inside only by means of a horizontal bolt. I thought it was closed with the bolt, since I seemed to be able to turn the doorknob as usual, but figured I was wrong in my assessment, as no one was in the house and so the bolt couldn't be locking the door. I tried the front door and the outside basement door, even though I knew they were locked because of my feeling that the bolt was locking the door. I checked all the windows, all locked. My brother was getting more and more impatient, as he had to void, so I finally told him to just "go" in the corner of the yard. (He was far from happy about this.)

About an hour later, my father came home, and I explained that we were locked out. He tried his key, and the door wouldn't open. As I had thought, the bolt had been locked! My father tried the other doors, all locked. He was quite incensed. Finally, he had to break the window of the basement door to enter the house. I was right on his heels when he entered the kitchen. The bolt had been slid into place, but in the upper slot instead of the downward one. This is very peculiar because the door, an old wooden one, had to be pushed in with one's full weight for the bolt to slide into the latch horizontally. Also, I guess, because of gravity, we always turned the head downward into the slot, instead of upward. And I guess that with the passing of time, and the warping of the wood, it was very difficult to push that knob into its upper notch. When I told my father that it was completely impossible for that door to be so locked from the inside, he replied that the dog had probably locked it! (My father should have worked on Project Blue Book!)

Later during that summer, I was out in the yard with C. It was just after supper. I was watering the vegetable garden when suddenly the water stopped. C. being in the vicinity of the outside tap, I asked her to stop fooling around and to turn the water back on. She insisted she hadn't closed the tap and went to reopen it. However, that was impossible. I went over to the tap and turned it all the way, in both directions, to no avail. I checked the hose. There were no kinks. I figured my father had turned off the water inside to do some work, but when I got inside, he was in the kitchen washing the dishes. I explained the problem to him, and he ran the kitchen tap to see if the city had shut off the water. The tap was running fine. So downstairs he went. The problem was that someone had shut the inside tap to the hose. My father had done all the work in that house, including plumbing and electricity. He had never shut that valve in his life. And now he was faced with a problem. The valve was stuck shut, and he was worried that forcing it open with a tool might cause a flood, as the pipe was so rusted he was afraid of its breaking. He was quite angry. He shut off the water main, and worked at that valve with oil and tools, till he slowly reopened it. He asked me several times if I had shut the valve. He kept on repeating that valves do not shut themselves off on their own. My father was a very calm and peaceful man who rarely got angry, but he was quite angry that night. He always got angry when things unexplainable occurred. Maybe the tap slowly closed because of vibrations over thirty years. But that water stopped flowing out of that hose suddenly, not slowly like someone closing off a tap.

Another time, I was alone with C. and the kids. It was the afternoon. C. said she was going outside, and I told her I had to go to the bathroom and would join her and the kids, who followed her into the yard. The bathroom door had a knob that had been broken for years, and it didn't even remain closed. We locked it from the inside with a hook. When I removed the hook, the door wouldn't open. I started pushing it, but it wouldn't budge. I yelled C.'s name. No answer. The dog started barking, and I started getting more and more nervous. No matter how hard I pushed, that door wouldn't budge, not even a bit. Now, I was twelve, but I've always been a hefty and strong girl. At fifteen, I would pick up my sister in my arms and carry her around. She weighed 120 pounds. I was stuck in that bathroom (which is really tiny, just enough room for a toilet and a person, no sink) for several minutes, when suddenly the door opened without my touching it. I was on the verge of tears, and ran out of the house like a bat out of hell. C. was with the kids in the laneway, about five houses south of my house.

One night, I woke up at around 3:00 a.m., for no reason. I also don't know why I got up and went to my window, on the south side of the house. It gave on to the side of the yard. It was a beautiful, windless, starry night. There used to be two full-grown Montgomery cherry trees in line with my window. No wind whatsoever. The next morning, we were up at around 8.00 a.m. I had breakfast while my brother was shaving. I then went outside. It was a beautiful sunny day, an all-day-in-the-pool-type day. But something was wrong. Something was different in the landscape, but I couldn't put my finger on it. I went back inside and told my brother that things looked different. He came outside with me, and after a minute or so said, "Mr P.'s tree is missing." So we went to see. He was our neighbour to the south. He had two full-grown *vinegrier*. (I'm sorry, I don't know the English name for the tree. Sumach?) One of them had been uprooted and laid about three feet from the hole. The branches and leaves were fine, except for a few leaves, but the trunk was completely twisted! Nothing else in the environment was disturbed. I've heard of mini tornados. Could that be the cause?

One evening, I was lying in bed waiting for sleep. My arms were above my head. Suddenly, I felt as if someone was pinching my thumbs between their fingers. I grew cold with fear. Believe you me, if I was half asleep, that wakes you up, fight or flight type of awake! I hadn't moved and started thinking I had imagined it. Then it happened again. I bolted up and looked all around, ready to fight the devil if need be. There was nothing in my room. I went back to bed, with my arms under the blankets, scared like hell. Some time later, there was loud banging on the basement door that leads to the kitchen. I sat up straight up in bed and waited. Nothing. So I lay back again. Right away, there was again this loud banging on the door. I sat up and called out to my parents to ask if they had heard it. They answered that they had heard nothing, that I had woken them up. I lay back down again and again I heard the same loud banging. But this time my parents heard it. I got up at the same time my father got up. I started opening my door, to go see what was going on. But as I was opening it, I saw my father in his undies with his pants in his hands. Now, he was born in 1913 and was a very prudish man. And their bedroom has only three walls (it's a tiny house) and no door. So my bedroom door gave directly on to their bedroom. My father saw me seeing him in his undies, but was so unsettled about the banging that instead of pushing my door shut, he started pulling at it while I was pulling at it to try to close it! I had to say, "Dad, let go of the door." He then let go. He put on his pants, and to my amazement, he not only checked all the windows and doors of the house from the inside, but also went out to survey everything from the outside! I was terrified something would happen to him.

The last event was by far the scariest. The kids were in their rooms. I was watching TV. It was around 8:00 p.m. I stared hearing heavy footsteps in the wooden staircase leading down to the basement. A footstep per second, very loud, like something out of a bad horror movie. I got up and was standing in the living room, watching the door to the basement. The footsteps stopped. Then the door moved as if someone was pushing it. (It could move like that a bit even when locked.) You have no idea how terrifying this was. I started to go upstairs to get the kids up, as I had decided to leave the house. (The hell with that!) I was halfway up the stairs, when our dog started barking loudly in the kitchen. I went back downstairs to find the basement door ajar, its bolt unlocked! I quickly shut it and put the bolt back on. Then Tchouky ran onto the front porch, which is closed in and has windows all around. She was looking at the south window on the side of the house, and would jump onto a La-Z-Boy while barking loudly, then run behind me with her tail between her legs, whimpering. She did this several times. I went back inside the house, fetched the kids, and ran back downstairs with them. At this point I was in a panic. I wanted to leave but didn't know how. The backyard was closed by gates four feet high and I knew I couldn't negotiate them quickly with two children. (There was a padlock on them.) On the other hand, I didn't want to go out the front door, as the dog was still wild, and I didn't want to put us in danger. I called my mom at the store and asked her to come home right away. She could hear the fear in my voice, and hear the dog wildly barking then whimpering in the background. She was home ten minutes later. That was the last incident. Then all the weird occurrences stopped.

Several years later, I found out about poltergeists. I was the right age, maybe these things were caused by me unconsciously. I don't know. I just know I never want to relive that summer.

In 1990—I've retraced it to November 7 by checking the Internet for sightings in Montreal—I was pregnant with my son. I hadn't quit smoking yet, which I did on December 28 of that year. My husband and I had had a second-floor apartment in a huge stone house at 63 8th Avenue in LaSalle. I remember eating souvlaki in the kitchen and listening to the American attack on Baghdad during the Kuwait crisis, and we were fearing another world war. Around 8:00 p.m., I left with my car to get cigarettes at a convenience store. I was driving north on 8th Avenue when something in the corner of my eye attracted my attention. At first I thought it might be something on my windshield, since it needed cleaning. (I'm not very good at keeping my car clean!) But when I realized that this thing was moving relative to my windshield, I parked the car and got out. Northeast of where I stood were seven or eight filaments or strings that were hanging from the sky perpendicular with the Earth. They were separated from each other by the width of two fingers. They were of different colours, orange, yellow, and red, and, if memory serves, blue. I describe them as light in colour, although I don't know why. They didn't shimmer, or glow, or blink. There was no variation in intensity. I probably think of them as lights because how else could they be seen in a dark sky? I couldn't detect any object they would be suspended from, nor any object hanging from them. They were stationary. I watched them for maybe five minutes, then went to the depanneur. I could see them still. At that point, I was on the corner of 9th Avenue and Centrale. I attracted several people's attention to them. I watched them for about ten minutes, then drove home. I told my husband about them, and we watched them from the kitchen window, which was on the north side of the house. Wanting to have a better look, we went up to the attic. Now, this house has an attic the size of the house itself, and the lowest part of the ceiling is three feet high. You go up by a full staircase with hardwood steps. We watched the filaments from there. I wanted to get in my car and try to get closer. Maybe that's why my husband said it was the northern lights. I argued that I had seen the northern lights as a child and they were nothing like this. I wanted to stay up and watch them as long as possible, but seeing his disapproval, I went to bed around 10:00 p.m. You could still see the strings. (I think the hypothesis that one marries someone like one's father is true!) The next day, the *Journal de Montréal* had a report about a UFO being sighted over a building in Montreal, but there was no mention whatsoever of filaments in the sky. How I regret that I did not get into my car that night and drive towards them! The other day, talking to my husband about this, he said that no way could they have been northern lights. I replied, "Then why did you tell me that's what they were?" He doesn't recall having said that.

I have a few more stories, but they are more of the telepathic type or premonitions. I'll write to you about them. Please feel free to include what you like in your book. I had a week's vacation two weeks ago, and having some time to read, started going over some of my old UFO books. That's what prompted my looking for newer ones and buying your book. I decided to write to you because if people don't tell their stories, then no one will ever know about these occurrences. Things not divulged can definitely never be explained. I am sure many, many people have stories, but never dare tell people about them.

Thank you,
Sylvie Loranger-Journeau

3.

July 19, 2004

Hello,

Thank you for the compliments. I will ask my mom if she can write her own account. However, if she does, it will be handwritten and in French, so I'll mail it to you. Her handwriting is very good though. Not like mine! Hieroglyphs are easier to decipher than my handwriting! I should have been a doctor! Here are some more events.

In the late 1940s, my father tried to make a go at farming. He rented out the house in LaSalle and bought a farm in St-Jude, Quebec. One morning, he got up and went to do *le train*, a French-Canadian term for taking care of the animals. When he came back to the house, he told my mom that in the barn the hens were all *juchées*, perched in line on a beam, and were singing "Le Libéra." This probably has an English term (although it's Latin) but I can't find one in my dictionaries. "Le Libéra" is a Roman Catholic chant or hymn for the dead, or so I was told. Now, as you know by now, a statement like that from my father is in itself an oddity.

They sat down and were having breakfast when they both heard a loud knock at the door. However, as one heard it at the front door, the other heard it at the back door. Apparently, both doors were visible from the kitchen table. They separately went to each door to answer, but no one was there. My father then circled the house, and saw no one. Neighbouring houses were miles away. Later that morning, my father did something he had never done. He walked to the road to check the mail. He opened a letter addressed to him (my mom always did this) and said that one line just jumped at him, as if highlighted (although there were no such pencils as highlighters back then). It stated that his Aunt Sylvina had died. She was his favourite aunt.

Now, I've heard my mom retell this story many times, and my father never denied any of it, although you could see that he was uncomfortable, and would try to make jokes.

In 1986 or '87, I dreamt of a man I hadn't heard of nor seen in seventeen years or so. He was a very good friend of one of my older brothers. His name was Ronald Francoeur. They were close friends in the late sixties. He must have been in his early twenties at the time, as my brother Roger was born in 1947. I never forgot this man, because, unlike "young bucks" my older brothers befriended, he always said "hi" to me and asked how I was, and would chat a little (with an eight- or nine-year-old!). He was very sweet, and he had same personality as my husband. (Interestingly, my husband's name is also Ronald.)

In the dream, I was standing on the sidewalk in front of my parents' place. Across the street, I noticed Ronald walking slowly, looking at the ground before him. He looked very sad. All happy to see him, I called out to him. He stopped, looked at me with this indescribable look of sadness, then lowered his head again and resumed his walk. When I woke up, the dream was still vivid in my mind, and I couldn't understand why I had dreamt of him. I had never dreamt of him in the past.

Several hours later, my mom called to tell me she had bad news. Before she could go on, I interjected, "Let me guess, Ronald Francoeur is dead." She asked me who told me, and so I explained my dream to her. The man had suffered an intracranial bleed caused by the rupture of a cerebral aneurism. He was kept alive for two days, unconscious, then died, the day before my dream. He was thirty-seven or thirty-eight at the time of his death. Why *I* should dream of him, I have no clue. Maybe because he left young children behind or recalled his youth after his death. Who knows? He did live on 7th Avenue close to Champlain in LaSalle at the time of his death, and I had lived on 8th, near LaSalle Boulevard. But I only found out about this after his death. And according to what I heard, he died at Sacré-Coeur Hospital, which is on the northern side of the island.

I've often had dreams of things that would happen the next day. Mundane things, like calls I would answer on the ambulance, nothing spectacular. But how can one dream of things that haven't happened yet, unless time is not as one assumes? One such event was really creepy. I was on standby at Bedford and Côte-des-Neiges. Being a quiet night shift, I decided to lie down in the back and fell asleep. I woke up suddenly after dreaming that I was on call for a man or a woman (I can't recall) who had jumped off an overpass onto the Décarie Expressway. A "jumper" is what we call them. The victim was still alive but was a severe trauma. Upon waking, I decided to get up and get back into the cab of the truck. I hate sleeping on an ambulance, as we never know when and what your next call will be. My partner asked me why I was getting up, so I told him about my dream. A few minutes later, we received a call for a jumper on the Décarie Expressway! However, when we got there, we couldn't find anything, even after patrolling the highway in both directions. My partner told me I was a witch!

In January of this year [2004], I had a strange dream that had the peculiar feeling of not being a dream. I can't explain what I mean, except to say that some dreams have a different feeling about them than others. Also, when dead relatives are in my dreams, it always ends up being a warning. I was at my parents' house and had decided to build a stream in their backyard. I started digging a hole. My father and older sister, both deceased, were in that dream. My father was far from happy about my project, but I just kept on digging. Gradually the hole filled with water, but having no water input, it became stagnant water. Suddenly, I was in front of a house I didn't recognize. Two people were outside, telling me that someone had died. They asked me if I wanted to go inside to see who was dead. I replied, "No thanks, I've seen enough dead people in my life," because of my profession. Two days later, one of my nieces, thirty-five years old, was killed instantly in a snowmobile accident. That was February 1. I still wonder whom I would have seen if I had decided to have a look at who was dead.

For three years, my husband (who is also a paramedic) and I teamed up at work. It was a very sensible choice, since we live forty minutes away from the office (Cavendish and Highway 40) in Montreal, especially with the price of gas soaring. Plus, we had the same days off, and after work, we could do other things besides talking about our day at work. We broke up our work team because of a herniated disc that I suffered, which led me to the decision to change my full-time job to nursing. Most people don't understand how a husband and wife could work together. Their reaction has always amazed me. Are married people supposed to be at war? Even the public was surprised. We would take care of an elderly person and, during the call, would talk about the fact that we were married, and they couldn't believe it. It was sweet, in a way, one couple taking care of another couple! Sometimes it led to confusion, though. I recall a car accident with multiple victims, and other ambulances hadn't arrived yet. I gave a KED to a police officer and asked him to take it to my husband. Oops! Old habits die hard, especially in the heat of the moment!

My husband firmly believes in God. He says he talks to him every day the way you would talk to an old friend. But although he was an altar boy for many years in the Anglican church, he hates talking about religion. He doesn't go to church. I think he hates dogmas, and that's probably the reason he loves the movie *Dogma* so much, as it makes fun of organized religion. Being an ex-student of anthropology, I've always been interested in religions, but should I start talking about religion, he says it just rattles him to no end. So I don't.

That is the reason why I was so surprised one morning while driving to work. He was at the wheel. It was a beautiful, warm September morning. The 40 started being jammed with traffic west of St. John's, but since we always left early, there was no problem. Besides, my husband is a very patient man, a very courteous driver, who rarely complains. When he sees someone driving like a nut, cutting off people and speeding, he says, "That's job security."

We were both silent, listening to CHOM on the radio. Out of the blue, my husband said, "And God saw this mess and was greatly displeased, so he destroyed everything." I froze, and had goosebumps. I had to bite my tongue not to ask him if he was prophesying. We never exchanged a word about it. We arrived at the office, checked our ambulance, and signed on available at 9:00 a.m. At 9:02 a.m., while driving to our assigned standby point of Bedford and Côte-des-Neiges, listening to the radio, we heard the news of an airplane crashing into one of the Twin Towers. In my mind it was a Cessna, probably because I had read once of a small plane crashing into the Empire State Building. Two or three minutes later, we heard of another plane crashing into the second tower. The rest is history. Only in the afternoon did my husband talk about the drive in. He said, "I will never, in my life, say anything like that again."

Two months earlier, I had one of those dreams that feels "odd." I was on a call for a multiple-victim accident in the curve where the 20 joins with Highway 13. I loaded a trauma patient on board and was told by dispatch to go to the Jewish General, which is odd, since it is not a trauma centre. I was driving, and worked with a fellow I've occasionally worked with in the past. When I started heading north on the Décarie Expressway, the highway became littered with debris. Suddenly, an airplane engine was coming right at me, and I avoided it by scraping the wall of the Décarie with the ambulance. That was just south of the Côte St-Luc overpass. Once north of it, the highway was destroyed, and sixty or more people were walking in a daze, all injured. I got out of the ambulance and told people I had to get to the Jewish General. I was told that the Côte-des-Neiges district didn't exist any more, that even St. Joseph's Oratory was now a crater. If that is a premonition, I hope to God that was a dream about the Twin Towers, and not something that will happen in Montreal.

Several years ago, my brother was visiting my mom, having a cup of coffee at the table. Suddenly, they both heard an incredible rush of water coming down the stairs from the second floor. They rushed to the landing of the staircase, to see nothing. At the same moment, the phone rang.

It was one of my sisters, who lived in a flat on David Street in Verdun. She urgently needed my dad, as a pipe had broken in her bathroom, and to try to stop the flooding, she had stuck her finger into the broken pipe!

Well, that's it for today, although I don't think there is much more to tell. Have a good day.

Sylvie Loranger-Journeau

4.

July 20, 2004

Dear Mr. Colombo,

Hello again!

I've found the little book which mentions *la grande noirceur*. I've stumbled on it right away. We have been renovating the basement of our house, and all the books had been in plastic bins, so I wasn't sure how much time it would take me to find this particular one. It is just a tiny book, of historical events, that I bought probably in the '70s (I cannot find a date of publication in it!), being interested in history and anthropology and such. (At the age of eighteen, I retraced my genealogy, with a letter of introduction from the Minister of Justice, by travelling to various villages in Quebec by Greyhound bus. [I had no car.] It was a very tedious affair.) The story my mother told us must have come from her grandmother, however, as the year of the event is 1819. Or, more probably, her great-grandmother. These things go down the verbal family storytelling, I guess, like myths do in nations. However, I'm not sure if there is a mistake in the date. It is listed as the same year as the foundation of the Montreal General Hospital. I know that the year of foundation is 1821. Maybe a charter was written in 1819 and the hospital built in 1821, I don't know. I'm sure these facts can be verified. Also, the drawing of the MGH at the bottom of the page doesn't look like the old MGH building (which was located on Dorchester [now René-Lévesque] east of St-Laurent), but more like Hôtel-Dieu maybe.

However, I may be wrong. Part of the old MGH survives, and is now called St Charles Borroméo, a nursing home. And an extension was built to the original brown stone building. Now, my memory of drawings of the old MGH (on the main corridor of the hospital on the first floor) is that of a square, stout building, not an elongated one. I'll check if the pictures are still there. (They could have been removed, as the ER is under renovation.) I will photocopy pertinent pages of the book today and send it to you by mail. The last entry in the book is of the year 1972.

Blessed or cursed, I have no idea. I feel I'm blessed, because I've had wonderful parents, I have a wonderful husband, and a thirteen-year-old son (who is already 5'10"), gorgeous, loving and very polite. I've never lacked for work, and am faring a lot better than most people on this Earth. I know I've been feeling kind of silly writing you about these events, which I guess is normal. But like I said, if these things are left untold, they can never be explained. I've also started having a hard time sleeping again. I know this is ridiculous, but at forty-three, I find myself going to bed the same way I did for years after 1973, making sure that my hands are under the blankets, and with a pillow over my head! These events really scared me, and I guess the fear is surfacing again, which is probably why I am writing to you every day, to get this over with. (Not to mention that I've had three days off.)

I'm not one to scare easily, in the sense that even when scared, I'll check out what's going on. In 1992, my baby was asleep, when I heard this terrifying howling coming from the back of the house. It sounded like a dog, but nothing I've heard before. I had no flashlight, and it was dark, but I went out to check things out. It came from the back corner of our yard, near a big tree (*un érable giguère*), some sort of maple tree I guess. I slowly walked to the scene of the howling, and then realized what was going on. This adult malamute dog (I still to this day have no idea who it belonged to) had broken his chain (a huge one) at the proximal end, and had been dragging about ten feet of it behind him. He turned around the tree several times, until he was caught there. Now, I used to be scared of dogs other than my own because I was bitten once.

But I felt sorry for this guy, and I didn't want him to wake up the baby. I started talking to him in a soothing voice, and slowly approached. He let me grab his collar and untangle him. I then removed the chain and let him go. Animals know when you are trying to help, and are, believe me, more cooperative and less dangerous that many drunks!

The blessed or cursed comment reminded me of another event. I was dating this guy who lived on Belec Street in LaSalle, about one kilometre from my parents' house, where I lived at the time. It was 1982, around 2:00 a.m. I got into a fight with him, and asked him to drive me home. Being an idiot, he refused. So off I went by foot, mad as a hornet. I have a wretched temper (which I get from my mom). And when I'm angry, common sense is gone. I'll confront a bull if need be. I was crossing the Aqueduct bridge at Shevchenko when, suddenly, I went from mad as a hornet to scared to death. This overwhelming feeling of impending doom washed over me (like you can read of in medical texts), but I wasn't having a heart attack!

I just couldn't get myself to keep on walking home. That's when I remembered my father telling me time and time again that, no matter what the time, and no matter where I was, I could call him, and he would come and pick me up. (Now, when I was eighteen, in the summer of 1979—I was born in September 1960—I left for LA on a Greyhound bus and travelled in the States by myself for a month, with no reservations. I did the same in 1988, touring Australia and New Zealand by myself, and so his coming to pick me up in those instances was, needless to say, out of the question!). So I checked my pockets for small change. Back then, you only needed a dime for a phone call. But I only had a penny. That's when I remembered a quote from the Gospels, of Jesus saying, "Whatever you ask of my Father in my name, if you believe it will happen, it will," or something of the sort. So I walked to a phone booth, and inserted the penny while praying and hoping I would have enough faith. As expected, the penny ended up in the change slot, but to my amazement, the phone rang at the other end, and after a few rings, my mom answered. My father came to pick me up. Now, having a sceptical mind, I thought to myself that Bell Canada was fooling the public and that a phone call could be made with a penny. So I tried, over and over again, from various phones, including the one I had used, to make phone calls with a penny. It never worked. Now, you may wonder why I didn't call the operator and ask her to reverse the charges, but back then, I didn't know one could do that with local calls. Believe me, I've tried this prayer and faith stuff many times to win the 6/49, but it never worked! I guess the phone had a malfunction, or I don't have enough faith!

In April 2004, I was alone at home and went into my son's room to water a plant. Suddenly, I heard a heavy sigh just behind me. I looked down behind me, thinking that my ever-faithful Scout, an Australian shepherd (who follows me on my heels, and once managed to sneak by even though I'm very fast at closing the gate between the kitchen and the rest of the house), had sighed behind me, but there was nothing there. I returned to my watering the plant, thinking I imagined it, when it happened again. At which point, I left the bedroom. I told my husband when he came home, as I was worried that things were starting again, and being especially concerned because it happened in my son's room.

Now these are very recent occurrences, and somewhat unprintable I guess. Last Wednesday, I was housecleaning. My son was in the basement. I had just finished cleaning the bathroom on the first floor and was putting away clothes in the bedrooms. I went to the bathroom, to find that feces were in the toilet bowl that I had just cleaned! It was a formed stool too big for a cat (I have four), and some diarrhea on the sides of the bowl. I checked the underside of the toilet seat, thinking that maybe the sewers had backed up (although that has never happened before), but it was clean, as was the floor. I flushed the tap, and the toilet blocked. I cleared it and washed the bowl again. I called my mom to make sure everything was fine, and she said yes, but that they expected bad news. On Sunday, around 7:30 (that would be July 11, 2004), she had been sitting on the front enclosed porch with my two sisters (the third one died of lung cancer in 1994), when the doorbell rang three times, over two minutes, with no one at the front door. Maybe it was a short circuit. We haven't had any bad news.

This last event was told to me by a fellow nurse, who had goose-bumps on her arms retelling the story. She was working the night shift in an observation room. She had just done a round, and all the patients seemed well. It is very hard to sleep for these patients, because of the noise, not to mention that some elderlies get the "night crazies," becom-ing confused at night. This elderly woman was awake. Her bed was positioned just in front of the nursing desk. This is what the nurse said: "I don't know why, I felt the urge to recheck that patient. I even felt her radial pulse, and found it to be in the 170 range." (Now, sometimes, nurses have a sixth sense about people. Someone will come with a his-tory that doesn't warrant keeping them in the acute care area, but on a hunch, the nurse, after triage, decides to keep them there anyway. Some time later, the patient goes into cardiac arrest!) She then rechecked the patient's full vital signs, and moved the patient to the acute care area, to be on a cardiac monitor. The patient started decompensating, and the acute care area being very busy that night, she stayed on to take care of the patient. (The other area was still covered by the second nurse.)

Not long after the transfer, the clerk informed the nurse that the patient's son was on the phone and said someone had called him from the hospital. She told the clerk to tell the man that she was too busy to talk and that if no one called him within an hour to call back. Now, she hadn't called the son, and neither had the doctor. Thirty minutes later, the son called again. This time she spoke to him. She asked him who had called. He replied that he had had two phone calls, one of which he was sure of. The first call, he had been sleeping, and he wasn't sure if it had been a dream or a real phone call. That's when he had phoned the hos-pital. But when told to call back in an hour if not called back, he had decided to stay up, and had fixed himself something to eat. Then the sec-ond call came in. He said there was a lot of static on the phone, and he couldn't make out what his mother was telling him, but he knew for sure it was his mother's voice. She then proceeded to tell him that her mother had gone into fast atrial fibrillation, etc. The son decided to come to the hospital. No one had called him. It may sound strange to lay people, but we do not call relatives unless a patient goes sour on us and the doctor decides that death could ensue. Phones are very hard to come by in that department. There was no phone the patient could have used, either in the observation room or in the acute care area. The nurse reconfirmed the son's statements when he arrived. The patient survived her crisis.

These are all strange stories that I cannot explain. I am not afraid of the dead, nor of cemeteries. My grandmother, whom I have never met, used to say, "Do not be afraid of the dead, it's the living you should be afraid of," and I agree with that statement, after taking care of a number of victims of stab wounds or gunshot wounds. I am sure there is a logical explanation to all of them, but, unfortunately, explanations that are not available to us yet, either because of our lack of knowledge or of science's refusal to investigate "where no man has gone before," to quote *Star Trek*.

Well, that's it. I've had enough. I think I've related to you all the stories I have. There may be more, when I talk to my mom, as I may have forgotten some. But I doubt it. I'll get back to you on that missing-time story. Thanks for your listening. I hope you don't think I'm a lunatic. But if you do, well, so be it. If I had logical explanations, I would not have written to you in the first place. Maybe someday, someone will find the answers, and we can all laugh together. Until then, all the best wishes to you and your family.

Sincerely,
Sylvie Loranger-Journeau

5.

August 9, 2004

Dear Mr Colombo,

"I'm back!" I hope all is well with you and your family. The weather is still very poor here in the Montreal area. It hasn't been a "pool-type" summer. Mind you, we have a twenty-seven-foot circular above-ground pool, and even though we have a passive solar-heating system, it's a lot of water to warm up, especially when it's always overcast. When I came home from work in 2001, after the company installed it, I exclaimed, "My God, a UFO has landed!" It had never really dawned on me how big this pool actually was! I guess women aren't very good at estimating dimensions. That and reproducing sounds, like animal sounds or mechanical sounds. Have you ever observed that? Men have a talent for that. Women sound ridiculous. Maybe it has to do with our greater capacity with speech. (I am not trying to offend men.) It has been documented in medical research that a higher percentage of men than women lose speech capacity after a CVA. Whenever I try to reproduce a sound, my husband says I sound like a moose in heat!

Okay, for the last stories. They are not spectacular, and it's up to you whether you want to include them or not. Here goes. I'm retelling the entire stories, feel free to edit as you please.

Around July 6, 1996, I was driving the ambulance on a transfer, a patient returning to her nursing home, Centre d'accueil Real-Morel, from the Verdun General. This was a 10-16 transport, meaning non-emergency, no lights, no siren. It was our last call, as I was due to end the shift at 23:30. She was an elderly woman, demented. Back then, Wellington Street became a one-way at about Regina, so I had to drive towards the entrance to the Champlain bridge and then take a street south (Henri-Dunant, I believe) to then turn west onto Wellington. I came to that intersection, which was a four-corner stop-sign intersection, came to a full stop, looked both ways, and started to turn westbound. The street lights were not working. The city of Verdun had recently enlarged Wellington Street at that section to convert it to a two-way street. My partner, as is mandatory, was in the back with the patient, sitting on the side bench.

Almost immediately after accelerating, I hit a wooden hydro pole. I felt an intense pain in my knee and, in shock, I heard my partner faintly calling from the back that he was bleeding. I called into dispatch 10-14 (accident) and 10-33 to follow (information). I hadn't seen any cars coming, but my first impression, since I had hit a hydro pole, was that a vehicle must have rammed the ambulance from my right (from the east) and pushed our truck into a hydro pole. Now, these were big trucks, top kicks, which were used for tow trucks and were not supposed (apparently) to be used for human transports.

Since my partner seemed to be in distress in the back, and I knew nothing of the state of the patient, and even though I wasn't sure my knee wasn't busted, I tried to get out. Once out of the truck, to my surprise and anger (I'll spare you the French religious curse words that came out of my mouth), I had hit a hydro pole that had been left about three feet from the new sidewalk, by the city of Verdun, without any orange cones, not even fluorescent paint on the damn pole! It was left in the middle of the street! I realized this when I saw a wooden hydro pole standing where it should be to the left side of the accident scene, beyond the new sidewalk, and then gazed at the hydro pole I had just hit. I rushed to help my partner, who had fallen into the stairwell of the side door, where his neck had hit the door's bar that we use to open the door from the inside, and controlled the bleeding. The patient hadn't moved from the stretcher. She seemed fine.

I called for two ambulances, one for my partner, who was complaining of numbness in his limbs and needed to be immobilized, and one for the patient, who needed to go to a hospital for exam since she was incapable of telling us if she was hurt. The accident occurred at 23:07. Believe me, I'll never forget. It was the only time I had an accident with an injured person. I've scraped paint off cars a few times, but that is to be expected when you drive an emergency vehicle five days a week in a big city. After both patients were transported, and I had finished my deposition to the cops, who kept on saying that I must have been speeding because of the damage to the truck (it had a fibreglass hood, and thank God we have black boxes on the trucks, which demonstrated that I hit at 5.2 kilometres per hour after leaving from a full halt, believe me, you don't want to hit those wooden poles at 100 K), I called my husband with my cell to let him know what had happened so he wouldn't worry if he realized I was late, as I had to go to the hospital myself for my knee, and then go back to the office to file more reports.

My son was five years old at the time. Jake had always been an easy baby and easy child, a sound sleeper who never woke up at night in his childhood. When I called home, around 00:30, I was surprised that my husband answered at the first ring. He should have been asleep. He explained that he was up because he had just managed to calm down Jake, who woke up screaming and crying in the middle of his sleep. I asked him at what time this happened, because it was so out of character, and he replied, "A little after 23:00." This has been the ONLY time Jake has ever wakened up in the middle of the night (aside from when he was a baby). Did he "feel" I had been in an accident? I'll never know. The patient had no injuries, my partner only suffered a laceration, and I was back at work three days later (thank God), and the truck had $7,000 in damages and was out of commission until September. Being a woman paramedic, several guys tried to tease me about the accident, about women drivers, and, off the cuff, I answered, "Well, as my old partner used to say, I drive just like a man." I started joking around that I would have to change my address to Les Poteaux instead of Les Coteaux!

In the summer of 1993, Jake was two years old and still sleeping in a crib. I asked my mom if I should transfer him to a regular bed, as I was afraid he might try to climb out and hurt himself. She told me that, except for one of her children, she had always transferred each child to a bed at around the age of three. I relied on her expertise. A week later, it was a hot humid summer day, and Jake was having his afternoon nap. I decided to go for a swim in our pool. I brought the Fisher-Price monitor with me. Jake has always been a happy child, who wakes up talking and giggling for a while. Being a nurse and a paramedic, the house was CHILD-PROOFED to the max. I even had inside hooks on the outside doors, but, obviously, couldn't have them all on if I went outside. It was the first time I went in the pool while Jake was asleep. At around 4:00 p.m., I thought I should get out to start fixing supper, but then decided against it since it was so hot. Ten minutes later, I felt the urge to get out of the pool. So I did. I put away the ladder and started to walk towards the house.

There had never been any noise on the monitor, and I checked it afterwards to find that it was working fine. As I was walking towards our driveway (the kitchen door is on the north side of the house and gives on to the driveway), I was surprised to see a toddler leaving my driveway and walking into our northern neighbour's yard. It took me two seconds to realize that THAT toddler in diapers was JAKE! He had gotten out of his crib, closed his bedroom door, closed the kitchen door, and was off exploring! He had never climbed out of his crib before. If I had gotten out of the pool later, I would not have even realized the baby was gone. Now, this was particularly dangerous as we live 150 feet from a CN railroad track where travel approximately a hundred trains per day! Two years later, my husband saved a two-year-old child by grabbing him by the diaper as he was about to walk onto the tracks just as a fast passenger train went by. (The track is now fenced off.) And Jake, being a true little boy, loved trains, and always watched *Thomas the Tank Engine* on TV. We also have the Delisle River about 250 feet north of the house. Coincidence? I don't think so. To me, it's a miracle. God told me, somehow, to get my a— out of that pool!

This is the last story. Jake, at seven, joined the Scouts. He only stayed a member for a year, not wanting to go back, probably because, at the time, he was mainly unilingual English, and the Scout group was French. That was 1999. He had an incredible opportunity, as it was the first time that Scouts Canada allowed a group of Beavers to go outside the country on a trip. They had organized a trip to La Martinique, and had had fundraising activities for the two previous years to finance it. We didn't think Jake could go, since he had just joined, but found out that, aside from the fundraising we did that year, we could send him for only $300 or $400, all included. Scouts Canada allowed the Beavers to go because the organizers were so reliable and had done such a great job. My husband wasn't too thrilled about it, but I convinced him that it would be a great experience for Jake. I got his passport and everything ready, only to find out that I was a lot weaker than I thought. I cried like a baby when he left and when he returned. It was a long week. You can imagine what goes through your mind in a week's time. We received a phone call, as planned, in the middle of the week to let us know everything was all right.

I had given him one of those disposable cameras with twelve exposures. No, he didn't take any pictures of UFOs. To my disappointment, ten of the photos were of trucks with different mirrors (unlike those that we have in Canada)! He had been fascinated by those mirrors! So much for the beach!

On his return, Jake didn't have much to say about the trip, aside from the fact that it was fun flying in a big plane (he had been on a small plane before), that it was very poor in Martinique, that the kids were nice. I think he had probably been lonely, and maybe resented us for sending him away. Several times, I asked him about his trip, and would always get the same answers. (Mind you, after a school day, when asked what he had done that day, he would inevitably answer, "Nothing much.")

During the week of his return, we were having supper, him and I, when, out of the blue, he started talking about the beautiful lights in the sky he had seen while on the plane. It was during his return trip, and he said it was still dark outside. (This was in March, and the plane had landed at Mirabel at 09:00.) I casually asked him about them. He said they were of different colours, red, blue, yellow, orange and beige, and that they would form different figures in the sky, sometimes like a star. I was stunned but acted matter-of-factly. I said that they were probably the lights on the wings of the plane, but he replied, "Oh no, mama, I could see those, but the other lights were farther and bigger." He was very matter-of-fact about the whole thing. I asked him if he saw them for a long time, and he replied that everyone on his side of the plane watched them for a long time (how long is unsure). He kept on talking about the beige one, that the beige one was especially beautiful. Now, maybe someone should inform the Fisher-Price company about the fascination of a child with the colour beige! I then told him he had probably seen planets. As soon as I said that, Jake became very excited and said, "Really? We can see planets, mama?"

I said, "Sure we can." So he asked me what they looked like. I told him they looked like stars but were a little bit brighter and bigger. He looked very disappointed and resumed his eating, while saying, "Oh no, mama, they weren't planets. They were much bigger than stars."

Exasperated, I asked him what the monitors said they were. He replied, "Other planes." Then I asked him what he thought they were. And, nonchalantly, he said, "Oh, I think they were just those UFO things they sometimes talk about on TV."

Just those UFO things! Now I do not claim that my son saw UFOs. I will never be sure of what he saw. A seven-year-old's observation during his second time on a large plane is far from reliable. But the candour is remarkable. He got excited at the thought of being able to see planets, and then disappointed when he realized that is not what he had seen, and then stated it must have been UFOs, just like that was the most normal thing in the world. Jesus said the Kingdom was here and that, unless we be as little children, we would not see the Kingdom. I have yet to hear of children talking about seeing the Kingdom. I think that what he meant was that, unless we have open minds as children do, we will never see the Kingdom, whatever the Kingdom may be. Now, don't get me wrong, although I'm not Roman Catholic any more, I'm very religious, but there are a few oddities in the Bible.

In closing, I think that the day when people are open-minded to UFOs and ETs, and when mainstream science stops being more obtuse than the Pharisees to protect their "Establishment" and control over what they think is knowledge (not to mention maybe their foothold on their personal rationality), and when the governments come clean (wow, what a utopian event that would be), then I think that THEY will make contact.

In the meantime, I praise your work and encourage everyone who has odd events or possible sightings to write you. There are many, many people who have stories but don't talk about them out of fear. I have had the sleep paralysis experiences that some researchers describe. I couldn't move, felt I was flying, and felt terror. I forced, and I mean forced, myself to wake up. I never saw aliens, never had any abduction experiences. I honestly wish I would see a UFO land. I think I would approach it in daylight. At night, I'm not so sure. Probably because of an animal instinct or taught behaviour that things are more dangerous at night. But it's a moot point, as I probably never will see a UFO land. That's too bad, as I sure would have many questions for them.

Sincerely,

Sylvie Loranger-Journeau

PS: Has anyone ever reported to you the Quebec legends of *la chasse-galerie*, in which people who had supposedly sold their soul to the devil would fly in airborne canoes at night? This might have an Amerindian origin to it; I don't know.

A Retarded, Deformed Thing

JIM GREENWOOD

Out of the blue, I received a phone call from Jim Greenwood. He had been given my name by Mike Filey, a photo historian who publishes books on Toronto's pictorial past. Mr. Greenwood had a strange story to tell and a photograph that he wanted me to see. I listened to his account of his experiences and his description of the photograph and urged him to type out the account and send it to me. Three weeks later, I received the letter that appears here. Make of it what you will. I have limited my editing to breaking up some of the sentences and adding some punctuation.

◆ ◆ ◆

Saturday, November 28, 1998

Dear John Robert Colombo:

The incident that I talked to you about over the phone three weeks ago, after talking to Mike Filey, who I thought did a program on the house but didn't. He wasn't interested in ghosts, but was helpful in giving me your name, knowing you would be interested.

This incident happened about twenty years ago, around 1978. The reason I am writing to you about this experience now is I was being visited by spirits last year after my dad died. Incidentally, this is the second anniversary of his death. I don't know exactly what it means, other than it was a warning from God. These spirits visited me here in Toronto and on Lake Kashwakamak, which, I think, is sacred Indian land. This visitation went on for four months, from June to September 1997, up north and in Toronto.

I want to iterate that these spirits were evil spirits because of what I've learned. I also want people to know there is a spirit world, which I have proof of. I have a photo of a spirit. I will send a copy of it to you. The Indians recognize it as the Bear Spirit. I had it digitally copied by a photographer because I didn't have a negative. The picture was taken by one of my aunts. In it is the image of a bear, also my mother, grandfather, and one of my aunts. The person that this incident happened to at 21 Grenville, his wife develops film for a major photography firm. She said she has never seen a picture like it. Psychiatric letters from Westminster Hospital in London, Ontario (a war hospital for Canadian World War I and World War II veterans—he suffered from shell shock and was institutionalized from 1923 to his death in 1975) state my grandfather was having auditory hallucinations in English, French, and Iroquois. He was being visited by spirits, in my opinion. He was a captain in the First World War in France. Incidentally, this picture was taken in 1948. I don't want to delve too deep into the subject. I only want to know the truth. I was not in good mental or physical health when all this happened. I was going through alcohol withdrawal at the time in '97. I also had over one hundred Bible verses memorized, which means a lot, believe me. I also believe in JESUS CHRIST as my Saviour and Lord. So much for the introduction. Now on with the story.

We were renting a sound studio on the top floor of 21 Grenville Avenue, one block north of College, off Yonge Street, right behind Fran's Restaurant and across from the coroner's building. A friend of mine had just got back from Florida from a win-a-week's-vacation for the best costume at a Halloween contest in a local bar. His mother had made it. She was at one time a seamstress. He had a lot to do with it too. His character was Gandalf from Tolkien's *Lord of the Rings*. He and his girlfriend won. He was the drummer in the band. There were five of us in the room when this incident took place. All of us were childhood buddies. We were all around twenty-two at the time. There were two brothers who lived across the street from me, one a guitar player and the other a conga player. One was a keyboard player who lived in the West End who was a high school buddy, and the drummer, the leader of the gang, whom I knew all my life and still know. As I said, he just got back from Florida. We had just picked him up from the airport. His girlfriend went home and we went down to the studio from Keewatin Avenue, where we all had grown up together. As the drummer said before this happened, he had a high sense of spirits, that "this place is haunted." Climbing the last flight of stairs to the top floor, he said it "gave you the chills."

We all came into the studio room. I was the soundman, lowest in the pecking order, the one least daring. The room had a tape area that was about five feet wide and twenty feet long, with a window and a door. The room was fifteen feet wide by twenty-five feet long, with a vestibule going out to the stairs. The room had a table at one end, with four chairs and a couch along the wall.

We were smoking pot that night. It was strange stuff because of its dark colour and strange smell, but that had nothing to do with what happened. I have never seen anything like it since, so the name we called it was "Demon Weed." I'm totally straight now. I go to church.

The drummer had a T-shirt on, I recall, with the Union Stars and Stripes flag and the Confederate flag crossed. He was setting up his drums when he cut himself on the high hat. I figure the month to be November. When he saw blood, he fainted. I don't know if it was jet lag or what, but when he saw his finger, he said, with an "oh no" expression on his face, "See you later, boys," and simultaneously he sat down on the couch.

All four of us were sitting at the table. His eyes went up into the back of his head and he started going into convulsions. His body would jerk forward violently and then he would become animate. Another personality had taken control of his body. The entity would stay long enough to show his or her personality, but every one was animate. This happened with his eyes closed. After the spirit would show its identity, the drummer's body would lurch forward and come back again, but this time with a different spirit. This happened over a two-minute period. I figure ten spirits passed through his body. Everyone sat motionless as this was taking place. I didn't know who the spirits were because I didn't know them, but I could recognize male from female. I think there was only one female spirit. But the last spirit that entered his body was unmistakable because it was hideous. It was that of a mongoloid child. Deformed, he became a mongoloid, a retarded, deformed being, so animate it changed his whole appearance. It made your skin crawl. When this spirit left him, he died. His teeth dropped and his cheeks went back and he sat motionless on the couch, leaning to one side for two minutes. After one minute, I got scared because I knew he was dead. So did the others. So I got up and grabbed his arm and shook him, calling his name, and one of the brothers, the conga player, said, "Leave him alone." So I sat back down, talking to him. I can't remember what I said—I was in shock. So were the others. So we sat and waited another minute, not knowing what next.

And all of a sudden he jerked forward violently and he was back in his body, but he was dead, I figure, for two minutes. For half an hour, no one could talk to him. He was in a post-traumatic shock. He said, after a while, "Leave me alone." Because I was so freaked out about what had happened, telling him what just took place, he was afraid he was going to go back into a fit. He was holding his head and was obviously in grief, and that was not like him, being a drummer. After a while, he started feeling better and we got into his car. We didn't jam that night, and he drove us home, up Yonge Street to Keewatin. He went for electrocardiogram tests after this happened, but they found nothing abnormal.

He told me that during the experience he left his body and was going down the tunnel. He went into another fit later at a party, when a dog bit him. The guitar player was there. I wasn't, so the guitar player thought it was an illness. The guitar player didn't want to talk about the experience either because he didn't want to accept it or put it down to an epileptic fit. But his brother, the conga player, remembers the mongoloid child.

I lost contact with the keyboard player. He was an exceptional keyboardist, but he got a little mixed up with transcendental meditation and never was the same. He didn't say much about it.

Just a note: The drummer moved up north to Huntsville and bought a 102-year-old house that I helped him to renovate. He's sold it since, but it was haunted. They called in a diviner, and this person said there were seven spirits in the house. I've talked to the guitarist recently. He now lives in BC with his brother, and he now knows what happened that night after all these years.

Yours truly,
Jim Greenwood

PART IX
GHOSTS FOREVER!

You don't have to believe in ghosts to appreciate them, or doubt their existence to be free of them. Ghosts belong to the category of experience, not to the category of belief or disbelief. The Spanish philosopher Miguel de Unamuno said in 1924, "The sceptic does not mean the one who doubts, but the one who inquires and searches, as opposed to the one who asserts and supposes he has found," and it's still true today. In the intervening decades, studies in folklore, psychology, neurology, and psychiatry have advanced our thinking on expectation and experience. Yet I think it can safely be said that there will be ghosts and spirits among us for as long as the human race is allowed to give expression to its hopes and fears, and as long as the stars in the heavens shine down upon us.

I Saw a Man Coming Towards Me

DORIE FRATESI-MURIE

I received the following letter from Dorie Fratesi-Murie, a resident of Sault Ste. Marie. It is a clearly written account of an experience that occurred three decades earlier but that still puzzles Ms. Fratesi-Murie.

We exchanged emails, and on the following day I learned a few additional details.

> *The city that this took place in was Sault Ste. Marie, Ontario. It was in July and I remember it was a very hot, hazy day and I had all the windows open. My fellow worker did not see anything as she was not there that day. However, I called her that evening and told her about the experience I had and indicated to her that it startled the life out of me and I did not intend to work alone in the future. It was the first time I had been in the attic. The reason I went up there was because a dentist had retired from the building some years before and his son told me there may be an old dental cabinet belonging to his dad in the attic.*

The experience is indeed puzzling, as well as the "confirmation" of the discovery in the attic.

◆ ◆ ◆

May 11, 2004

Dear Mr. Colombo:

I have recently read your book about Canadian ghosts. I enjoyed it very much.

I am going to relate an experience I had about thirty years ago. I worked in an office that was in a house that had previously been a medical clinic. Prior to that, it was a doctor's residence. At the time of the incident, there were two offices in the building, a doctor upstairs and my office downstairs. An office at the rear of the building was empty.

About three o'clock in the afternoon, I was alone, busy finishing up a project, and was intent on my work when I heard footsteps coming from the back of the house. I looked up in surprise because the back door of the building had been tightly locked for years and was never used. I saw a man coming towards me, carrying a small child.

I smiled at the man but he did not seem to notice me. I noted that the child had his head leaning on the man's shoulder with his face pressed into his neck. I could not see his face but I was amazed to see that the boy (for somehow I knew he was a male child) had an old-fashioned brace on his leg.

Now I became very curious and took a good look at the man. I noticed he had on a Harris tweed jacket. There were leather patches on the sleeves at the elbows. As he neared me, I realized that he was going to turn and go into a room with no exit where we kept supplies. To exit the building, he would have had to turn the other way and go out the front door. I said, "Sir, the door out is to your right."

He never looked at me but continued on into the supply room. After a few moments, when he failed to reappear, I got up from my desk and went into the room to see what he was doing. To my horror, the room was empty!

Completely shocked, I tried to reason out what I had just witnessed. Could he have been up at the doctor's office and came down the old back stairs no one ever used? I went upstairs and inquired from the doctor's secretary as to whether they had a patient who had a small child with him. She said there had been no one of that description in their office. Who was he, I asked myself? How did he disappear from a room with no way out except past me? I had to accept that I had somehow had an encounter with something unexplainable. I could not really understand what had happened and it remained a mystery.

However, I still had a shock coming to me. Before we moved to another office building, my fellow worker and I made a trip to the attic to see if there was any old furniture. (I am an avid antique collector.) There, in the corner, covered with dust, was a little child's brace. We looked at each other and quietly descended the stairs, a very shaken pair of individuals.

As a footnote, I might add that the man I saw was solid and sturdy-looking. He did not look like an apparition at all. But I now must conclude that he must have been one!

Yours sincerely,
Dorie Fratesi-Murie

My Ghost Stories

THERESA ROSS

Ah, the wonders of books! The wonders of email! On August 24, 2004, I received this email from Theresa Ross, of Oshawa, Ontario. The email is self-explanatory, except that the various incidents described therein defy ready explanation. I immediately replied to Ms. Ross to thank her for taking the time to send to me this account of her unusual experiences (which I have reproduced here as she has written them with a minimum of copy editing) and to encourage her to ask her cousin in Nova Scotia to share with me and my readers her own eerie experiences.

I am not sure what to make of Ms. Ross's experiences, except that I am certain that she is faithfully recounting what she remembers and what she recalls of the other people's conversations that she is repeating in good faith. These are family accounts, or stories, or memorates, as folklorists know them. It is not unusual for youngsters to have imaginary playmates. Indeed, it is quite possible that these playmates are more than imaginary, for it has been argued that children are more sensitive than adults to psychic phenomena.

Whatever is the case, Ms. Ross has a whole series of extraordinary experiences to share with the readers of this book. And it should be noted that she receives a complimentary copy for herself and another for her cousin in Nova Scotia!

◆ ◆ ◆

August 24, 2004

Hello, my name is Theresa Ross. I just read your book *True Canadian Ghost Stories*. I loved it. I have a few stories myself. The first takes place when I was a baby. We lived in a town called Springhill in Nova Scotia (1977). From what I am told, my aunt was babysitting me and could hear me laughing in the next room. She came to check on me and saw that the cradle was rocking as if someone was swinging it and I was looking up at "someone."

A few nights later, Mother woke up in the night after hearing a crash. She woke up my father and told him to go look. He said there was nothing out there. This happened for the next few nights.

My mother did some digging around and found out that the people who owned the house before had a son who was killed in a car accident out front of the house. We all assume he was my cradle-rocker.

Another time, when I was older, I remember my mother telling me about my imaginary friend. I would blame her for everything. When my mother asked me what her name was and what she looked like, I said her name was Tammy and she was dressed in very old-fashioned clothes.

At that time I wouldn't have seen pictures of the period of clothing that I had described, around the 1920s and '30s. She must have been a ghost. I was only three or four.

We later moved here, to Ontario, and in '92 moved to Caesarea. My mother and I hated going into the basement alone. If one of us had to go down there, we had to get the other one to stand at the top and wait. It was an awful feeling. I would run as fast as I could to get back up the stairs.

One night I was asleep on the couch in the living room. I heard one of the bedroom doors open and then the bathroom door close. Neither door opened again, and I felt like someone was walking through the living room and into the kitchen. I wasn't long going into my bedroom and shutting the door. I asked my mom and stepdad the next day if they had gotten up in the night, and they said they had not.

Another time, in the same house, my mom was alone. It was evening and not raining. She happened to look up at the mirror in the living room and saw two tear-shaped drops sliding down the middle of it. Then they stopped. She left it like that until my stepdad came home and he took the mirror down. There were no water spots on the wall and no leaks anywhere.

A few days later my sister and I were in a serious car accident. Was it a sign?

When I was nineteen, I moved to Oshawa, Ontario. A friend of mine and I rented a house on the corner of Adelaide and Mary. I figured out very quickly that we were not alone. My closet door would lock for days. If I went out to the bathroom in the night, the attic door would be closed. Upon returning to my room, it would then be open. In the morning I would awake to find it closed again and locked. At times when I was the only one in the house, I would go up to the bathroom and find toilet paper shredded and tossed everywhere. My friend had a very large Rottweiler that was terrified to go up there. I lived there only a month or two, then I was gone. My friend wasn't too far behind me.

I also have a UFO story. A few years back, I was dog-sitting for my sister, and our cousin was with me. I heard the dogs going nuts. When I looked out the window, there was a car in the driveway. (She lives in the middle of nowhere, with one or two neighbours down the dirt road.) I went to wake up my cousin, and when we came back to the window, the car was gone.

However, I remember looking into the sky and seeing this glowing green light hovering, and then all of a sudden it shot across the sky and disappeared. I looked at her and she looked at me. Neither one of us could speak. It was odd. We slept together the rest of the night.

I hope you find these stories interesting, and if you ever want to use them in your books, please feel free.

You can also contact me. I live in Oshawa, Ontario.

My cousin in Nova Scotia also has experienced her own strange happenings and I will ask her if I can recount those as well.

If you do use these, will you let me know so I can purchase the book?

Thank you for your time. Hope to hear from you soon.

Theresa Ross

A Ghostly Experience

KELLEY IRWIN

I received the following email from Kelley Irwin, a correspondent unknown to me, on June 24, 2004. "A Ghostly Experience" is her account of seeing a vision of the late Kurt Cobain. After reading it, I find myself wondering how common such experiences are. Performers have a habit to entering into our emotional natures and striking deep chords there, whether singers or not! I wrote to Ms. Irwin and asked about the message she wrote under the influence of the pop singer and composer.

◆ ◆ ◆

June 24, 2004

Hi, Mr. Colombo:

I'm currently reading your book *The Midnight Hour* and find it fascinating, as I do with anything that has to do with the supernatural, UFOs etc.

I'd like to tell you about an experience I had ten years ago when I lived in North York. I and my then six-year-old son lived on Bartley Drive, in the Victoria Park and O'Connor area of Toronto. We'd lived in a walk-up apartment since July 1991 and there had never been any occurrences before or after the one I experienced in September 1994. I no longer live there, having moved to Hastings, Ontario, in 1995.

To start this story, I'll go back a few months. In April 1994, Nirvana lead singer Kurt Cobain committed suicide. I heard about his death on the news and felt sorry for his wife and little girl. Other than that I never gave it or him another thought. I wasn't into his music at that time anyway, I was more into Aerosmith and Guns n' Roses.

September 1994 rolls around, school starts for my son and we get back into the school routine, nothing exciting, just day-to-day life. One day I was sitting at my kitchen table, which was in front of a large window, and you could see into the living room, down a short hall to the bedrooms from this area. It was during a sunny day. I happened to look up and standing in my living room, close to the hall, was Kurt Cobain. I just sat there looking at him, more in surprise than anything else. I wasn't afraid, tho'. He had his head down a bit, then turned and walked down the hall and disappeared into my son's room. (He was at school.) When I say he disappeared into my son's room, he just sort of faded away at his door.

As I said before, I wasn't into his music and knew nothing about him. I later discovered that the clothes I saw him in were what he was wearing when he died. He had on a pair of faded, torn blue jeans, a brown, button-up sweater that was sorta fuzzy and a pair of white and blue sneakers. After seeing him, tho', I became very interested in him and his music. I also write poetry, but after seeing him my writing increased tenfold. I even have a letter I wrote that was basically dictated by Kurt, explaining why he killed himself. A lot of it, I found the facts matched after I did some checking on him. I also have become a fan of his and his music, as has my son, who also learned to play guitar. He also plays it left-handed, the same as Kurt Cobain did. He has a right-handed guitar that he plays upside down left-handed. It's quite unique.

Well, I hope you enjoy reading my experience, as I've told very few people about it. If there's anything else you'd like to know about it, please let me know.

Thanks,
Kelley

To my request for further information about the contents of Kurt's letter, I received the following detailed response on June 26, 2004:

Hi, Mr. Colombo:

I must say I was surprised at how quickly you got back to me. I figured a few days or so—you must be a busy man.

Anyway, you asked for some more info on myself. Guess I'll start at the beginning. I was born in August 1961 in North York and given up for adoption. I was adopted into my family in December '61. I was the only child at that time. My brother was adopted in 1964. I just remember him coming home. My mother still lives in the house where I grew up, in Scarborough, the Brimley and Lawrence area. I had a fairly normal childhood until my parents split up when I was ten. There's a year I don't remember because of this; I obviously blocked it out. My mom then met my stepfather two years later and they remained together for about ten years before they split when I was about twenty-one, twenty-two. I moved home at that time too. I graduated high school in '79 and got my first full-time job a few months after and left home around the same time.

That job lasted a year and I was out of work for a year before getting the next job, where I was at for nine and a half years before the company started to go under and I was laid off. In between times, I had married, having met my (now ex) husband at my second job—we married in '86 and my son was born in '88. We lived in the basement apartment at my mom's when he was born, but after I had lost my job moved into the apartment at Bartley Drive. In '93 my ex up and left, no explanation (not even to this day), so it was my son and me. By the time of seeing Kurt we'd settled into our own routine. It was also in September '94 that my dad passed away. I hadn't seen him in about five years, but was at the hospital when he did pass on. I didn't want him to be alone at the end. He was an alcoholic and lived in a rooming house in downtown Toronto. His death did upset me, but as I knew the life he was living I also felt a sense of relief, since every time I heard about some older man being found beaten or dead I was so afraid it was him. So with his passing I didn't have to worry, he was in a much better place.

In March '95, my divorce was finalized and by then I'd met someone else. I also moved to Hastings in July of that year and was engaged. Unfortunately that didn't last and by July '96 I was on my own with my son. We once again managed. I got involved in his school as a volunteer and he enrolled in the Cub Scouts. In the summer of '97 I met another man, but he was visiting from down East so after he left I wrote him off until he surprised me by moving to town with his son in December '97. We have remained together since then. He's heard of the Kurt story and does believe it. He's about the only person other than my son and his youngest who've heard the story.

I guess that's about sums up my life, the condensed version anyway. I have serious health problems at the moment and am currently awaiting a double lung transplant that will be done at Toronto General Hospital. This has nothing to do with smoking, tho'—I have never smoked a day in my life. Some doctors think the damage to my lungs was due to a prescription diet pill my family doctor in Scarborough gave me in the early '80's. I'm still trying to find out the name of the drug.

I hope this isn't too long or boring. As for the letter, I have to dig that out of my files. I don't leave it lying around. It's too hard to explain it to people and pretty well no one knows of it. Try to explain a letter written by Kurt after his death—hard for a lot of people to believe.

I'll get that info as soon as possible. Thanks for getting back to me.

Yours truly,
Kelley

The Ghost of University College

CLARA BLACKWOOD

I met Clara Blackwood at a poetry reading at the Victory Cafe in Toronto. She introduced herself and said she had enjoyed reading my book Haunted Toronto *and that, if I was interested, she would like to send me an account of her sighting of a ghost at University College, University of Toronto.*

"The building's said to be haunted," I said, "by the ghost of the stonemason Ivan Reznikoff."

"I know," she replied.

"Yes, I'm definitely interested!" I responded.

"I wrote a poem about the experience too," she added. "Would you like to see it as well?"

"Most assuredly!"

"I'll send them to you."

A couple of weeks later, on July 11, 2004, the account in prose and the account in a poem duly arrived. Here they are.

I should add that Clara is a poet of interest. Her first poetry chapbook, Under the Dragon's Tail, *was published by believe your own press in 2002; a second one,* Visitations, *was launched in the fall of 2004; and her work has appeared in a number of literary magazines. From 1998 through 2004, she organized the Syntactic Sunday Reading Series in Toronto. She writes both prose and poetry with great precision and clarity, and is studying English and religion at the University of Toronto.*

◆ ◆ ◆

July 11, 2004

It was the fall of 1995. One evening I suggested to my boyfriend that we explore the U of T campus, which would be quiet, dark, and almost deserted—a good place to end a date.

After circling the University College building, we decided to relax and sit down in the middle of the open field north of the College. We were laughing and joking around when, all at once, our mood dramatically altered and I felt my blood pressure drop. The conversation came to a halt.

Simultaneously we turned from each other towards the wall across the field.

Immediately I saw a tall, shadowy figure, in profile to us, moving along that wall. He was like a projection, strangely flat but also charged and fluid. A melancholy feeling accompanied him. I had a strong impression that he was from another time and was patrolling the premises looking for something. Indeed, he held a lantern, also of translucent grey, resolutely in front of him. Each time he reached one of the ground-level windows, of which there were many, he would disappear entirely as though entering it, and then reappear right outside of it. This happened again and again. When he reached the last window, he vanished for good.

I turned again to my boyfriend; his eyes confirmed everything I had seen. Overcome by a kind of rapture, I could barely get the words out: "We've seen a ghost!"

Accustomed to the uncanny, my boyfriend merely shrugged; his apartment was haunted, and he had already had many such encounters.

Visitation, University College

I can see us
sitting in the dimly lit field
at the College,
when a sudden chill came on,
unhinging the moment.
Together we turned and stared
at the many-windowed north wall.

Across that stone exterior
an apparition walked,
six feet tall with beard, long coat
and guiding lantern—
translucent hermit.
He was electric, fluid—
arising at one window,
vanishing into another.

Rapt, I breathed,
"We've seen a ghost. *We've* seen a ghost!"
You, calm, familiar
with ghosts and spirits,
gave a shrug,
remained untouched.

No other witnesses
except the leafless trees.

True Supernatural Occurrence

"VLAD"

Email is a fast medium—pretty well instantaneous. There are three emails here, all dated July 3, 2004. The first and third come from "Vlad."

I read the first one shortly after it arrived and was intrigued. I found myself wondering about the sobbing and the chuckling. My correspondent called himself "Vlad," so I sent him my own email, included here, and in it I requested further information. The third email is his response. All this correspondence took place within little more than half a day.

I have reproduced "Vlad's" two letters as I received them, with some routine copy editing (including exchanging the lower-case "i" for the upper-case "I" and deleting my correspondent's full name and street address).

Let me add that East York is part of the Greater Toronto Area.

I think it is appropriate to note that experiences like the one described here are far from being uncommon; indeed, they are a lot more common than we might imagine. They are also scary. One loses a night's sleep over them, and then puzzles about the experience for weeks, months, years, and even decades to come.

I am grateful to "Vlad" for sharing this incident with me and my readers. Perhaps the gentleman known as Bruce will read this account and write to me at the address on the last page of this book.

◆ ◆ ◆

1.

July 3, 2004

Dear Mr. Colombo:

I have always been open to the possibilities of things unknown to us existing in this world. But if, prior to July of 1998, you ever asked me if I believed in ghosts, demons and such, I'd most likely have said "no," because I never, ever experienced anything of that nature, and frankly, I believed that modern science had all the answers already.

All that changed on a hot, muggy Toronto night in July of 1998. I was alone in my ground-floor apartment in East York, soundly asleep. Suddenly, a loud, sobbing sound came from the kitchen. I woke up, trying to figure out if I was dreaming. The sobs sounded again, accompanied by the sounds of shuffling feet. I froze.

The kitchen is adjacent to the entrance lobby, so my first thought was far from supernatural: Being on the ground floor, I thought I'd simply forgotten to lock the door and some poor girl had escaped from her attacker into my apartment. I feared that the attacker might follow her inside and I braced myself for a very dangerous situation.

The sobbing sounds continued for a few seconds and then stopped. I got up slowly, not knowing what to expect. I went to the kitchen and turned the light on, expecting to see the poor girl huddled on the floor. You guessed it—there was no one in there! That's when I got real chills. I checked the door quickly and it was locked! Now I was very frightened and it entered my mind for the first time that the event might be truly otherworldly. I turned on all the lights in the apartment and sat down, lighting a cigarette, trying to figure out what had happened. Just as I was reaching the conclusion that I had experienced what they call a "lucid dream," a loud, evil, gremlin-like chuckle came from the kitchen! I was beyond scared at that point. It was around 3:00 a.m. and I spent the rest of the night smoking on my couch, waiting for the morning light.

I am still in the same apartment and nothing like that has ever happened again.

Now, the real twist in this story: A couple months ago, I was watching the program about so-called night visitations on the Discovery Channel. There was this gentleman from Toronto who was telling almost the same story, complete with the evil chuckle in the end. The gentleman's name was Bruce, I think. I debated whether to try to contact him but decided not to. Now I'm at least sure I'm not crazy and that what happened to me was real and really supernatural.

Please let me know what you think of this experience... and feel free to use it any way you wish to. Just don't use my real name, for obvious reasons.

Thank you very much,
Vlad S., Toronto

2.

July 3, 2004

Dear Vlad:

Thanks for your account. It is well told and truly puzzling!

I will use it in my next book, but I do need some further details, some for publication, others not.

Not for publication: I need your full name and mailing address (to send you a copy of the book when it appears in a year or so).

For publication, could you supply some more details? How old are you (generally) and what's your line of work (generally)? What is the street address of the apartment building? Have you had other experiences that are out of the ordinary?

I'm curious!
Best,
JR

3.

July 3, 2004

Dear Mr. Colombo:

I'm still in the same building, different apartment. It's located in the Pape and Cosburn area, East York.

I wouldn't want to give you too much info about myself for publication because people would recognize me and wouldn't understand that I'm not nuts (you know how it is) because I have a somewhat exotic job in the music industry and people would easily guess that's me, given the street number. Please refer to the building as in the Pape and Cosburn area. At the time of the incident I was thirty years old. I don't use drugs, rarely drink and I hadn't had a single drink that night.

I continued to live in that apartment until the year 2000 and never experienced anything out of the ordinary since that night. There is one more interesting detail: You might remember that in my building in 1996 (I think, you can do a research of local newspapers, but I can't recall whether it was in '95, '96, or '97) there was a gruesome murder on the fourth floor where a fourteen-year-old boy was murdered and dismembered. Maybe there is a connection, but at the time I was on the ground floor. I don't know.

As per my other experiences, I have seen a UFO twice as a child, but that did not occur in Canada and it was not very spectacular, just distant lights in the night sky that moved erratically, doing manoeuvres which no machine from this earth can do. The UFOs were very high in the sky and both times there were many witnesses.

Thank you very much,
Vladimir S.

The Ghosts of the Casino

KRISTINE DOUCETTE

In late January 2004, I received a three-page letter from a young woman unknown to me. Over the next month, I corresponded with her and elicited some further details. Here is a consolidated version of her original letter to me.

This is the first time I have heard of ghostly occurrences in one of Canada's casinos.

◆ ◆ ◆

The Ghosts of the Casino

I am a twenty-six-year-old woman. Over the years I think I have worked almost every job imaginable, but I have never before come across anything like this. In the workplace it's usually your boss you worry about watching you, not ghosts!

I worked as a security guard at the Casino by Vanshaw, which is located in Medicine Hat, Alberta. I had started in March of 2003. As soon as I had started to work at the casino, members of the staff started to tell me ghost stories. These were apparently accounts of experiences some of the staff had had working nights inside the empty, dark, closed casino building itself and at the adjoining lodge.

At first I thought these stories were some sort of initiation. I then started to notice that it wasn't just the security staff that was telling me these stories. It was the staff of the entire complex—casino, lounge, and lodge staff. Needless to say, I was starting to get a little nervous. Every direction I would turn, someone would have another story to tell me.

Now I am going to tell some of these stories to you.

Scents of a Woman

One of the cleaning ladies was cleaning the ladies washroom in the casino. It was roughly an hour after closing. She was going about her duties. She had just set all her supplies on the counter. As she began washing the sinks, she sensed someone watching her. She slowly turned to look behind her at the stalls. Out of nowhere, a large black shadow flew past her and out of the washroom. The cleaning lady stood there frozen for a moment, then drew a deep breath. She then smelled a strong musky perfume. She dropped what she was doing and left the building.

Is It Safe?

One of the casino's games technicians had started her shift at 4:00 a.m. She had just cleaned all the quarters out of the machines. She set a big bucket of them on the counter, then bent down to open the safe. She put in the combination and turned the lever. It didn't open. She figured she had made a mistake, so she tried it again. Again, nothing. She didn't understand how she was making such an error, considering that she had been doing this for a couple of years. She took a deep breath and tried it yet again. Again, nothing. At this point the woman was so frustrated that she yelled at the safe. Just then, the door of the safe swung open. The lady shook her head, put her hands on the counter for balance, and stood up. She took one look at the counter and jumped back. All the quarters were now spread across the counter and arranged in little triangles.

Face to Face

One of the security guards was on the graveyard shift. It was about 3:30 a.m. and he decided to watch some television. He sat down in the lounge, turned the TV on, and got comfortable. He was watching for about fifteen minutes when he saw something out of the corner of his eye. He then turned to look at it. There was someone peeking at him from around the corner of the kitchen. The security guard informed the person that the casino was closed. The guard got up to let whoever it was out of the building. The person vanished. The guard then checked the exit where the person had just been, but it was locked. Not just locked, but dead-bolted from the inside.

The Lady in White

Another one of the security guards was working the graveyard shift one night. It was about 4:00 a.m. when he decided to get some reading done. He was sitting at the security desk reading his book. He glanced up from the book. What he saw stunned him. About ten feet in front of him stood a woman. The woman had long blond hair and was wearing a long white dress. For a moment she stood there, looking at the ground. All of a sudden she looked directly at the guard and began to cry. The guard put his book down and got up to go speak to the woman. But when the guard rose, the lady just disappeared. He searched the entire casino, top to bottom, but found no one.

Child's Play

One of the night auditors was working the graveyard shift. It was about 3:00 a.m. when he had started to get a series of calls from angry customers in the lodge. The customers were saying that someone had knocked at their doors, and when they would answer, no one would be there. The clerk figured someone's kids were having fun in the lodge. After receiving about eight complaints from the same wing, he went into the camera room to check the surveillance tape. He watched the tape and saw all of the customers opening their doors and peering into the hall. The clerk watched the tape a couple of times but saw no one at all in the hall.

The Voice

Unfortunately my graveyard shift had arrived. I was really freaked out, but I put my fear in the back of my mind and went to work. I worked three of my five shifts with no problems. I then thought I was in the clear and the casino and lodge were not haunted. My fourth shift changed my mind dramatically. I had just completed my 4:00 a.m. check of the casino. I thought I would go and watch some TV in the lounge for a while. The lounge had the most comfortable chairs. I turned on the TV and got cozy. I didn't find anything interesting on TV, so I called a friend. About three minutes into our conversation, I saw a dark shadow pass not three feet in front of me. I took a deep breath and told myself it was all in my head. Then I saw it again. Okay, now the hair was starting to stand up on the back of my neck. I ignored the sensation and told myself I was just scaring myself. I then tried hard to focus on the telephone conversation. That's when I heard it plain as day and loud as thunder. I heard a voice. The voice was deep and dark. I turned to my right in hopes that someone was just playing a very mean trick on me. No one was there. My body froze, and every hair on my body stood on end. I hung up the phone on my friend, got out of my chair, and shot out the back door. I didn't even realize what it had said to me until I had calmed down some time later. It had said my name.

Postface

"It is a field in which the sources of deception are extremely numerous. But I believe there is no source of deception in the investigation of nature which can compare with a fixed belief that certain kinds of phenomenon are *impossible*."

—William James, letter to Carl Stumpf,
January 1, 1886, in *The Will to Believe* (1897)

"Professor Openshaw always lost his temper, with a loud bang, if anybody called him a Spiritualist; or a believer in Spiritualism. This, however, did not exhaust his explosive elements; for he also lost his temper if anybody called him a disbeliever in Spiritualism. It was his pride to have given his whole life to investigating Psychic Phenomena; it was also his pride never to have given a hint of whether he thought they were really psychic or merely phenomenal."

—G.K. Chesterton, opening sentences of the short story
"The Blast of the Book," in *The Scandal of Father Brown* (1935)

Acknowledgements

The assistance of researcher Alice Neal and librarian Philip Singer is gratefully acknowledged. Ever helpful were fellow investigators Dwight Whalen, W. Ritchie Benedict, David Skene-Melvin, and Ed Butts. Dr. Cyril Greenland and Dr. David A. Gotlib offered insights into societal and psychological contexts. From the first, Tony Hawke encouraged the collection and the publication of mysterious accounts. Anna Porter of Key Porter Books suggested that a sequel to *True Canadian Ghost Stories* was in order. The manuscript was smoothly edited by the talented Janie Yoon. My wife, Ruth Colombo, like a guardian angel, hovered over this project as she has all the previous ones.

Readers who have witnessed strange events or had eerie experiences, and who are willing to share accounts of them with the readers of my collections, are invited to write to me care of the editorial department of the publishers. I may also be reached through my website, *www.colombo.ca*, and my email address, *jrc@ca.inter.net*.